Where Have All The
FLOWERS
GONE?
An American Story

Where Have All The
FLOWERS GONE?

An American Story

Christopher Lee Bowen

ARPress
ILLUMINATING IDEAS.
EMPOWERING VOICES

ARPress

45 Dan Road Suite 5
Canton, MA 02021

Hotline: 1(888) 821-0229
Fax: 1(508) 545-7580

Ordering Information:

Quantity sales. Special discounts are available on quantity purchases by corporations, associations, and others. For details, contact the publisher at the address above.

Printed in the United States of America.

ISBN-13:   Softcover   979-8-89330-392-6
                     eBook   979-8-89330-393-3

Library of Congress Control Number: 2024903117

TABLE OF CONTENTS

FOREWORD

Gauguin titled his Tahitian painting: *Where did we come from? Why are we here? Where are we going?* An un-Tahitian line of questioning. Those lightly clad and uncomplicated islanders were content to enjoy what is at hand and not question much of anything. Unlike us, well upholstered and inwardly uptight, who question everything. Our Western search for God, meaning, and explanation for why we are here is like breakfast in a failed marriage. All questions, accusations, resentment on one side of the table, silence on the other.

Of the 31,000+ days I have lived at the point of this writing, which people, events, places should I chronicle? Through selection I end up with a story, a capsule compared to what is left out. This is a chronicle, more on the comic than tragic side, of the people I knew, worked with, played with, disliked, loved, lusted after, let down or was let down by, admired, mocked, made me happy or at least content, damaged me, or elevated me. In order to provide a sustained narrative and an acceptable level of continuity, I leave out many byways, detours, characters, events and dead ends which might serve as footnotes to this story. This is not a documentary that might require, even benefit from exhaustive detail.

We all have a story to tell. Most of us don't bother telling it. That is sensible. We all face eventual oblivion. We may strut and fret our way around for a few decades, but when we 'pass' as the euphemism goes, we are un-remembered within seventeen days and mostly forgotten ever after. Save yourself the bother. If told, your story or mine might survive for a while, but will eventually disappear as well, like the flowers, young girls will have picked them every one. No matter. This is my story.

BEGINNINGS

I was born 16 February 1938 in St. Luke's Hospital, Manila, Philippines. Keeping me company in the adjacent maternity ward was Mrs. Douglas MacArthur and newborn Arthur MacArthur. My father, Captain Robert Oliver Bowen, US Marine Corps, served on General MacArthur's staff, where he occasionally encountered Lt. Colonel Eisenhower, who at that time had no additions to the family to deal with.

Newly weds.

Lt. Bowen.

But enough name dropping. Years later I read claims that we are born free (Rousseau) and created equal (Jefferson), two great fallacies on which two of the greatest events in history were based: the French Revolution

1

and the American Revolution. Neither myself nor Arthur were in the least free, dependent entirely on the Philippine nurses who, in my case, saved my life. And I was definitely not equal. Mrs. MacArthur and son received constant care and attention, whereas my mother Alice and I were at death's door after a Caesarian delivery, I in an oxygen tent and she exhausted and sewn back together after surgery. My father was about to go on maneuvers, when a Navy doctor, who apparently enjoyed the sadistic perks of his profession, brought him to my oxygen tent: '*Say farewell to your son. He probably won't be here when you get back.*' Although this was my mother's second try, she had lost twins in a 1936 miscarriage, my father may have welcomed the prognosis. He didn't want the competition.

Which brings up another source of complaint. We don't choose the epoch nor are we responsible for the society into which we are born. We are, in a sense, victims of and at the mercy of adults whose luck or stupidity contributed to prevailing conditions within which we have to survive, with their help of course. In 1938, Hitler pulled off the Anschluss with Austria, Spain was embroiled in Civil War, Russia was undergoing the Stalin purge, a year earlier Japan had begun its assault on China, Germany was headed to Munich, and the US was still reeling from Depression with worse to come on all fronts worldwide. My arrival was hardly noticed. I remember nothing of the Philippines. Reportedly I sat on a dead 25-foot python (much smaller ones sometimes were kept in attics to subdue the cat-sized rats), swam in the Pacific, provided cute photo ops for my parents, and survived my birth trauma. In 1940, we returned to the States, passing from New London Connecticut to Quantico Virginia finally to Kinston North Carolina, early in 1942, near Camp Lejeune where my father trained in the 'swamps' of North Carolina for the Guadalcanal landing August 7.

My sister Linda was born May 9. Aunt Christine (Jenny) Sundvall, a restless horny 20-year-old facing the prospect of a man-less home front, visited us, ostensibly to help Alice, but mostly to check out the departing Marine talent. 'Help' an oxymoron. Hormones took charge. William Langfitt, son of a Pittsburg steel executive and officer in the USMC, in hot pursuit of Jenny made for chaos in the two-bedroom apartment we occupied.

With the prospect of battle and legal homicide in view, Robert's sadistic side was in full swing. Slapping my hands and saying *'No, No, No'* as I reached for whatever was available. Perfectly normal 4-year-old behavior but provoking to the former 13-year-old drowner of cats employed during summer at the Chelmsford Massachusetts pound, a perverting experience. I ran away half a dozen times in downtown Kinston to get away from him. Each time found by police who gave me ice cream cones, desire for which the ostensible and only acceptable explanation for my repeated behavior. The truth would be too untimely. I was relieved when suddenly and beyond my wildest hopes, Robert was no longer there.

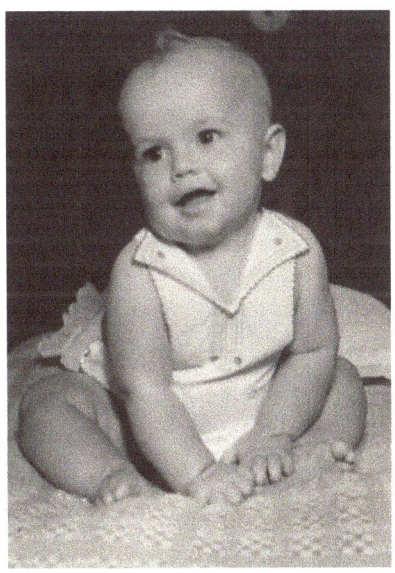 

Gerber candidate?   *Worst over, 6 ½ months old*

SEATTLE

On August 7, 1942, the Marines landed unopposed on the beaches of Guadalcanal, our first land attack since the naval victory at Midway. Major Bowen commanded the 3rd Battalion, 5th Regiment, 1st Marine Division. A number of books on that campaign include a photo of General Vandergrift's command staff, Robert included. There are photos of Robert and his Battalion staff, plus a few individual shots. Apart from lines showing positions and arrows showing movements on campaign maps and descriptions in historical reports after the war, we learned little about Robert's time in the Pacific. He once mentioned that he was in a foxhole and saw the head of a Marine in the foxhole next to him blown off by a mortar shell. He also mentioned that

November 6, 1942
Matanikau River, Guadalcanal, Solomon Islands
3rd Battalion, 5 Regiment USMC
Command Post

1) Capt LD Spurlock Bn-3. 2) Maj Bolt Barba Exec. 3) Maj RO Bowen CO.
4) Lt AF Dill Bn-1. 5) Capt VF Croizat COMg. 6) Cpl Disbrier. 7) Pfc McLean.
8) Capt S Sullivan CommAFF. 9) Cpl Totty. 10) Lt J Naylor MortorFMF
11) Lt Barrett M-Co.

Guadalcanal

his carbine jammed and he pulled on the bolt moving his head abruptly just as a Jap bullet went into the tree he was leaning against, exactly where his head would have been. When on Henderson airfield with another officer, he looked up and saw a Jap Zero flying over the tree tops headed right at them. They didn't bother to run or seek cover, they just waved at the pilot, and he waved back. Probably out of ammunition or maybe just professional courtesy. My mother, Jenny, newborn sister Linda, and I went to live with Fritchiof and Gerda Sundvall, my maternal grandparents, at 827 33rd Street in Seattle. We had tin drives, paper drives, and an air raid warden in tin hat who checked our blackout curtains every night so Jap Zeros couldn't attack us. Blimps trailing steel cables floated everywhere over the city protecting the Boeing aircraft plant. We had the '40 Buick. With Robert in the combat zone in SE Asia, we got extra ration coupons for gas and other items in short supply. Hollywood kept up home morale with films like *And the Angels Sing*, starring Betty Hutton. America was great then! If you weren't there you will never know how great. That film gives an idea of the spirit and spunk that won the war and made us unbearable, I mean unbeatable. I started 1st grade in 1943. Alice took me crying and screaming to the school. After thirty minutes I was running around chasing the girls even into their bathroom which landed me in the classroom corner with a dunce cap, a shaming exercise in the presence of fellow students. Teachers did that sort of thing in those days. But my way with the girls was compensation, as I had my first girlfriend in 1944, a tradition I followed at every new location to which we moved.

Sundvalls were a tumultuous group, never a dull moment. Uncle Alf was the center of confusion in the period 1942-1944. He was a celebrity in Seattle in the 1930's and early 1940's. A noted tenor, he participated in radio broadcasts of religious services and secular celebrations, sold recordings of religious hymns (the Lord's Prayer a particular favorite) and popular songs, was frequently engaged to sing at parties and weddings. Strikingly handsome, he was popular with the press and the ladies. Alf had discovered his inner tenor in High School, where he wowed the

Alfred Fritchiof Sundvall

girls in a class performance of Sigmund Romberg's musical *The Student Prince,* a rank he tended to appropriate in daily life. He attended the University of Washington for a semester then pursued a career as church tenor, making successful recordings of favorite hymns, especially *O Holy Night,* which enjoyed good local sales, tending to peak during Christmas Season. At 6'1", well built, a clothes-horse, with peak lapel double-breasted suits, white/brown Florsheims, and looks to stun the inexperienced, he was a favorite with girls, at least until they got to know him well, which took long enough to make possible early harvest of rewards later withdrawn. His emotional zig-zags projected just that element of bad-boy risk and danger to excite and attract devotion and passion in the willing victims. In 1941, Alf auditioned for the tenor part on the Jack Benny radio show. Swedes were hot (think Garbo, Bergman, Bjorling). Corporate talent scouts heard about his reputation in Seattle as a popular singer and came to check him out. Dennis Day, a safely compliant Irish tenor got the job, fortunately for Benny. Dennis had the simple directness that would complement Benny's amiable flow of dialog and song. Alf, a perpetual steam boiler likely to explode at any and invariably inconvenient occasion brought on by imagined slight or insinuated hostility was temperamentally unsuited to the Benny style.

Alf told me he fucked the wife of an Army private (then dodging Jap bullets in the South Pacific) on a pew bench in the entryway of the Swedish Covenant Church in 1943, though I never could sort out the physical logistics of the act taking place on a Church pew. Alf was 4F, disqualified for military service (although he did qualify for Air-raid Warden complete with natty blue uniform), which placed him, as part of the male domestic remnant in an enviable, and deliberately unreported to preserve GI morale, position to take advantage of lonely ladies during the war years.

No Eric the Red or Sven Bluetooth, my grandfather Fritchiof Alfred Sundvall nonetheless inherited the wanderlust gene common to coastal Swedes. Born 1886 near the seaport city Sundsvall on the east coast, he had the 'elsewhere' gaze common to Swedes who yearn for high seas and distant Shangri- Las. A dreamy lad, rather short for a Viking, but stocky, sturdy, green-eyed, brown hair, he always seemed to be surrounded by girls in school and family pictures. He was good looking and, as was typical in peasant/landlord societies, a myth that he was the bastard son of the local Count Sundsvall added spice to his otherwise commonplace background.

Fritchiof Gerda

There were sufficient examples throughout Europe and Russia of such dalliances that this possibility had some statistical support, however improbable. His surname helped sustain the dwindling hope for advantage such a liaison might entail. After school he joined the merchant marine and sailed to Central and South America, as far south as Buenos Aires. His pocket notebooks record nothing to suggest travel to exotic lands, only pedestrian accounts of expenditures for food, knives, shaving cream, hotels, pencils, down to the last Swedish Krona. Not that he lacked imagination. He was a dedicated if slow reader, liked to paint in oils, and, when permanently settled in Tacoma after retirement, enjoyed correspondence chess with buddies back in the homeland. Gerda Nilsson, born 1896, was raised with an older brother and sister on a farm in south central Sweden near Malmo. A tale of woe amplified and augmented over the years, she often complained about hard labor, fresh farmhands, and desperate conditions. Early photos show otherwise, she being nicely dressed in white high-collar blouse with cameo and full length skirt, buxom and rather cute. In company with her sister, she arrived in Canada in 1910 to begin their expatriation in Ottawa with their older brother, Otto. Alfred Nobel, a Swede, invented dynamite, an efficient means for rock removal that greatly expedited mining and tunneling projects worldwide.

Unfortunately, Gerda's older brother working on mining projects in Ontario was blasted into unrecoverable pieces by Nobel's invention, an unintended fratricide from one point of view. Alfred did establish the Nobel Prize, perhaps in expiation for the collateral damage of his invention. Otto's death left the sisters stranded for a time. Eventually they moved to Vancouver British Columbia where a colony of Swedes welcomed them. Gerda's sister later moved to Connecticut, but by that time Fritchiof had married Gerda in 1914. Alf was born in 1915, Alice in 1917, and Jenny Christine in 1922. Alice and Jenny attracted attention. This photo shows Alice around 14-years old, plump but cute with a nice smile. Not sure the sailor is interested in her or the girl behind her, but his interest would have been one of degree not exclusion. Jenny Christine, born 1922, eluded Gerda's malign influence largely because she was Fritchiof's favorite and was extremely good looking, of which she was obviously aware. Even at 13-years she had the body and poise that gave her advantages with men, invariably coquettish and sexually savvy. In May 1944, I came home from school, and was told a surprise awaited me upstairs. With visions of a pony or Schwinn bike propelling me upward I ran to my mother's bedroom, then froze as I looked at the unsmiling Robert in uniform. I panicked *(He's back!!!)*, and ran from the room. This time no ice cream and no where to hide.

Alice

Jenny

QUANTICO 1945

Robert was transferred to US Army Fort Benning, Georgia, where in late 1944 he instructed recruits in jungle warfare. In 1945, he transferred to Quantico where he trained recruits in the same likely engagement.

Shoo fly pie and apple pan dowdy
makes your eyes light up and
your stomach say Howdy!

That song, the first I distinctly remember, was popular in 1945, and is associated with a birthday party in Quantico at which I, age 7, ate too much cake and got sick. The cake was some kind of almond flavor I have since been unable to smell or taste without gagging. Other than the mournful trumpet playing taps every afternoon, when Marines slammed on brakes and jumped out of staff cars, ran out of barber shops half shaved, or abruptly heeled on streets and sidewalks turning to the flagpole in salute, I had no further recollections of music's command over the human spirit.

The Axis lost the war in Europe, but the war against Japan dragged on. VE day in May was welcomed but the prospect of a land invasion of Japan dampened enthusiasm. Estimated 50,000 dead likely to defeat a fanatical Japan on the ground made the endgame too unappetizing to contemplate. Two friends and I emulated the war games with as much real equipment as we could scrounge. My playmates in Quantico during the last year of WWII were Beau Butler son of Colonel Beau Butler, the fifth in a series of career Marine officers, Southerners, graduates of Virginia Military Institute (General George Marshall a distinguished graduate), who formed the elite of the USMC, and Chip Woodrum, son of an officer from Mississippi who accumulated war souvenirs by the trunk load, the Japanese bayonet Chip is holding part of the trove. We acquired helmets and other gear to play war in imitation of the only

10

game in town, but in our case almost catastrophic. Chip and I opened a chest of Jap souvenirs in his father's garage. We found a

Beau Butler, Me, Chip Woodrum.

Japanese rifle with ammo, loaded the rifle and then paused not sure how to fire it and a bit afraid to. We decided to mount the rifle, butt on the ground, barrel resting on a box about 12-inches high, pointed out the garage door toward the street that ran by the house. We tied a string to the trigger, reluctant to pull it ourselves, sat behind the box, nodded OK, and pulled the string. Exactly at the time we fired, the Commandant of the base drove by in his olive drab command car with 2-star red flags flapping off each front bumper directly in front of the rifle. Fortunately, the rifle was elevated sufficiently that the bullet went above the vehicle. The Commandant was spared being the last Marine casualty of the Pacific War, and nothing came of the event thereafter.

I attended the base school, 2nd grade, had a finger painting displayed in the school corridor, along with twenty others, but somehow flunked. How one can flunk 2nd grade remains a mystery to me to this day. What possible sadistic academic requirement could be imposed on a 7-year-old that would justify so drastic a judgment on his intellectual capacity? Residual adherence to the Puritan emphasis on punishment and austerity toward children? Consider John B. Watson who wrote *The Psychological Care of Infant and Child, published as late as 1928, in which he offers guidance to mothers: 'The greatest threat to the child is too much love. There is danger lurking in the mother's kiss. Don't hug or kiss the child and never let it sit on your lap.'* This '*spare the rod and spoil the child*' *perversion of child* care would never make it in Tahiti.

Parents, having passed the same stages as the ones their children are passing through, forget or willfully suppress their memory of the state of mind and capacity for mischief of the very young. Adults assume a level of moral 'innocence' in the young that is so totally at odds with fact as to lead to comic occasions. But they impose through 'school', intellectual imperatives that should be adjusted by age and experience rather than by grade and theoretical expectations unreasonable to achieve. At 7-years of age I was perfectly capable of murder (the Jap rifle incident), albeit more inadvertent than intentional, but not up to handling the complexity of a school to their satisfaction. An opportunity to illustrate this precocious inclination to amorality occurred with a girl school mate, daughter of a fellow officer and occasionally invited with her parents to visit our quarters. I recall even at seven years certain pleasurable sensations in the erogenous zone, erotic arousal at so early an age entirely excluded from parental and most adult assumptions. Another revision in the Puritanical vision of childhood innocence so cherished in our culture involved the sharing of girls in these disruptive impulses, total abstinence and indifference by girls assumed by parents, at odds with all experiential evidence. The girl in question was three years older than I, a millennium of experience by comparison. Rather good looking, obviously by now somewhat advanced in such matters, and seemingly taken with me to the extent that contact was not at all proscribed. She initiated certain embraces and touching that were both novel and pleasurable beyond my then very limited imagination in these matters. She made sure to close the bedroom door where we were, as the parents believed, secure in our innocent pastimes. After several visits, my mother began to smell a rat and sense forbidden irregularities. She once abruptly opened the bedroom door at a point where the girl and I were quite properly separated, fortuitously as it happened, but she said emphatically: *'Never close this door when you are in here!'*, clearly an admonition provoked by some subconscious remembrance of dark and forbidden events in her own childhood. That December, I played Joseph in the church nativity enactment with convincing piety admired by onlookers unaware of the latent sexual rascal I had become.

O Holy Night.......

NEWPORT

My father was assigned in 1946 to the Naval War College, Newport, Rhode Island. We shared a four-plex apartment building with US Navy Commander Harold Funk, son Danny, daughter Brenda, and wife June. I attended Miss Collings school downtown, the elite grade school for children of the Newport social register. Newport's Mansion row was the epicenter of social life outside New York, a familiar milieu for readers of Edith Wharton. Miss Collings was a terror, entering a classroom unannounced, harrowing barrage of questions regarding the times tables: '*6x7, 9x8, 7x4!!!!*' She gave a special award, a 20-volume miniature set of the books of the Bible, to those who could recite the books in order. I won one! The math teacher smelled of tobacco but was a wonderful attentive instructor, so my math skills improved considerably but from zero any improvement might seem remarkable. Our French teacher, Madame Lelong, about 60-years old, in long black dress, *pince nez,* very elegant and especially attentive to the daughter of a mansion family, Alison Beaudreau, who already spoke French fluently, having a French nanny. Madame produced the same play every year, every student assigned a part but the lead this year assigned to Alison, I merely a *poulpicon* (fairy) chorus member. All spoken in French to demonstrate achievement calculated to reassure parents of their investment. I had entered 4th grade, having made up qualifications for 3rd grade over the summer of study that somehow in turn made up for flunking 2nd grade, a twisted academic recalculation of my status still entirely unclear to me.

How, why, I ended up taking tap dancing lessons remains unclear as well, but I was enrolled by my mother in the local Fred Astaire Dance Studio. Robert liked Bing Crosby and Fred Astaire. Fred and Gene Kelly gave tap a certain cachet, and the Negro tap era of Sammy Davis was not yet in play to diminish (more likely extinguish) its prestige. To this day I can't imagine myself hoofing it, but I apparently got good enough for the teacher to call on me to demonstrate for new students the progress one could make in just four months. I had no initial prejudice against tap, probably enjoyed it for exercise and improved agility, but was abruptly disillusioned by Dan Funk, then taking piano lessons, when the idea of tap dancing was presented as so infra dig as to be laughable. Danny irritated me for no directly explicable reason. I could see the truth in the piano preference which made me even more irritated.

His mother June had a peculiar relationship with him, he seated on her lap, she holding him close, kissing him on the lips, a sight that instinctively repelled me. Harold Funk was a Naval air pilot, had many kills in the Pacific, drove a Cadillac, and was acceptable to June's family, they being wealthy Los Angeles business people who introduced flavored potato chips to American homes (cheddar, jalapeno, garlic, blue cheese, etc.). Harold reminded me of Roy Rogers, almost a look-alike, and the same wholesome Western manner. I suspect his sexual appetites were modest, June perhaps seeking affection with Dan to replace expectations unfulfilled elsewhere. Which leads to the strangest encounter of my 9-year life. Given our proximity and our fathers attending the Naval War College, Dan and I were often together to play and fool around. Once he asked if he could suck my penis. I assumed I had one and knew about it, but never had it been explicitly mentioned as such in any context. The girl in Quantico had shown some interest in it but did not actively seek to engage or otherwise explore its potential. That Dan should make a direct request of such astonishing nature was totally unanticipated. I, however, complied with his wishes having already felt the pleasant sensations that anatomical appendage could provide. He sucked me, I liked it, and apparently, he did too. Was this some effeminacy induced by his mother's kissing and fondling, a passive sexual orientation induced by maternal abuse? But there are certain limits drawn by biological endowment. He asked me to suck his penis. I refused. No argument of reciprocity had any effect on my aversion to the prospect. I was definitely biased toward girls, as my Quantico experience showed, and I began to feel very odd and uncomfortable around him. Fortunately, Robert was reassigned to China, we moved to Tacoma, and any further complication with this matter was averted.

TACOMA 1

From July 1947 to February 1948, we lived in a rented house on Browns Point, just below the Sundvall residence Fritchiof built after retiring, dubbed 'Sundvallia'. Located at the top of a hill, it had a view of the Olympic Mountains and Puget Sound from the living room to the north, and Mt. Rainier from the bathroom in back of the house to the south. He and Gerda had eight Rhode Island Red hens and one rooster, not sure if breeding was in mind, but not long after our arrival the rooster was marked for consumption. The hens were large, very large, and pecking order was strictly maintained by daily skirmishes. Fritchiof fed them corn. Abundant lizards in the surrounding wooded landscape provided protein. The hens had names. Henrietta I particularly remember for an interspecies confrontation that revealed a level of astuteness not commonly associated with chickens. Henrietta was marked for consumption on the ground that she hadn't laid an egg for nearly a week. She was publicly scolded (in the presence of the other hens lined up to witness the proceeding) and the message apparently was understood. That evening before dinner we heard a clucking at the back door of the house, located at the top of a 15-step staircase. We went to the back door and saw Henrietta and an egg. She saw us, turned and waddled back down the steps, a considerable effort on her part that earned her a reprieve from capital punishment. The hens had witnessed on a number of occasions Fritchiof beheading a fellow hen, once loosing his grip such that the hen ran around headless for three minutes before the jig was up. The rooster was defended by the hens with great ingenuity. They would surround him when Fritchiof came with the axe, giving him time to hide under the 1934 Plymouth. Alas, time and the odds were against him, and they lost their stud two days later.

I attended Dash Point School 5th grade, an undemanding institution about which I only remember a girl contortionist about 8-years old doing a pretzel with her female parts, albeit clothed, prominently displayed above her smiling face. Alf showed up, one of his intermittant returns home from San Francisco, and we went fishing, he is smelling of garlic clove which he chewed to lubricate his vocal cords. Polly Ekberg, a family friend from Seattle, retired to Browns Point on the Sundvall recommendation, buying a house just below theirs. She was perky, smiling, very attractive, slim, in great shape, never married and had a pension, a combination that attracted Alf's interest, but she was not about to reverse a lifetime of independence for such a risky fling.

The momentous event of this interval was piano lessons with Adele Carlson, married to a successful businessman, living in an elegant mansion in North Tacoma. A Steinway grand in the living room and an upright in a practice room where she taught students, reserving access to the grand only after diligent practice demonstrated commendable progress. I have always responded to beauty, the thing I value most, so seeing this dark-haired, blue-eyed Greta Garbo of the Pines shifted my gear of endeavor to top speed. She was cool and gorgeous, hard to take my eyes off her. I sensed that my adulation penetrated her otherwise distant professional but agreeable manner toward students and parents. I had ditched the rather absurd pursuit of tap-dance glory, for the much more rewarding prospect of the piano repertoire, about which I sensed the importance but in fact knew nothing. My disadvantage was that I had never touched a piano, knew nothing about the keys, the pedals, the entire magnificent contraption that the Italian Christoforo invented around 1700. No matter, we started with the most elementary introductory material, undoubtedly excruciating to teach, but with my rapt devotion, made tolerable as an investment toward more rewarding results to come. They came fast, due mainly to my maniacal application and motivation to sit near her, breathe her scent, feel the warmth of her body, the gentle touch of her hands, imagine prematurely the lovely and strikingly prominent swell of her, albeit well-upholstered, breasts, engulfed by the beautiful rapturous seduction that is teaching. At $5 a lesson I have never had a better bargain. I did satisfy her requirements such that after five lessons I was taken to the holygrail and thereafter performed as acolyte at her place of worship on the instrument of her choice. Once you have played a Steinway grand, nothing else will do.

Alf married Christy Kennedy, Irish daughter of a Police Captain in Seattle, and they moved in with Fritchiof and Gerda, Alf unemployed and Christy not quite able to support both. Fritchiof had a bedroom in the attic. Gerda had a bedroom on the main floor. Alf and Christy had the bedroom next to Gerda. Such a juxtaposition of Calvinist Puritan and randy newlyweds was combustible. Gerda heard bedsprings and moans and shrieks of pleasure in a disapproving silence that raised tensions to a boiling point, while Fritchiof snored away upstairs after his nip of Jim Beam, indifferent to the drama unraveling beneath him. Every Saturday Fritchiof and I would drive to town in the Plymouth to buy chicken feed, then go to nearby movie theaters, he to see Jeanette Macdonald and Rudy Vallee, and I to the other theater to see grade B westerns. We met after, headed to the Plymouth, stopped briefly in front of a local bar, he went in for a snifter, then together home. This rather pointless existence finally ended in January 1948, when Alice received word that we could join Robert in Qingdao. The most popular song of 1947 was *'I'd like to get you on a slow boat to China'*. Life sometimes imitates art, at least in this case, as we drove to San Francisco in our 1940 Buick and boarded a Navy supply ship, pretty much fulfilling the dream of the song.

CHINA

We sailed from Pier 25 in San Francisco in February, a 21-day trip to Guam, Yokohama, then Qingdao. We had a below deck cabin with shower and 18-inch round porthole. On the main deck was a large room with tables for games and sofas for chat. Outside there was a railing below which the Pacific raged, an infinite green sea. A major draw was the ship snack bar where ice cream bars were readily available. Protecting us was a Marine PFC, short, stocky, armed with a .45. I talked to him a lot during the voyage, but remember practically nothing except his recurring reference to looking forward to fucking Chinese girls. I fell in love with the daughter of a fellow passenger on their way to meet her Navy officer husband stationed in Japan. Love included discrete walks around the deck, maybe a kiss or two, and expressions of devotion. In Japan I bought her a Geisha doll. Never saw her again.

We were not allowed to leave the ship in Guam because there was an epidemic of mumps among the local population. No great matter, Guam being the most sordid unappealing island in the entire Pacific. We then sailed toward Yokohama arriving at dawn, stunningly beautiful Mt. Fuji appearing above the fog as we passed the Dragon Islands leading to the mainland. We visited Kamakura and the Buddha overlooking the former prison camp that had held American captives. Tokyo was completely flat, no buildings standing, just a network of cleared streets. The submissive behavior toward Americans was at first alarming and then gratifying, such esteem unearned became rather agreeable. Three days later we sailed for Qingdao.

I lived in Qingdao China from March to October 1948, the most significant event of my life. After arriving at port, we took a staff car to the Officers Hotel. I saw a young girl, no more than 13- years old, lying in the gutter crying, a rather shocking experience for me, moved to help but having no idea how. We were taken to our new house in a housing area built by the Japanese during their occupation of Qingdao and the Shandong Peninsula (1919-1945). Ours was a 2-story house, three bedrooms upstairs, living room, dining room and kitchen downstairs. Behind our house was a separate building for servant quarters. The neighborhood was large with many houses similar to ours. Open sewers ran in the gutters. We didn't have piped water. A large water truck delivered 200 gallons a week to a storage tank on the roof. The streets were unpaved and lined with trees that had been cut back to within an inch of their lives by Chinese to obtain fuel. We had a double garage which we shared with the neighboring Navy family.

Jingle Bells was my best friend and constant companion. He was an orphan of the war and revolution ongoing, just one of millions whose lives had been disrupted or destroyed by the prevailing insanity. The Marine regiment occupied a former Japanese compound, fenced by a terracotta wall 10-feet high and 5-feet thick. Marines found Jingle Bells singing the eponymous song at one of the gates and a Sergeant agreed to take him. I met Jingle Bells at school, learned that he lived five blocks from our house, so we could easily meet and together roam the surrounding venues of Qingdao. We were the same height weight and age, 10-years, so comparably able to horseback ride, swim, and roam the beach areas of the city. And of course, essential to any association, he spoke fluent English.

Horseback riding became my major pastime. The Navy paid for a stable, located along Zhanshan Dalu, managed by a Cossack Colonel from the Tsarist army, a refugee from the Russian Revolution. I forget his name but he was one of the most impressive men I have met. At least 60-years old but fit and handsome, well groomed, moustache, he sat bolt upright in the saddle without discomfort. He dressed as a Tsarist officer, which he had been, in immaculate shined boots, tan riding britches, green tunic and peaked hat. He was modest, friendly, good natured, dignified, gracious, a perfect officer and gentleman. I enjoyed his company and conversation in heavily Russian-accented English although I remember nothing about it other than instructions for proper horsemanship and general rueful remarks about the current political situation that went over my head. His horses were well groomed, he regarded horses as a charge to be treated with respect and even reverence.

The colonel gave lessons, holding a rope tied to the bit as the horse went round in a circle and I bounced uncomfortably on top. After a few lessons I got the hang of 'posting' and eventually we went for rides outside the compound down the dirt roads of suburban Qingdao. On one of our rides, I saw a boy in my class come tearing by at full gallop. The Chinese stable about a mile from my house kept horses for the races at the Qingdao racetrack every weekend. You could rent horses at the stable for $1 an hour. The Colonel looked disapprovingly at the boy and noted that he was abusing the horse. You should never work up a lather, etc. I thought otherwise. The Colonel would allow at most a brief canter, never a gallop, whether to preserve the horses or insure my safety

I didn't know. Sometime after that ride I ended lessons with the Colonel and started going to the Chinese stable with Jingle Bells.

Every Saturday morning, I left my house, met Jingle Bells, and walked to the stable for a 2-hour ride. If we assume the best, we tend not to realize how uncommonly surprising the best is. At no time in my many ventures with Jingle Bells to shops, neighborhoods, outlying hills, beaches, did the Chinese threaten, intimidate or cheat me. Maybe the great decency of their culture toward children accounts for it. I could easily have been kidnapped, held for ransom, sold into slavery, all much later retrospective assessments of the worst that might have happened but didn't.

The stable workers and the owners of the horses were friendly, laughing, engaging. A goat once butted me in the rear, an icebreaker about which we all laughed heartily. Various breeds of horse were on offer. I once got a plow horse that wouldn't gallop or walk, just doggedly trot, at considerable discomfort for me. My favorite was #40, an American quarter horse, who would walk or gallop or stop. Our best ride was the peninsula located just four blocks from my house. Jingle Bells and I would ride to the beach, head for the peninsula, and amble up the road that ran around the peninsula, fairly leisurely until we reached the top of the hill and faced the 200 yards of dirt road ahead. I then kicked #40 and he took off like a .44-caliber bullet, full gallop, hell bent for leather, Grade-B Western style, with me bouncing in the saddle loving the greatest thrill there is, riding a horse at full gallop into oblivion. Some vendors brought donkeys to the neighborhood, providing very young kids a chance to ride for .25 cents a pop. Unfortunately, donkeys are notoriously horny and often get hard-ons nearly 2-feet long. On one such occasion a group of five kids aged 4- to 6-years stared in mute astonishment as the owner holding the reigns of a donkey with left hand and beating the donkey's backside with a stick in his right, both turning rapidly in a counterclockwise circle, the donkey fleeing the stick under contradictory sensations of erotic arousal and applied pain.

Americans took over the old German School, large brick with auditorium, stage four feet above the basketball-court floor. We sang *Cielito Lindo* and other songs every morning, our Anglophone White Russian teacher directing. I remember nothing about classes. The recreation activities included high jumping, something I was fairly good at, able to jump four feet over the bar. During recess we went to the playground where one rather fat 8th grader having procured porn photos showed us a Russian couple in a state of unmitigated delight demonstrating a number of positions. A few ingenious male students taped mirrors to their sneakers hoping to see girls' underpants. I remember the photos but didn't participate in the peek-a-boo.

Top row far right.

Conflict was always possible. In my case it involved our neighbor Navy Commander's son, an irritating and aggressive little shit. He shot holes with his bee-bee gun in my mother's brassieres hung out to dry on our clothesline, an unaccountable provocation suggesting deeper emotional disturbance. One way or another, as retribution I challenged him to a boxing match at our school, a regular feature of talent shows arranged by our ubiquitous White Russian. The big day came. I was in shorts, sneakers, towel around my neck, nude to the waist, outfitted with boxing gloves that weighed a ton, led onstage to wild cheers, predominantly soprano. We waited. The audience got restless, blood lust percolating, churning expectations, male testosterone rising, females getting moist with anticipation of male blood sweat and muscle, when to everyone's crushing disappointment, the White Russian announced that Johnny was sick and couldn't make the event.

Piano was still in the picture. My mother arranged lessons with Miss Weaver, an English lady of 65, former British consulate employee, who retired in Qingdao. Plump, pink and white, fluffy grey hair, charming smile and ebullient British personality, living in a chunk of the Cotswalds inserted in the middle of Qingdao, doilies, horse hair-stuffed armchairs and sofa, bric-a-brac, Royal Doulton figurines, Persian rug, flower garden, white picket fence. She had a relic upright piano capable of only approximating the tonal demands of the music. Her emphasis was on physical dexterity. We did an exercise every lesson. Hands together in a steeple formation, move each finger on each hand down. After two lessons we explained regretfully that we could not continue.

My next teacher was a stunning improvement. Anastasia was White Russian, about 25-years old, dark hair, dark eyes, beautiful, pensive, well built, in white button blouse and tight blue skirt, red fingernails, lovely lavender scent. She would sit on the bench turning pages of *Intermediate Piano Classics*, in itself a flattering assessment of my ability, making notes on the pages, as I felt the warmth of her body, the top blouse button often came undone to reveal the marvelous fullness and curve of her breasts. I was ravished and played with erotic desperation. We had about ten weeks of lessons. We arrived one day in September to find she had left. Trains out of Qingdao were covered with refugees headed for Shanghai. Anastasia probably got an offer to leave China for Taiwan, Hawaii, who knows where. I was disconsolate. Beautiful Anastasia, Anastasia, Anastasia…*mon amour.*

We lived about three blocks from the Soviet Consulate, a large walled compound, ominously quiet and menacing. I had met a Soviet kid, son of a consulate housekeeper. They lived literally in a hut outside the compound walls, with dirt floor and large iron kettle for whatever goulash she prepared for supper, like some parody of rural 16th Century Russia. He was suspicious, even hostile at first, didn't say much, probably carrying out his NKVD spy assignment, but gradually warming up under totally nonpolitical American friendliness. He invited me to his hut. I felt sorry for him and gave him comic books to cheer him up. I learned a lot about the Russian stone face that conceals underlying doubt, inferiority, and craving for friendship. But there was an exception.

Most weekends in summer a group of five Soviet teenagers walked by our house to the Russian beach. I was 10-years old, they were 13- to 16-years old, bigger and very indoctrinated. They invariably shouted, '*Yankee want to fight box?*' I was totally unaware of the Soviet 'threat' and obviously I was not, at ten years, physically endowed sufficiently to meet such a challenge. I was furious and fearful. Fury won out. Battles are won by Strategy and Tactics. Emotion and impulse usually fail. And in the end surprise and superior force contribute most to ultimate victory. This is a good theory, but to confront and deal with an immediate threat doesn't always allow for much deliberation. I do not remember how and by what mental process I engaged in this skirmish. One Saturday the Soviet kids passed by my house, made the same contemptuous challenge and went on to the beach. I had by then identified means and methods and went inside up to my parents' bedroom. I can't remember how I knew but I did know that my father kept his general issue .45-caliber Browning pistol on a shelf in his closet. I got a chair, climbed up, took the .45, and went back to the front yard, waiting for the Soviet forces to return.

The Browning .45-caliber side arm has a history closely related to the USMC. When the United States acquired Spanish colonial possessions after the Spanish-American War, we inherited the Philippines, then in social turmoil caused by rebellious inland jungle tribes. Marines were assigned to subdue this insurrection. The territory in question was thick jungle foliage, not open terrain. The tribesmen would often attack at close range, hidden until then by foliage. Marine pistols were at best .38-caliber. At close range a tribal attacker could machete a Marine even if he was able to fire a shot directly at the attacker. The Marine Corps needed a pistol that had such impact as to stop and even throw back the attacker. Browning was assigned to design such a pistol. A .45 can blow your head off, slam you back ten yards, and definitely terminate even a running charge. The only problem for me was that it weighs nearly four pounds, really heavy for a 10-year old. So here I am waiting for the enemy, my weapon concealed in my belt, figuring my odds. On schedule the Soviets return up the road, see me and shout *'Want to fight box, Yankee?'* or *'Afraid to fight Yankee?'* When they were opposite me, I pulled the .45, held it with both hands, and decisively with appropriate menacing expression pointed it directly at them. Response to challenge is unpredictable. Some will irrationally attack or equally flee. No telling what five bigger boys would do when opposed by a 10-year-old shrimp. I had in fact not speculated on their response, so intent was I on the impression I hoped to make that I supposed it would be to my advantage, not necessarily. I was relieved and surprised at what happened next. They flew, not ran, flew as fast as they could possibly fly away from what must have seemed certain death, not considering that if I got only one of them the other four could have overpowered me, taken the gun, and finished me off. I learned more about international relations, power politics, and gang warfare in that encounter than any class or textbook could possible teach. I also learned how to deal with Russians. A lesson I have not forgotten.

A boy at school invited a number of us to his birthday party, followed by a rickshaw ride to a Chinese opera theater, the coolie running at an even pace in front of me, I gently bobbing up and down in the rickshaw, a marvelous, pleasant ride but later reconsidered when I learned of the short life span such exertion imposed. The opera was amazing. We entered a small but very ornate building like a large garage. The stage was about two feet high. Dragons and banners hung from the walls and framed the stage. The orchestra had a bench on one side of the stage, Chinese violin, tambourine, flute, drum. Sunflower seeds and tea served for refreshment. The audience was Chinese, who looked in disbelief but amiably at us seven American interlopers. The opera began with men wearing dragon masks, wielding swords, shouting and singing (hard to distinguish which at any one time) while prancing and dancing to the accompaniment of bells, whistles, horn, drum and Chinese violin. The hero didn't wear a mask but was made up as if he had one. The thick lipstick and red, green, yellow, black makeup seemed weird to us. He fixed his eyes on our group, going through what must have been stylized expressions of anger, rage, and remorse, throwing his sword around and swishing his red and gold robes and streamers that hung all over him, while the Chinese in the audience occasionally mumbled or clapped perhaps in acknowledgement of a virtuosity we were not trained to appreciate. The performance lasted about an hour or so. I loved it. The kid's parents were obviously imaginative to have thought of sending us to this arch-typical Chinese event, one unlikely to occur to my parents. It was a great treat and wonderful bit of lore to take home to the States.

One advantage to China duty was servants. Inexpensive, capable, grateful for employment and income. Some imaginative officers hired several including cooks. Robert was unimaginative. Our servant Wang did everything. If we did anything he could do he would throw a tearful repentant fit, wondering what he did wrong. Eventually we decided that doing nothing was best, and began to like it. His wife and two kids lived in a small mini-house out back, servant quarters in Japanese days. Seeing his wife suckling her newborn was an erotic occasion unavailable in the States, breasts being a forbidden fruit concealed with desperate efficiency.

Wang and Linda

In August 1948, Chiang Kai-shek introduced currency reform to curb inflation and restore stable economic conditions. The new rate of exchange was four yuan to $1. The exchange of old currency was 1-million yuan to $1 dollar. Before the reform, we got bundles of 1-million yuan tied together in squared shaped packets and carried them to market downtown, where stalls set up on sidewalks provided an astonishing variety of goods. One waited to the last minute because the exchange rate changed every few days, yuan depreciating vis a vis the US dollar. Our servant Wang accompanied me, able to bargain on my behalf. Of great interest were the large number of baseballs and baseball gloves, obviously obtained from Marine/Navy supplies. The going rate for a screw was one baseball glove, the large number on display indicating the volume of trade in the respective commodities. No questions asked, no questions answered.

A large number of Methodist missionaries lived in Qingdao. For that matter, Chiang Kai-shek was Methodist. He had converted to Methodism in 1926 when he married a Soong daughter, a very influential Nationalist family. Her father had studied at a Methodist School in North Carolina, returned to China, was active as a missionary and eventually a businessman and political leader. Madame Chiang studied at Wellesley Women's College near Boston. Missionary kids attended our school and only toward the end of 1948 did I understand the difference between their position and mine. Many missionaries decided to stay in China after the US military evacuated in the late fall of 1948. They were worried but kept talking about faith and *Jesus will provide*. Many of their kids were sent back to the States, some decided to stay. Eventually all of them returned to the States. They spoke fluent Mandarin, and many took advanced degrees at Princeton and other universities, joined faculties and became 'experts' on China in Federal intelligence agencies and the Foreign Service. Mao was consolidating forces outside Qingdao, but he had no intention of provoking a US response by attacking the city. In fact he liked and respected the Marine Corps. A special contingent of Marines was sent in the early 40's to help Mao train troops for guerilla war against the Japanese. Our total defeat of Japan and the Atomic bombing were especially appreciated in China, where Japan to this day is despised for its atrocities in Nanjing and elsewhere.

The currency reform lasted about six days then inflation reduced the yuan to 1 million to $1 by mid-September. We were ordered out of Qingdao in October. Teachers hired for the school departed early, parents of students taking over. A lovely blond lady, mother of a 5th grader, took over our class, explaining the ongoing turmoil to our great satisfaction. The adult world was collapsing into chaos, no homework

28

assigned, liberation from all rules and constraints ahead. We loved it. End of October we prepared to leave. An officer held a farewell party for about fifty of our American contingent. He had a cook who prepared a dozen Chinese specialties, 1000-year eggs, lobster, sea bass, jowzas. At the end of the dinner our host brought him out for appreciative applause. The cook cried, the host cried, we all cried. Servants and employers knew the future under Mao was not likely to be pleasant. The fable was nearing its end. One wednesday morning we got in a jeep and headed for the US Navy Cruiser. It was already bitterly cold. I was wearing a Russian style fur hat with fur earflaps. As we approached the dock, I saw a Chinese boy about my age cross the street. He timed his moves so that he could grab at my hat as we passed. He touched it but couldn't grab it. I looked at him, he waved and smiled, I smiled and waved back. I never saw Jingle Bells again. Korea, Great Leap Forward, mass starvation. What became of him? The wonderful Chinese people faced an unpromising future. My destiny lay elsewhere.

Zai jian Zhongguo, zai jian.

TACOMA 2

Alice, my sister Linda and I lived at Browns Point from end of October 1948 to August 1949 in a rented house about two blocks from Sundvalia. I attended Tacoma Middle School, taking a bus from Browns Point downtown every morning and back every afternoon. We had a fair number of girls and boys 10- to 14-years old, with a bus driver about 50-years old notably unappreciative of the turmoil American youth experience and can inflict. The girls were of course docile and quiet, but about seven boys were notably provocative. A crescendo of disruption began at first with occasional shouting and running from seat to seat. The driver would shout for them to sit down and be quiet. At first, they did. But as the weeks went by things escalated to the point that the boys would hold the upper hand bar railings and rock the bus side to side, while students toward the front of the bus attempted to block the driver's view of the culprits. They rocked the bus so effectively that the driver had difficulty keeping on track. He sometimes stopped the bus and went back to intimidate the culprits, by this time in his opinion to include practically everyone on the bus. Eventually he lost his temper and shouted and threatened and even grabbed a few collars and shook the boys attached. By January a school warden was assigned to ride the bus with authority to hold offenders for juvenile detention. Total calm ensued but the era of turmoil was truly invigorating.

The school was OK. A biology teacher had a glass cage with a rattlesnake on his desk, an alarmingly constructive influence on class attention and conduct. Shop class was run by an arch-typical 85-IQ older guy in carpenter overalls who had us making napkin holders and darning knobs, skills of dubious use in later life although learning to use a jig saw, lathe or chainsaw was not entirely futile. I confronted a Negro for the first time, clearly from another world of graft and opportunism who equally out of his element, tended to exaggerate his already well-formed talent for imposition. He was constantly asking to borrow money, something we had very little of.

I remember getting a bee-bee gun for Christmas. I practiced shooting at flying sparrows, invariably missing, but unfortunately on one occasion I did hit one midflight and he fell dead to the ground. I was sick with remorse, truly. I resumed lessons with Mrs. Carlson, able to more fully appreciate her considerable physical charms than nearly two years earlier. Uncle Alf by now divorced or about to be, returned from San Francisco from time to time to live with the Sundvall grandparents. I went fishing with him a number of times but never caught anything edible. In August, Robert returned to the States from China, reassigned as director of the Third Marine Reserve District headquarters in Chicago, a new scene for romance and adventure, and some misadventures as it turned out.

CHICAGO

We arrived in Chicago from Tacoma on September 10, 1949. Lovely warm but not stifling day, bright sun, trees green and dappled, the most beautiful city in the United States, adjacent to Lake Michigan, seeming more like an ocean without restless waves, no land as far East as one could see. First called Checague by French trader Robert de la Salle in 1679, a corrupted version of the local Indian word for garlic, an abundant savory in the area, Chicago was incorporated as a city in 1837, burned down in 1871, and has been rebuilding ever since to its current population of nine million, third largest in the Nation. Each of the great cities in the US commands a regional socio-economic watershed around which surrounding cities and areas are organized: Boston, New York, Chicago, Atlanta, New Orleans, Dallas, Los Angeles, San Francisco, Seattle, Philadelphia, and Washington D.C. But of them all, Chicago is the greatest. Stockyards, railroads, finance, industrial headquarters (Boeing, Caterpillar, Kraft-Heinz, McDonalds, Sears, United Airlines, Walgreen Drugstores, All State), meatpacking plants focus of the Muckrakers, organized crime and prohibition (Al Capone et al.), architectural and infrastructure innovation (the first skyscraper, elevators, Frank Lloyd Wright), Poetry Magazine, Chicago Art Institute, Chicago Symphony, Chicago Opera, University of Chicago (Rockefeller's gift, an exact copy of Oxford), Northwestern University. Our city of muscle and drive and sense of 'can do', the 'real' bootstraps America.

We moved into a new triplex at 4954 North Leavitt Street. Joe Melin, a Swede, built that and two single-family homes adjacent. He was a worker, builder, and possessor of a family recipe for 'grog', handed-down for generations, a mixture of bourbon, plums, other fruit, herbs, and secret amendments in percentages strictly concealed. The concoction was heated for 20- minutes at 80-degrees, bottled in glass canning jars, and left in a cool dark place to do whatever chemical magic it undergoes for three months, just in time for Thanksgiving/Christmas/New Year celebrations. Joe was an agreeable landlord and generous with the grog.

He reminded me of Fritchiof my grandfather, a bit short, sturdy, with a lilting by-yumpin-yiminny Svensk accent. His backyard was a party zone to which neighbors were invited, one of whom we met shortly after moving in.

Our neighbor in the house next door, Ralph Baumgartner, was Chicago. Big, burly German, shock of thick white hair combed back, robust, bottle nosed, barrel-chested, full lipped, rugged vigorous face, inexhaustible energy, he had a Senator Dirkson voice once described as honey over gravel and looked like a rougher version of the Senator as well. Ralph had a dick like a fire hose (I once saw him sleeping nude as our guest), a warm engaging insistent personality, could drink like a fish to 2 AM, go to bed and get up at 5:30 AM, every morning! He was born 1892, an orphan, grew up in the brawling no-holds-barred no-inch-given pre-WWI Chicago. Raised in an orphanage, he and his 'brother', not by blood but by association, ran away age 14 and began the street-life hustle that molded his character and forceful personality. He enlisted in the Navy in 1917, deserted in 1919, and got a dishonorable discharge as well as a wife. Returning to the streets of Chicago, he tried a number of jobs, possibly not all legally certified. Ralph was an avid swimmer in Lake Michigan. He met Johnny Weismuller then a lifeguard at Oak Street Beach, and frequently swam with Johnny far out to 'sea' and back. Both ambitious Krauts. Johnny got to the 1924 Summer Olympics and eventually to the movies as Tarzan 1932. Prohibition began in 1919 and the entire gangster era ran until Prohibition was repealed in 1933, Chicago the epicenter of its more notorious personalities. The 1929 St. Valentine's Day Massacre, John Dillinger shoot out, Al Capone, Irish and Italian mob rivalry. We never heard much about what Ralph was up to before WWII, although he dumped the wife, or she dumped him during those years. In 1949 he was successful owner of a construction business, homes, apartments, probably how he and Melin got acquainted. Ralph dressed well, elegant sport coat, classy shoes, drove the latest model Cadillac, even let me take the wheel once. Dressed up he was a formidable guy. He told the story of how a mafia grunt came to his office, told him he needed to pay protection. The thug was predictably big and ostensibly tough, but no match for Ralph in weight or determination. Ralph got up from behind his desk (clearly intimidating the unwelcome guest) picked up the thug literally off the ground and threw him out of his office. He wasn't bothered again. Ralph wanted to remarry but forgot about the first wife, they had not officially divorced. There was a bit of a legal tussle sorting out where #1 was, apparently conveniently died in 1939, so the wedding went as planned.

I attended Amundson High School, a very large reasonably pleasant brick building, with slack academic standards, and pretty girls. One girl in our singing class was exceptionally well developed in figure as well as vocal ability. The teacher (male) once called on her to demonstrate how to sing a passage. When she was through, he asked the class: *'What two things did you notice most'* leading to an understandable outbreak of laughter and appropriate but flattered blushing on her part. Charmaine Brautigan also attended Amundson, another anomaly in the mythical image of American schools: disciplined, dedicated students, equally dedicated teachers. Charmaine's mother was a principal 'performer' at Minsky's Burlesque downtown, a favorite watering hole for visiting salesmen and other rogues of the road. Charmaine's older sister already had followed the mother onto the Minsky roster, Charmaine to follow her as soon as she reached her 16th birthday, legal age to end schooling and begin life as we know it. Such abandoned career planning intrigued me, short-term calculations of fugitive rewards not within my personal list of criteria. Charmaine was, even to put it favorably, horse-faced, her body a bit slim even bony, her butt a bit under-padded, her primary and outstanding assets being a pair of very large tits that hung temptingly from her erect body, which she emphasized on every occasion. Given a less than blistering intellectual endowment and the attractions of her physical endowment confined to one area of anatomical advantage, her gamble for success at Minsky's was on further consideration not entirely irresponsible. Within the work environment and clientele associated with her prospective occupation, stunningly endowed tits could easily offset deficiencies elsewhere, especially in the nocturnal, ill lit settings in which she would be likely to appear. I was nonetheless surprised when she disappeared the following spring, intentions fulfilled so I assumed.

Apart from a recital by Tagliavini in 1949 (he being the hot new tenor from Italy) that my mother took me to, I heard mostly popular music in the Chicago years. I remember *Bacia me, I bacia you and everything goes crazy* sung by Rosemary Clooney over a loudspeaker in a movie theater, Johnny Ray singing *If your sweetheart sends a letter of goodbye* making Cry a hit in 1950, his sweetheart on his side of the ledger. Doris Day sang *A guy is a guy wherever he may be,* her girl next door voice combined with the pleasantly lascivious lyric was especially stirring. I went to a 'concert' with Tom Steinbock held at a large movie theater one Saturday afternoon where Vaughn Monroe sang *Ghost riders in the sky.* The Ink Spots were on television and Eddie Fisher sang *Oh mine papa*, a ghastly song that made him unaccountably a star. I was watching Arthur Godfrey's show when he fired Julius La Rosa and the latter gave him the finger, hard to edit visuals on TV, sound much easier. I remember tango songs from Chicago days--*Kiss of Fire, I get Ideas.* Nat Cole, in his peanut butter voice, recorded *Unforgettable.* A girl told me about *Shake rattle and roll* but I hadn't heard it and I didn't register the birth of rock and roll.

The pattern of my love life first took shape in Chicago. We attended a Methodist Church, which had a denominational coed Summer Camp at Lake Geneva. Rates are $50 a week for room, board and activities, which included various sports, inspiring daytime talks and evening bonfire song fests. I was 12-years old in 1950, my first camp experience. Boys stayed in cabins at the west end of the camp, girls in cabins well away to the east end of the camp. Obviously, they hoped for the best behavior but provided obstacles against the worst. College students were hired to supervise each cabin, prepare and serve food in the cafeteria and direct recreational activities.

It is hard to imagine how adults could be so unaware of the essential depravity of boys 12-years old and up. A great deal of acting and dissimulation on my part, a great deal of willful overlooking on theirs. My first pairing was with a more physically arousing girl, this time a girl from South Chicago with what must have been a genetically inherited sluttyness so obvious and magnetic that even the supervisors' efforts to overlook were seriously challenged. At 12-years old she had quite respectably large breasts and a well-rounded bottom, no doubt provoking encounters that left no doubt in her mind of the appeal of her endowment and predictable male responses thereto. Her speech matched her bodywork, a prematurely wise slouch and banter. She did let me feel her tits and even get my hand in her pants and finger her, but her reply to attempts at further involvement was equally earthy: *'I don't want to be a mommy with no poppy.'* Not poetic but an accurate assessment of the consequences.

So much for Tuesday/Wednesday. The fugitive gratifications of lust were soon disposed of in favor of a Grace Kelley look-alike, 12-years old, blue eyes, blonde hair, beautiful beyond description. Another boy had gained her attention early in the week, but I was so taken by her beauty I came saw and conquered to the extent of prying her away from my competitor, an admittedly rather unprepossessing guy who at the final departure said to me: *'Take good care of her.'* Pathetic! Thursday evening, I sat next to her on a bench near the lake, sang popular songs, kissed her once or twice. On Friday night I went with her on the farewell cruise around the lake, infatuated by her beauty. Saturday, we parted, never to see each other again. But my ideal was implanted like a template in my mind. From then on, I only wanted to meet my soul mate and marry. No hanky panky, no living together, nothing but marriage. I departed from this ideal a number of times, but it was finally fulfilled miraculously in 1965 by Renee Engel and sustained until her death thirty-nine years later in 2004.

My experience of religion also took shape at the Methodist Youth Camp. Since my family first took me to Church to be baptized, I have been at intervals and to varying degrees in communication with Jesus. Probably true of most Europeans and Americans given 2000 years of Christianity, a Semitic form of psychological complication not native or even compatible with the character of Indo-European tribes from whom we derive. An alien introspective obsession with God, guilt, salvation, conscience, belief and eternal damnation has twisted the simplistic Indo-European calf-burning form of Man-to-God bribery for favors, help or absolution so beautifully embodied in Nordic and Classical mythology. Even then they only burned the parts of the calf that were inedible, a presumably sly reduction in the tariff required to entice divine providence. They could deceive the Gods in little ways, Christians can't even hide.

Age 13, 1951, at Methodist Youth Camp on Lake Geneva, Wisconsin, standing on a hill overlooking the lake, warm breeze wafting shoreward, following an inspiring sermon by visiting minister Akhbar Haq, Indian Christian from Pradesh Province (near the Bangladesh border), a Christian tribal region converted by British missionaries, a sudden warm feeling ran through me and a sense of Jesus' presence. He was there, my buddy, watching over me, personally, not just me as part of some mob of unruly teenage misfits. This personal attachment remained through years of indifference to formal church attendance, a belief that he was like an uncle up there clearing hurdles, foiling ill doers, indicating the right path ahead. Not directly intervening but steadily guiding. This 'bodyguard' view of his role was sustained even in the face of historical research disproving divine or other claims. My belief was supported by a reading of the Biblical
reported words of my hero, compelling in their originality and poignancy. Much of the New Testament reporting had been revised for purposes of orthodoxy, but the authentic sounding words remained in pristine untarnished truth. No other religion would have allowed a Thomas to be reported saying: *'Lord I believe, forgive my unbelief.'*

36

My ultimate conciliation was that I didn't care if he was divine, virgin born, or divinely engendered. I didn't care if there was life after death or not, the clinching argument for many. I don't want a life after death. This one is wonderful and horrible enough. I enjoy it on the whole but eternal oblivion has greater attraction than endless bliss. I might cut a deal if I could spend all my time visiting past places, people and events, Shakespeare at the Globe, Caesar at the Rubicon, the first performance of the Marriage of Figaro, Anchises and Aphrodite going at it, that sort of thing.

In 1949, television was coming in, a neighbor across the street first to buy one, their lovely daughter obligingly inviting friends to sample the new mania at spin the bottle parties from which her parents very considerately absented themselves. Sampling their daughter (one got to kiss the girl the bottle stopped at) was infinitely more rewarding than the early nonsense programming of the tube. With one exception, *Kukla, Fran and Ollie,* possibly the most charming show ever produced on television, this by the local public WBBM station. Kukla was a boy doll, Ollie was an alligator, and Fran Allison was their friend and interlocutor, a lovely lady, beautiful endearing and young. She said in an interview that the puppets were so real to her that seeing them hung up shocked her. A Swede impresario did the voices of both puppets and wrote the script for each show, which Fran did not see but responded to their conversation spontaneously as if for real. It was magic and went national. Howdy Doody also came along, a silly Saturday morning clown show to keep kids occupied and allow hung-over parents to malinger in bed a few extra hours every week.

I took ROTC at Amundson HS, headed by a staff sergeant, equipped with .22 rifles for target practice on a 30-yard indoor rifle range, and M1 rifles for parade drill every Friday. We got standard issue uniforms which we wore on Fridays for the drill and to class. The ROTC classes were outstanding. The sergeant served in Europe in WWII and had access to captured enemy films, especially Japanese. We saw Jap soldiers using Chinese captives for bayonet practice. We saw films of Jap soldiers beheading American prisoners. Appropriately enough, in June 1950, hardly nine months after we arrived in Chicago the Korean War broke out as North Korea invaded South Korea, Dean Acheson, Secretary of State, largely responsible. He had delineated the absolute line of defense against Communist expansion in Asia, but did not include South Korea. Naturally the Communist Kim regime in North Korea assumed they could get away with a swift move, contrary to Stalin's wishes, and achieve a *fait accompli* to which no opposition other than the usual face saving protests would be mounted. Thus began the first of the many winless wars, expending lives and fortune to end up *status quo ante bellum,* an idiotic policy we continue.

Largely disarmed by Republican budget cuts and left with outmoded WWII weaponry, the United States and the United Nations troops were pushed back to the Pusan peninsula, humiliating defeat for the West, another triumph for the East. Our 2.8-mm antitank bazookas bounced off the Stalin tanks of Kim's troops like ping pong balls. We finally got 3.2-mm bazookas that could penetrate and nailed them. Our air force was at first ineffective, then became decisive. General Ridgeway's Inchon maneuver trapped the North Koreans and then drove them back to the Chinese border, which provoked Mao to infiltrate and then assault the United Nations forces back to the 38th parallel where things remain today.

But the real war was going on in the United States, not Korea. Since his speech in West Virginia in 1949 charging Communist infiltration of the State Department and other parts of the federal government, Senator Joseph McCarthy of Wisconsin unleashed a pent up outcry against the entire New Deal failed policy. Communism on the advance, Democracy on the defensive. Republicans denounced appeasement as Truman refused General MacArthur's request to bomb Chinese installations north of the Yalu River. Stalin was totally against the Chinese intervention and North Korean offensive, so when Truman through secret diplomatic channels warned Stalin that the US would use 'THE BOMB' on China if they didn't end hostilities and negotiate peace, Stalin lowered the boom and said he would not defend them if they didn't comply with Truman's request. Calls to nominate MacArthur for the Republican Party and support for MacArthur's request to bomb north of the Yalu, led to virtual hysteria in favor of nominating Mac to the Republican ticket in 1952.

We were involved to this extent. Bill Mott, Robert's Naval Academy roommate, came to the Naval Station in Chicago in 1951 to produce instruction films on military court procedure. My father was head of the Midwest Marine Reserve serving six states as the mobilization for Korea began. Many mafia capos came to visit him on behalf of their sons who wanted to get into the officer training program of the USMC. The Republican Party was dominant in the upper Midwest, a long tradition of Isolationism and America First had found resonance in the area. So when Mott was recalled to Washington in 1951 to accompany Admiral Radford to Asia for Truman's firing of MacArthur, we felt somewhat part of the show.

Firing Mac was equivalent to a political A-bomb. Rage! Consternation! A war hero 5-star General cut down by a Kansas City haberdasher sell-out UN toady President. Colonel Robert R. McCormick, owner of the Chicago Tribune, gave weekly lectures before Chicago Symphony broadcasts, which I listened to regularly. His choleric denunciation of Truman and the Democrat traitors in Washington rang throughout the Midwest and was joined by millions. MacArthur began his return to America (he had been out of the country since 1937!) to enormous acclaim, limousine parades down every city center, Chicago one of the greatest, where two million lined the streets waiting for his motorcade to Soldiers Field and his address to the Nation. I happened to be in that parade as member of the Amundsen High ROTC, marching with dozens of other similar units down Michigan Boulevard, glancing left to catch sight of the General, without success. Some are born great, some achieve greatness, and some have greatness thrust upon them. I didn't even get to see it.

In November 1950 we got the Sears Roebuck Christmas Catalog. Much excitement selecting possible gifts, an annual treat for millions of Americans from that iconic and now defunct bit of Americana. Precursor to online shopping, it had dishwashers and boots, bicycles and bee-bee guns. It had dresses and winter coats, bench tools and pajamas. All with photos and illustrations of seductive appeal, as these hats from the 1925 catalog, for the rural and urban lady of fashion. A beautiful corny charming period in the history of American retail magic. America!! Nothing like her.

Jim and Florrie Wells, members of a large and charming British expat community in Chicago, moved into the apartment below ours shortly after our arrival. A kind of Jack Sprat combination, Jim tall, lean, moustached and handsome and Florrie short, fat, unbeautiful and jolly, he in trim Savile Row and she in flowery large dresses. Incredibly generous, Jim gave me a complete set of mint Wagner Opera series stamps, the first stamps issued by the Hitler regime in 1933. He sold advertising for a trade magazine, traveling five states chain smoked, played Montevani records, drank gin and bourbon by the case and could stay up to 2 AM chatting. His English friends were like a cast from a '30's film. Ralph fit right in because he was a mixer. Robert bonded with Jim Wells over Harry Lauder records, both singing *'When I meet McKay and McKay meets me'*. Robert had served in Australia with British and ANZAC troops, so the bond went deep, a partnership of booze barbecue song and revelry.

I took piano lessons with Miss Stumpf, about 60-years old, pork pie hat with dotted veil, trim grey suit, bony sturdy hands and figure, echt Germanic, blue eyes, pale, wrinkled features, just about as far from Anastasia and Mrs. Carlson as you can get. The main advantage being that she came to our apartment, we didn't have to go to hers. No erotic imaginings to spark effort, I nevertheless respected her thorough approach. My first assignment was *Hark Hark the Lark,* by Schubert, on the presumption that I would play it at her annual student recital attended by admiring parents. This kind of accountability was new, alarming, almost disabling. It never occurred to me that I would ever have to play for anyone but the teacher and myself. I went along with *Hark* because she recommended it, I had no alternative in mind, and the way she played it made it sound interesting. Unfortunately, the more I tried to play *Hark* the less I liked it, and not liking something is an insuperable obstacle to success. After four vain weeks messing around with *Hark*, she replaced it with Mozart's *Turkish Rondo* something I really got into. It is a popular encore piece and many amateur pianists learn it by heart. I didn't, but I did get enough of it into my fingers to make a respectable stab.

I started lessons with Miss Stumpf in October 1949. The recital was scheduled for April 1950. It was held in a church gymnasium, folding chairs for the parents and friends, the victims seated in the first row in ascending order of Miss Stumpf's estimate of students' proficiency. I was about eighth of fourteen, the show moving from least advanced to most. The first five sounded much better than I thought I was, an alarming progression that rendered me nearly paralyzed by the time Miss Stumpf said: '*Thank you Miss Albers, and now please welcome Christopher Bowen, a student of only six months, who will play for you Mozart's Turkish Rondo.*' Terrified, moving on autopilot, I went the bench, sat at the grand piano and attacked at a faster tempo than usual but somehow managed to get to the first variation without mistakes or complete breakdown. I was stuck for a moment at the second variation, when Miss Stumpf quietly said D flat, which triggered what recollection I had of the piece and launched me into the rousing final cluster of fortissimo octaves. Big applause, I returned to my seat, as if falling breathless on the beach after an exhausting 400-meter swim. I paid more attention to the last few students who were astonishingly good. The last, her prize student, was so far as I could judge already concert level. He played Chopin's Polonaise op. 53, no. 6, in A flat major, a bravura display of technique, interpretation and virtuosity that was received by a standing ovation. Miss Stumpf didn't just teach piano, she produced artists. I was part of the post recital party where audience and students gathered for a buffet of treats and soft drinks, and was more or less included in the general adulation that greeted all of us students, but more relieved than exulted.

Alice was not impressed with Amundson High School. She felt more was needed and enrolled me in North Park Academy, a denominational day school presumably more academically rigorous. At Amundson, I signed up for Spanish, the only language listed, but was sorely disappointed. The teacher couldn't speak a word of Spanish and we in fact heard not a word of Spanish the entire year, with the exception of a few records of greatest hits. It was more a review of Spanish tourist sites, cultural features, and cursory history, plus an introduction to traditional Spanish costumes. In fact, I remember nothing of the slightest academic interest from the entire year at Amundson HS.

North Park was more academic, our Spanish teacher could speak Spanish and taught us the verbs, nouns, adverbs and grammar requisite to mastery. Geometry taught by a very tall lanky suit with thick glasses and a sour expression, though not old, was intelligible. He also taught Bible History, the only class in which I received an A. As a private school with some reputation, it attracted sons and daughters of affluent families living in Park Forest and north suburbs far from our apartment on Leavitt. I did attend a few parties at fellow student homes but contacts outside school were too difficult to be regular.

Tom Steinbock attended our Methodist Church. His parents, much like my mother, felt Amundson HS was not a suitable place for Tom and sent him to North Park Academy. In retrospect such parental involvement in their son's education seems incongruous. Tom's father was announcer for stock car races at Soldiers Field, comparable to auctioneer at a cattle sale, requiring no known academic achievement to succeed. As a result, we walked to school and back on weekdays and hung out on weekends. He was restless and quirky, obsessed with sex and seduction, but too homely and physically unprepossessing to make much headway in that direction. He had a friend, Bruce, God knows where or how they met, from Arkansas, 19-years old, who had a job as sheet metal worker at a Chicago plant. He owned a Hudson Hornet, and was a sex magnet, muscled, cute in an Audie Murphy way. We three hung out, greatly expanding our territory in the incredible Hudson (must have been one of the last in existence). Recollection is imprecise, but we did find girls who were interested in going to the local drive-in movie theater. Unfortunately for Tom, we often found the girls two at a time, girls' preferences and choices negotiated as subtly as possible to avoid offense to the losing male party, who invariably was Tom, I being much preferred by comparison. Bruce in the front seat, me in the back with our respective *amiga*, telling jokes, singing popular songs, the speaker hung on the front window, followed by heavy petting and kissing, greatly extending my list of partners and technique, although not reaching home plate.

My alternative hobby was stamp collecting. I often visited a stamp dealer in a commercial area not far from our house. He was American but seemed more European, talked a lot about Marshal Petain and other Vichy France personalities currently being tried for treason, the War and Hitler, and on and on but of interest since those subjects were new to me. Jim Wells gave me the Wagner Opera series of stamps, first postage stamps to be issued by Hitler in 1933, something that impressed the dealer. I always bought something with my paper route money, but he seemed to enjoy the company more than any purchases I might make, willing to chat as long as I did.

Chicago had three newspapers, the morning Sun Times and the afternoon Examiner and Herald Tribune. I had a paper route delivering the Sun Times, every morning up at 5 am, bicycle to the pickup shed six blocks away, take the 56 papers, and ride to my route about six blocks in another direction, collect in person every week for the subscriptions, all amounting to about $8.75 a week income. Terrific for building a work ethic, since ethics is about all you get for such monumental effort. But I didn't know enough to think of this as a disproportionate return on investment of my time and besides I needed the money, Robert's generous allowance of .50 cents a week barely able to cover my cigarette expenses. The route included several four-story apartment buildings, my subscribers usually on the third or fourth floor. I would throw the paper up to the respective floor with remarkable accuracy motivated by the unpleasant alternative of walking up as many flights, which I had to do when collecting, made worse if the client was not at home and second trip necessary. Such relentless and arduous dedication built character, not necessarily with regard to morality, but rather to persistence. I became a bulldog, never let go, never give up.

Winter mornings after a snow were magical. A blanket of unbroken snow covered the parks, front yards, streets. The streetlights provided a yellowish glow, the Moon spread silver magic over the large park fields, the quiet was deafening, no cars no snowplow nothing at 5 AM. Parks were flooded in winter to provide ice skating. In spring Chicago was stunning, rich green lawns and parks, blossoming trees in fresh vibrant green as well, blue sky, clean crisp air softened by the moisture from the Lake. Summers were warm but not often above 85 degrees, Lake cooling at night, long days, time for softball, swimming, playing catch. I love that city!

Political year began in 1952, a donnybrook of partisan rivalry, accusation, recrimination, confusion. Stevenson a domesticated animal against the great warrior Eisenhower, just cutting in ahead of the greater publicity hound MacArthur, a bit too presumptuous for the Republican establishment led by Ohio's Senator Taft. The Korean War was ongoing but headed for negotiations, Senator McCarthy was in full swing, the Midwest and especially Colonel McCormick was up in arms against the betrayers, commies, degenerates of the Roosevelt/Truman era, Soviet atomic bomb in 1951 traced to spies at Los Alamos, Containment or Liberation the debate about Eastern Europe, with communist advances in all European countries driving the move for NATO and other alliances to counter the Soviet moves worldwide. The Democrat convention was televised, the first time, and I remember FDR Junior in particular as an extremely well-tailored, elegant speaker. Stevenson photographed seated cross-legged with a hole in his shoe pretty much summarized the 'effete Democrat' argument against Democrats: don't let them cut the pie another four years for a total of 20 years since FDR's victory in 1932. Eisenhower ran on change and change is what we got.

So did Robert. He was assigned commander of the 5th Regiment 3rd Marine Division to report to Camp Pendleton in August. The Marine Corps was small. Three Divisions, 15 Regiments, 75 Companies, 225 platoons, combat command assignments amounting to 1 Lieutenant General Commandant, 3 Major Generals, 5 brigadiers, 15 Colonels, 75 Lt. Colonels or Majors, and 225 Captains, for which competition was merciless, the only ones that matter. Major Bowen commanded

3rd Batallion 1st Marine Division, at Guadalcanal, Lt. Colonel Chesty Puller the 1st Batallion, and Major Shoup the 2nd Batallion in the first counter assault against the Japanese. Having served in that campaign with Puller, the most decorated Marine in its history, and Shoup later Commandant drew special consideration. Each officer has a record established by annual fitness reports from commanding officers. Each officer knows personally all the other officers, and reputations lead to preferences. To be selected for a battlefield Regimental command places you in line for general grade. As close to military heaven as you can get, one of the chosen ones. The pressure to succeed is tremendous. And a Division commander has the right to approve or disapprove candidates for his subordinate officer positions. Major General Pepper commander of the 3rd Marine Division must have selected or approved of Robert.

We packed to go to California. I spent my last night in Chicago with a friend, Dave Tarnow, lying on the grass in Winnemac Park, talking about the future, me regretting leaving the great city, no idea what California would be like. Around 10 PM he had to head home, we shook hands, said 'See ya'. He then walked down Leavitt toward home. I watched him for a few minutes and then went in, sad, doubtful, anxious, and somewhat eager, accustomed to departures, leavings, partings with unknown meetings and adventures on the road ahead. I never saw Dave Tarnow again.

CAMP PENDLETON 1

I lived at Camp Pendleton August 1952 to July 1953, midway between Los Angeles and San Diego, at the tag end of the Korean War, but still very much in play. I attended Fallbrook High School. The cars were beautiful, the girls made your head spin. Sex was the target but love was the goal. I found love, many found neither. Poignant. All the hormones ideals lust hope in a stew pot of emotional transformation. I think of all the guys who died in Korea and a decade later in Viet Nam. All those dreams and longings buried in Korean dirt or Viet Nam mud. All the whiny teeny plangent songs and early R&R, Elvis just coming in, Everly brothers in the wings. Joyce de Leon from Louisiana who married a local mechanic swinging her lovely ass down the school corridor, open, free, uncomplicated, generous, friendly. Two classmates, one died the other shattered in car crashes, cars being the vector for tragedy and freedom. America! Nothing comes close, nothing can beat her, she is our destiny and our salvation.

A yellow school bus picked up six of us every weekday morning at 7:00 AM in front of the base movie theater located opposite the Officers Club. Hank our driver, at least 60, wore thick glasses that magnified his pale-blue vacant eyes like fish in a tank. He had close-cut gray hair and the mummified look of someone used to regular schedules and wordless repetitive work. His oversized plaid flannel shirt flapped as his thin bony hands worked the large steering wheel, the door crank, the yard high gear stick with the large black knob. Joyce de Leon swung onto the doorstep: '*Mornin' Hank. Ya'll drive carefully.*' She said that every day and our group laughed every day at the thought that this timid mute could ever do otherwise. Also, every day Hank looked momentarily perplexed, as if trying to think what he had done to lead her to conclude his driving involved significant risk. Hank presented problems of intellect, memory and comprehension. How can one be surprised by a remark heard every day, at the same time, from the same person? Is his memory reflexive rather than active, such that an interruption of the automatic performance of duty leaves him momentarily disoriented as if he had got on a bus for Des Moines and found himself in Istanbul. After the interval required for him to decide that Joyce's remark fell into the general category of jokes, a terrain he had never been tempted to enter, he rearranged his features into what must have been a smile, an expression to which he was so unaccustomed that he looked finally more pained than amused. Joyce would move down the aisle, swinging her hips, toward the back of the bus and thrust herself into a seat. We followed her, leaving six rows of empty seats toward the front of the bus.

We amounted to myself and five girls. Pricilla Allen, a senior, daughter of a Marine Colonel, Ellen Blake, a sophomore, whose father was a Navy doctor, and others I no longer remember.

Hank drove out of the officer residential compound onto the base highway headed for Fallbrook, past barracks, jeeps, and MPs snapping to attention as staff cars stopped at gates and checkpoints. Our antique yellow bus with Fallbrook School District in black letters on the sides and back, equipped with assorted red and yellow lights and stop signs flashing and flapping when Hank turned switches and pulled levers as we stopped at intersections, looked like some madcap circus vehicle bearing the King of Misrule through convoys of olive drab jeeps and trucks full of rifled Marines headed for maneuvers. Hank eventually left the built up base areas and headed across the rolling chaparral countryside toward Fallbrook. He stopped at the crossing of the rail spur that ran along the eastern limit of the base. He opened the door, looked and listened, shut the door, then drove the last five miles to the school. From September to June we never saw or heard a train. The base speed limit was 15 mph in built up areas and 35 mph elsewhere. Hank kept well within those limits, so the 25-mile trip to Fallbrook took nearly an hour.

Joyce turned up at Camp Pendleton last week of July 1952. Her father, Lt. Colonel De Leon transferred from Kinston North Carolina. The family was from Louisiana. Joyce had black hair, large brown eyes, a receding chin, loose full lips that suited her Southern drawl, and a kind of slatternly way of shifting emphatically from one hip to the other when standing or walking. I first saw her at the officers' pool. She wore a one-piece bathing suit that showed a well-endowed woman's figure that accentuated the swivel. She was 17, moved confidently, talked endlessly. I loved her, not for herself but what she represented that I could never be. We took part in Fallbrook High School activities--I played junior varsity football--and we were part of the social life, albeit at some inconvenience residing so far away. But we were nomads, had lived lots of places, and felt destined for better things. Joyce didn't seem to share any of these prejudices. She joined immediately the local student community. She looked completely at home wearing jeans and going around in cars with local guys. I first saw her driving with Leach, who quit school in December to work as a mechanic at the local gas station. With car, job and money Leach was a serious prospect in the avocado wonderland of Fallbrook society. He was driving when his car overturned and killed his friend Steve Bell a sophomore at the school. We didn't see much of Leach after that tragedy. I saw Joyce at the pool sometimes, but for the most part she wasn't part of base life. I did see her driving around with Leach. She looked like a Fallbrook local wrapped around Leach in the front seat, smoking, talking animatedly. She seemed to be at home cruising back roads, her back swing also looked more sassy. We all concluded she had by then 'gone all the way', a practice speculated on in theory but entirely beyond our confirmed experience.

In May 1953 I heard that Joyce and Leach had married. For some reason, that bothered me. I have no clear idea why. Joyce was not especially attractive. She had a good body but wasn't as lithe and toothsome as other girls. Maybe it's that she was uninhibited. She seemed to have discovered how to be happy with no more or less than what she was, where she was, with whom she was, ready to act on what she felt without reservation, calculation, or second thoughts. She had the courage of biological fitness which is spontaneous rather than the courage of conviction which is reflective. She seemed to enjoy present physical well-being unspoiled by concerns for the future. In China a boy had obtained some porn photos of a well-built Russian couple shown fucking, happily smiling, enjoying the gift God gave them. Maybe that's the kind of happiness Joyce reminded me of.

Coastal California in the 1950's was paradise. Dry, clean, baking heat moderated by ocean breezes, grapevines over lattices in patios and gardens, palms, Monterey pines, California oaks scattered over the Palomino-blonde hills, orange-blue-yellow Bird of Paradise and sweet-smelling honeysuckle, chaparral brush and wildflowers, a benign environment that made 360 days a year livable. San Diego and Los Angeles were separate, not the unbroken urban sprawl it became by the 1970's. Fallbrook had an asphalt county road that ran through town as the main street, all others were gravel over dirt. The High School was built in 1950, ranch style, corridors open to the outside, grape vine wooden lattices, rooms with wide windows, usually open, and two outstanding teachers, Mr. Ravn and Mr. Trask, who coached the tennis team. Mr. Ravn made no athletic claims, rather dressed every day in a tweed suit, dress shirt with tie, his right hand forefinger and middle finger stained dark yellow brown by cigarettes that he chain smoked when not in class. He looked like a cross between James Mason and Charles Boyer, dry baritone voice and engaging humorous style. One might expect on first impression that such an urbane sophisticated gentlemen would prefer an upscale large urban High School, not a provincial back water like Fallbrook. Shallow thinking. Teachers in California were well paid, and it is likely that Ravn and Trask received a 'hardship' bonus for working in a rural backwater. Admittedly there were intellectually challenged students, and the Indians were not working toward soaring prospects in the areas of law, finance, business. But most of the students were above average in IQ and ambition and responded well to academic instruction. The main thing was the teachers could buy marvelous houses and live extremely well with the prospect of handsome retirement and appreciating home values for the indefinite future. The chaparral brush made for a meal ticket every fall, when high school students and unemployed firefighters were hired to 'fight' the annual conflagrations in the State. Santa Ana winds from the scorched Valley came roaring across the foothills creating tinder conditions. California Department of Forestry, US Forest Service, and county fire departments hired seasonal firefighters and provided much welcome taxpayer-funded local income, enabling the agencies to justify substantial firefighting budgets and staff, supported by California Congressmen and State legislators whose constituents voiced frequent and emphatic support for the fire program, a perfect circle of advantage. About one in five 'wildfires' in California are arson, some of them started by prospective firefighters who want an earlier start to the fire season than Nature may intend. Anything that extends the season is acceptable to all parties and supported by the public whose homes and businesses are at risk in severe fire seasons. Firefighting was especially important to local Indian reservations.

Many Indians, most overweight, attended Fallbrook High School, providing heft to increase the lethality of the football team. Every Fallbrook male was on the team, about fifty boys, whose deployment from the dressing rooms of local High School competitors in Chula Vista, Escondido, Palomar and other towns took so long and amounted to so many opponents as to discourage our opposition, we hoped. I played wing back in a single wing formation. No great talent but I could run fairly well and keep my knees chopping through the line, making tackling more hazardous. At our only home game I was the hero, making two touchdowns and setting up a third. Few experiences are more addictive and elevating than public adulation. If you haven't experienced it you have no idea. To have people in the stands screaming 'Chris' and jumping up and down as I made a touchdown and win the game is indescribably tribal. The aftermath of girls' smiles and looks of admiration is an equally sweet post-game amplification of the event extending as far as the next game and new glories that supplant earlier ones. But the sheer thrill

Kennedyesque at 15-years old.

of acclamation is unforgettable. My career aspirations were taking shape. I subscribed to *Atlantic* magazine, having read a copy in the school library. How, why it got there I have no idea, unless Ravn, the most likely culprit, ordered it to provide a bit of New England Ivy League finesse to the California easy going view of things. I began to assimilate an 'Eastern' bias without any clear idea of how that should manifest itself. I was particularly obsessed with vocabulary, acquiring wordage to express with devastating precision and charm the thoughts I expected someday to acquire and share. I was equally dedicated to piano, having advanced under Miss Stumpf's instruction. We found a teacher in a neighboring town. Mr. Chastain lived in a ranch-style open-to-the-outdoors house on a level spot in the ambling hills of Vista, California. Lattices, grape vines, large patio off the main living room, bird of paradise, all the usual suspects. Dream house! He had a small grand piano, if that isn't an oxymoron, and an approach to instructing that irritated me in ways I could not then explain. Applying a later view to a past situation, I confronted the corrupting and demeaning influence of the notion that if something pleases many, it is as good as anything that pleases few. In theoretical terms, Hierarchy (quality ranked from superior to inferior) vs. Equality (no distinctions in value or quality). Under this program, the Supremes are as good as Mozart because they provide the same pleasure in music just to different, in fact many more, people. People are equal, ergo their preferences are equal. It is the bastard view of people who say *'I love all kinds of music.'* Such catholic taste (sic) is democratic but grossly wrong. Mr. Chastain had a book of 'concertos' reconstructed into simple chords and accessible keys. The general themes and melodies were retained but offered in versions easily accessible as compared to the original compositions. I preferred to play the authentic version less well than a travesty quite well. After three lessons we
discontinued the association.

My front teeth were knocked out in basketball practice when the coach had us dribble with eyes shut. Two Navy dentists stuck them back in place so no permanent damage was done. We had a local sheriff show a movie and discuss marihuana, its evil influence and consequences. A female itinerant instructor in sex education deployed by the State Board of Education used two white dolls to explain the process and warn about the evils of sexually transmitted disease. I worked as a lifeguard at the Officers Club pool, wives in bikinis, kids running around, nobody drowned. In May 1953, Major General Chesty Puller looking like a 5'6" bulldog, the most decorated Marine in its history, showed up at the club for a day. He had been fired by Truman for his comment to troops in Korea: *'I want a Congressional Medal of Honor if I have to kill every one of you to get it.'* Understandably unsettling their parents. He rose to Major General from the ranks so no varsity finesse impaired his fighting spirit or tempered his exhortations to valor. I overhead a girl say about me: *'I'd like him to rough me up.'* I did and she liked it as well as I did. I found a wallet in the men's locker room. Checked the contents to identify the owner. Found two photos of a hunky guy at least 18-years old in the driver seat of his car, his enormous thick 9-inch long dick fully engorged. The wallet belonged to an 11-year old kid, son of a Lt. Colonel. I returned it to the kid without comment. You just never know! In June we hosted a Fallbrook High graduation party for Priscilla Allen at the base. She was headed to University of Arizona in the fall. Classy and smelled so good on the bus I always tried to get a seat near her. A fairly jolly occasion at the club. A number of Indian girls from Fallbrook High, ugly fat, showed up with a 5th of bourbon, got drunk, and sat on the ground outside the club legs spread skirts pulled up, more or less inviting male attention. I thought of how whisky made winning the West from the Indians a lot easier. In August 1953 we moved to Tacoma Washington. To this day I have no idea what became of Joyce de Leon.

TACOMA 2

Robert had shipped out with the 3rd Marines to Korea and my mother, Linda and I returned to Tacoma, always a bad idea but driven by the hopeless irrational bond Gerda instilled in all her victims, I mean children. I attended Stadium High School, an impressive granite pile overlooking Puget Sound, with 12-foot ceilings, huge auditorium, football field, and remarkably talented teaching staff. Miss Pratt taught creative writing and public speaking. She had two competing students with opposite speaking styles, Doug Blankenship, light-brown curly hair, stout, sturdy, deliberate and good at algebra, and me, slender, animated in-your-face melodramatic speaking style and lousy at algebra, no deliberation in sight. Emotional irrational vs. rational logical. I had heard Hitler speeches and figured that in the short term on the spot with no future preference to inhibit commitment, the dramatic emotional appeal would win. It usually did, at least in terms of student reaction to my filibuster vs. Doug's laundry list.

By some total misunderstanding, I got into the Brock Scott trio, an inadequate attempt at forming a dance band, Scott on drums, me on piano and another guy I have forgotten on saxaphone. I was incapable of improvising, had to have written music in front of me even to have a slender chance of getting through a number. This restricted range of possibility meant we had to find songs I could play. Not entirely unworkable but almost. For the school talent show we arranged to play for the girls' chorus line *'Ain't Misbehavin'* for the musical accompaniment. My choice since I figured I could get through it more or less. We rehearsed, the girls singing while doing the can-can thing and other presumably provocative but well within the bounds of propriety steps. It came off pretty well to loud applause. My reputation as Mr. Music gaining a few notches on my piano bench. I also accompanied a friend for two solo pieces, *Moonlight in Vermont* and *St. Louis Blues*, including a pathetic piano riff whose deficiencies were overlooked or possibly unnoticed in the erotic swell of coed admiration. You could almost feel the 'fuck me' arousal of teeny bopper wild applause under the influence of male assertion. Flawed simulation of rock and roll concert acceptable absent the real thing. Gordon Trubshaw was the school MC, class comedian, and cynosure. A gifted ad-libber, fat and funny like Jackie Gleason, he had a complex life, orphan, skid row alcoholic age 15, recovered to return to high school, career goal, burlesque comedian leading to Big Time if lucky. He made a career in radio in Alaska, married Miss Alaska, and died happy in 1985. I met him at the Philatelic Society of Tacoma show in 1954. To my surprise he was an avid stamp collector, specializing in the US 1861 1-cent stamp. I remember him fondly.

Robert returned to Tacoma in January 1954, ruined, bitter, angry. Lyautey, Marshall of France, was asked, *What is the most important requirement for a successful military leader?* He answered: *De la gaîté, de la gaîté!* Robert was grim, fatalistic, angry, a deficiency hard to overcome. He was reassigned to Camp Pendleton, head of the Officers' Club, something equivalent to janitor in the 10-story edifice of combat Marine hierarchy. I stayed in Tacoma at my grandmother's house on Browns Point to finish my senior year and complete my application to Georgetown University.

CAMP PENDLETON 2

I finished my senior year at Stadium High School in Tacoma and returned to Camp Pendleton in June 1954, where my father, having failed miserably as Regimental commander in Korea, had been reassigned as head of the Officers' Club, not merely a demotion but a humiliation in the hermetic world of the Marine Corps. No dignity or prospect remaining, he applied himself to cultivate his ruin, while I, having to spend three months to September in this Eugene O'Neill family collapse hoped to get the Hell out in September and go to WDC and Georgetown. I worked (sic) again as lifeguard. A buxom blue-eyed blonde looking very Dutch with her bob haircut, a bit plump but not in any way disqualifying, got my attention. Nancy was daughter of a Naval Commander. She often babysat for the wife of an officer serving in Japan. How the wife got to stay in base housing is unclear to me. Perhaps her husband was on temporary assignment and expected to return to his regular assignment at Camp Pendleton. She apparently enjoyed a freelance love life often staying out all weekend with fugitive love interests. So Nancy stayed overnight with the kids she babysat. I got to dating her at the wife's quarters, no interference. Nancy liked to be stroked, spreading her legs and moaning appreciatively. I got to be buddies with David Laird, son of a Navy Captain, tall, intelligent, articulate, well-tanned and owner of a '41 Plymouth. The officers club had a combo Saturday nights. David and I would sit behind the combo drinking gin and tonics and enjoying the jazz. We also went to jazz spots in San Diego, once seeing Dave Brubeck and Chet Baker. We also went to Tijuana for a day, ate a grilled steak, turned down 75 offers for 'a good time', and returned unimpaired to the base. Summer over, I caught the Southern Pacific in Los Angeles heading East to Washington D. C and a new life, I hoped.

GEORGETOWN

I lived in Washington D.C. from September 1954 to August 1977, absent a little more than four years (September 1958-October 1962), two years in Grad school and two years in the Army. This was the period of Washington transformation from a temporary WWII encampment to permanent Imperial Capitol. The 1950's began with the Korean War. Eisenhower won the Presidential election in 1952. Earl Warren's Supreme Court overturned Plessy vs. Ferguson in a 1954 ruling that 'separate but equal' for segregated Black/White schooling was unconstitutional. Russia got the A-bomb in 1951, which gave credence to Joe McCarthy's claims of communist infiltration of the US Government, and Russia sent Sputnik to the Moon in 1958 sparking turmoil. Kennedy was elected President in 1960 and began vast expansion of federal agencies, their granite buildings and countless staffing crowded and at the same time diminished the former leisurely ambiance of a not especially efficient city. National aspirations for Education, Housing, Welfare, Smithsonian, National Gallery of Art, Kennedy Center, NASA all incarnated in glass and granite. Congress got a new office building as did the Library of Congress. One thing I most missed was the great electric trolley system, replaced by buses as part of the Eisenhower highway and GM-led (What's good for GM and its buses is good for America) push for lucrative increases in such oil consuming transportation. But the quietus came with the regional subway system constructed between 1964 and 1974, which dug up streets throughout the city and blocked access to downtown for a decade driving all the charming venues of diversion, arts, and dissipation to suburbs. At the end, Washington was a city of hustling careerists in over-priced housing and over-paid jobs headed no one knew quite where, much like the country at large. But I digress.

In 1954, military style barracks littered the Mall and the Tidal Basin, housing wartime bureaucrats in what were considered, mainly by Republicans, to be temporary and soon to be eradicated quarters. CIA had buildings along the Basin near the Lincoln Memorial and 15th street Bridge. The Navy Department had buildings in areas where the Viet Nam Memorial now stands. On the Mall, at the base of Capitol Hill, in front of the Department of Health and Welfare, wooden barrack-like buildings housed the overflow of bureaucrats from that agency. In short, the town was an unsightly mess. Eisenhower was elected in 1952 to put an end to New Deal aberrations in law and government expansion. The intention was to return to a place of Northern Charm and Southern Efficiency, eliminate the liberal, read socialist, encroachments of FDR/Truman drift away from American values. Though neither charming nor efficient, Washington was very interesting if you knew where to look and who to look for. I did and I did.

I left Los Angeles in September 1954 on the Southern Pacific passenger train headed for Chicago. Much of the scenery I had already seen on our family trips cross country to my father's new assignments in different locations as a Marine Corps officer. The passenger cars were well appointed with large wide windows making the overnight, seated, tolerable. The Porters' Union organizer was father of Congressman and Oakland Mayor Dellums, encountered two decades later. The arrogant Chicago-based Black porters made merry ignoring the White passengers in the dining car, snack bar, anywhere they possibly could until sufficiently generous tips were placed in the change tray. The Civil Rights movement was underway so this opportunity to lord it over White passengers was a fringe benefit they enjoyed immensely. In Chicago I visited family friends, Jim and Florrie Wells and Ralph Baumgartner, and our former neighborhood. Even had a chance encounter with a girl from our former church, one I had once felt up without much resistance in the choir cloak room. She asked what I was doing and was impressed or perhaps annoyed that I was headed in a relatively promising direction. For an instant I flattered myself that she was looking regretfully back to that cloakroom 'no', when a 'yes' might have led to better prospects now. You can't go home again as I learned again and again. After two days of old times, I took the Baltimore and Ohio passenger train to Washington D.C. I arrived at Union Station carrying a large suitcase containing a Robert Hall dark grey suit with an extra pair of light gray trousers, more appropriate to less formal occasions, but totally unsuited as it were to the Brooks Brothers world I was about to enter.

Unpleasant experiences have to be interesting or consequential to be remembered in detail, so memory of my struggle by streetcar from Union Station to Georgetown and the eponymous University, focus of my aspirations for a foreign service career, consultation with a welcoming advisor as to accommodations available, and eventual placement in a room with bath but no kitchen in a narrow townhouse near Wisconsin Avenue is at best cursory. Once settled in my depressingly furnished room, I called old family friend Rosemary Mott, referred to as Romey from now on, who lived in a large elegant three-story manor house in Chevy Chase, the residential locus of corporate and political power elites in the Nation's Capitol, fittingly close to the equally prominent Chevy Chase Country Club, a playground for teas, dining, dances, events, and political deal making at the highest and most enviable level.

If you weren't a member, you had no opportunity to share weekend golf, party, and other forms of leisure with the movers and shakers that make a mockery of Civics courses taught in High Schools, totally accurate as to the formal structure but totally misleading and erroneous as to the reality of power politics in the United States.

My father graduated from the Naval Academy in 1933, of which branch of the military, FDR, former Undersecretary of the Navy in WWI and a devoted civilian sailor, was especially fond. I have a photo of FDR and the graduates in dress whites at the impressive setting. I can't spot Robert Oliver Bowen in the blur of white tunics, but rest assured he was there. Only half his class was commissioned, due to the Depression and cuts in Military budgets. Robert an average student ranked near the middle of grade distribution, but sufficiently above the mean to make the cut. For reasons largely emotional, he joined the Marine Corps instead of the Navy, an ineradicable tendency to seasickness being a more socially acceptable explanation. To give up the stunning dress whites and blues of a Naval officer would be inconceivable otherwise. Bob's roommate was William Chamberlain Mott, as unlikely a pairing of opposites as might be imagined. Mott was from New Jersey with prominent family connections. He was 6'1", presentable looks, fit and loquacious, ambitious and amorous. Poor Bob was an uptight, very fit, 5'7", dogged student, with not much imagination, a lot of subdued anger, no social aspirations and very narrow ambition to be a 'Marine', with all the death-wish emotional baggage that can entail. Mott wasn't commissioned partly because he was severely near sighted and wore thick classes, a useful excuse for disqualification in times of austerity and cutbacks. Robert went on to marry, serve on General MacArthur's staff in the Philippines, and train for the Guadalcanal landing, where he served as a Major, 3rd Battalion commander of the 1st Marine Division.

Mott pursued a less risky and much more rewarding course. Naval career at least temporarily denied, he attended law school at George Washington University, simultaneously engaged in diligent pursuit of coeds at prominent women's colleges. Daughters of business and political, elites were suitable pickings and having some social credentials of his own, provided Mott a deer park in which to flex his powers of attraction. Rosemary Sutherland Baker (Romey) attended Sarah Lawrence College, fell madly in love with Mott, and they were married in 1938. Her father died when she was 3-years old. Her mother remarried John Watson Morrell whose brother, a Gulf Oil executive, served as executive liaison to the Undersecretary of the Navy for oil procurement. Since the Navy ran on oil, he was a major player in the FDR defense administration.

With power comes privilege. Through this contact, Mott was commissioned in the US Navy as a Lieutenant and assigned to the White House as personal aide to FDR himself!! In later years, as a public speaker for rent, Mott invariably told the story of when he was pushing FDR's wheelchair and got stuck near some filing cabinets, whereupon FDR said: *'Young man, are you trying to file me?'* Winston Churchill's White House visit in 1943 provided material for embellishment of Mott's role, its importance not explicitly claimed but sufficiently implied for his audience to draw inaccurate but flattering conclusions about Mott's contribution to ultimate victory. Such anecdotes gained him lucrative invitations to speak at Rotary and other venues throughout the country, a much needed income supplement as it turned out. In 1947, he and

Romey divorced, she receiving $200 month in alimony and child support, derisory today but sufficient then to impose a major burden on Mott's Navy income. He hustled for advancement as member of the Navy Judge Advocate General (sic) staff, and later became Judge Advocate General, a one star Rear Admiral position. In 1951, Mott accompanied Admiral Radford to witness Truman's firing of General MacArthur, another source of anecdotes for his burgeoning public speaking career.

All this by way of explaining how I was rescued from tenement oblivion by Romey. I said a while back that after settling into my room, I called her. She drove to Georgetown, immediately settled with the landlady, recovering my initial payment, and brought me to their Chevy Chase mansion. Far more significant, her mother, Mrs. Morrell, as member of the Sulgrave Club, that epicenter of Social Register/Wives of Prominent Politicos events and causes, learned that Miss Janet Fish, an American aristocrat if ever was, wanted to take on a student roomer in her Georgetown townhouse, presumably to provide security to assuage her elderly (then 71-years old) paranoia regarding imagined threats of burglary and mayhem. Upon Mrs. Morell's recommendation I became a tenant in Miss Fish's very compact 1100-square feet townhouse at 1624 32nd Street Georgetown: two bedrooms, one shared bathroom (a source of some tactical challenges) upstairs, a small garden patio off the living/dining room, and a slot kitchen downstairs. A large old farting Labrador, in constant and unsuccessful territorial competition for proximity to the fireplace with a scruffy fat cat, completed the family portrait.

Miss Fish (1883-1970), no one ever called her Janet, was a member of one of the most distinguished families in American History. Her ancestor Nicholas Fish served with Alexander Hamilton in the Revolutionary War. In admiration for his distinguished friend, Nicholas named his son Hamilton, a first name handed down generation by generation ever since (still ongoing!) in the Fish family. Nicholas married Elizabeth

Stuyvesant, descendant of Peter Stuyvesant, Dutch Colonial governor (1665) of New Amsterdam, adding quadrants to the family crest. Miss Fish's grandfather, Hamilton Fish, served as Secretary of State under U. S. Grant. His distinguished career included completing terms of the Alaska Purchase with the Russian Imperial government, then destitute for cash to pay for French railroad construction to bring Russia up to European standards. Allan Nevins wrote a biography of the Secretary, a copy of which Miss Fish placed prominently on her living room coffee table. As an aside, several Russian *Knyaz,* translated roughly as Prince, but more like Count as to number and prominence, accompanied the Russian delegation to negotiate the Alaska purchase, including Knyaz Cantecuzene who married US Grant's daughter in 1880. I worked with their grandson in a Russian intelligence unit of the Defense Intelligence Agency in the 1960's. Seven degrees of separation indeed!

But back to Miss Fish. She had an aura of *noblesse* that inspired an involuntary impulse to curtsey or bow in deference, without any outward title or position that might trigger gestures of subordination. One felt deferential and protective of this elegant and beautiful woman. A central casting aristocrat/patrician, tall (5'11") lean, invariably in a black dress extending to her ankles, with black lace up boots, her only adornment a gold *pince nez* on an equally thin gold chain around her neck. She was a bit near-sighted and tended to tilt her head backward as if to focus when speaking, her beautifully arched nose, even brow, somewhat pinched mouth exuding class and privilege and natural superiority without any sense of condescension or self- importance. She also stooped forward a bit given her height when addressing people of average stature. She was kind, gracious, seemed slightly bewildered at times given her age and slower synaptic processing of incoming impressions. Her voice was aspirate and firm, louder than required, mainly because her hearing was somewhat impaired so she spoke as much to make her voice audible to herself as audible to the person she was talking to. On the phone she was even louder given her anxiety that she might not be heard if she diminished the volume of her already amplified normal voice. Also, she had been head nurse for twenty years requiring exceptional vocal power to be heard and obeyed. Miss Fish came of age in the late 1800's when phones were still a novelty in domestic life. People at first thought they had to shout into the speaker in order to propel their words to the destined end of the line. She would most be suited to a mid-Victorian setting, a period in which her family in upstate New York were well established among the Stuyvesant, van Rensselaur, van Buren and other Dutch patriarch families, to include the Roosevelts and Delanos, all of whom were neighbors. Washington Irving immortalized their mores customs and attitudes, van Winkle being a satirical poke at any pretentiousness they may have acquired. Much of their wealth came from land and land speculation as well as the Clipper Ship trade with China and other lucrative sources of income.

FDR's father made his fortune during ten years in Shanghai as a member of a trading company, accounting for FDR's love of China and hatred of Japan. These patrician families took months-long holidays on the Continent, lived in affluent but diligently improving disciplined leisure, supported cultural institutions and acquired valuable paintings and other paraphernalia to adorn their spacious mansions in the City and the Hudson River Valley. FDR spent much time in Germany and other parts of Europe as his parents traveled extensively throughout Europe. The Fish progeny spent much time in schools in Germany and Switzerland.

Miss Fish's younger brother, Hamilton Fish (1888-1991), Harvard Law graduate, earned a Silver Star and the French Croix de Guerre for valor in WWI. Ham (as he was called within family circles) was 6 feet tall, weighed 200 pounds, and presented a challenge *mano a mano* to most men he dealt with. He was elected to Congress 1920-1944, a prominent Republican Congressman. He worked with Speaker of the House Longworth, a notably heavy drinker and womanizer, to investigate communist infiltration of US labor unions. Longworth married Alice Roosevelt in 1906, last daughter of Teddy, a social star for whom the song, *Alice Blue Gown* was written, a few years after the 'Teddy' (Roosevelt) Bear made its appearance. Alice much later became a regular guest at Kennedy's White House dinners. Noted for her stiletto wit, she once told another guest: *'If you can't say anything good about anybody, come sit by me.'* Ham Fish became a scourge of the New Deal in the 1930's, its Satanic leader and near neighbor FDR, and everything his treachery to his class had led to. FDR's famous taunt of *'Martin Barton and Fish'* in the kickoff to his 1940 campaign for re-election made Fish a National pariah, in part for his sympathy for Lindberg and Isolationism regarding the war in Europe. His objection to US entry into another European War was well justified given his war-time combat experience of blasted bodies and the evident failure of the war to achieve lasting peace as once hoped. Why repeat the same mistake? However, after Pearl Harbor he was as patriotic as any in supporting the war effort. Ham Fish promoted anti-lynching legislation in the 1940's and civil rights legislation in the 1950's after he left Congress. A bit of a curmudgeon, in 1986 his grandson Ham V ran for Congress as a Democrat so Ham III actively opposed his election, calling him a communist.

Miss Fish was as formidable character as her brother. She volunteered as nurse on the front lines in WWI. Like her brother, she received the Croix de Guerre and was inducted into the French Legion of Honor for valiant service at war hospitals in Nogent-sur-Marne and Biarritz. Edith Wharton and Henry James also received such honors by the way. Legend has it, like most legends based more on gullibility than proof, Miss Fish had a love interest abruptly terminated in the Battle of the Somme, where her swain was obliterated by a German artillery barrage, providing a fitting, touching and certain end to any further, if indeed there had been any former, moves toward matrimony on her part. Miss Fish pursued a post-war career as nurse, first at St. Mark's Hospital in New York City and later as head nurse (well prepared by dealing with blood and guts in WWI) at Emergency Hospital in Washington D.C. where she served nearly 20 years before retiring to 1624 32nd Street, my new home away from home. She never married, but at the time I stayed in her townhouse she was dating Senator Green from Connecticut, more a social than amorous pairing, both at an age to preclude any marital urgency or search for shotguns. The concept of devoted love for a lost lover persisting to death was generally accepted in Victorian times, since the queen herself wore black ever after Alfred's demise and of course never remarried. Miss Fish had an elevated position in the New York Social Register and often served as chaperone at dinner dances and comings out, including the coming out ball given around 1921 for Clare Booth, described by Miss Fish as the most beautiful debutante she had ever seen. Capable and ambitious, Clare wrote for fashion magazines, wrote a popular play made into a movie in 1939, *The Women,* with Norma Shearer, Joan Crawford and Rosalind Russell, and eventually married Henry Luce of *Time/Life/Fortune* fame and influence. She also served as a Member of Congress and later as Ambassador to Italy, where she succumbed to an illness finally traced to poisoning from lead paint on embassy windows rather than Soviet sabotage as first reported.

In contrast to the pre-Civil War landed fortunes of Miss Fish and family, Romey and her Morrell family came from the post-Civil War Industrial stage of aristocratic formation in America, when entrepreneurs formed corporate empires: Vanderbilt/railroads, Carnegie/steel, Rockefeller/oil, JPMorgan/banking and finance, Mellon/Alcoa and Gulf oil, the latter being the economic pyramid within which Morrell fortunes were made. The managers and legal firms that served and represented these corporate megaliths provided an extended family of wealth and influence closely interwoven in a web of clubs, schools, colleges, vacation homes (e.g., Newport Mansions), thoroughly covered in the novels of Henry James and Edith Wharton. Miss Fish and Romey, daughters of divergent generations of America's elite, were necessarily dissimilar in character if not in advantages. The graceful and effortlessly imposing Miss Fish was not in the least comparable to the energetic decisive and assertive style of Romey. Miss Fish exuded quiet authority, gaining voluntary compliance. Romey and her like lacked that imposing presence and fought for every inch they intended to take. Think of Kate Hepburn as a prototype of the thrusting privileged society girl of the 1920-1950's. Despite individual distinctions, Romey and her generation shared a common ability to articulate opinions of which they had many, and deal with any situation or person with assertion and only faintly veiled command. This strong ego endowment and the fact that she was an only child made Romey a marvelous committed friend and a formidable temperamental adversary. She tended to impose her way unless insistently opposed, and tolerated opposition not well.

She and Mott confronted each other once too often and he decided to divorce her in 1947, ending their11-year marriage. The settlement ran in her favor. She kept the children, and he paid alimony and support as explained above. But the disadvantage and perhaps explanation of the assertive character of upper class girls was that they were still excluded from careers and professional aspiration, having to employ all their ability and talent in striving for the success of their husbands. Husbands favored docile submission. They were unprepared for active intrusion in the ups and downs of their business and family decisions. Problem was that Mott probably married her more for the social and political advantages her family offered and was not tolerant of her persistent directions on career, social and family matters. Romey never got over the humiliation of divorce and Mott's continuing success largely empowered by the entrée her uncle provided him. Gnawing resentment led her to drinking and sexual adventures sometimes involving Chevy Chase police who were mainly trained to discretely extricate their distinguished residents from the undistinguished circumstances into which on occasion they fell. Under the influence, Romey would cruise the streets in search of ready and willing males often to be left .03-alcohol content passed-out in her car, police then calling her mother to rescue the prodigal daughter. I remember an occasion when I accompanied her to pick up her son Adam who was attending an evening dance party at Sidwell Friends School. We were parked in a secluded area. She sat sideways in the driver's seat with her knees up and legs parted as if to invite advances preliminarily acceptable. Such a departure from the decorum of loyal family friend helping son of absent parents was a bit disconcerting for me at 16 years. More intelligible in retrospect than at the moment of encounter.

In September 1954 I moved into 1624 32nd Street and began my freshman term at Georgetown School of Foreign Service. Why and how Georgetown? Without getting too autobiographical, my father at no point helped me select and evaluate career choices. More obstacle than helper, he left me to my own devices which were mainly intuitive. If I heard about something promising I readily explored it. But the precise sequence that led to choosing a career in the Foreign Service is unclear. My choice of Georgetown School of Foreign Service (SFS) was more or less obvious since the school itself was eponymous with my career preference. The Student Counseling library at Stadium High School in Tacoma, Washington, my fourth and final high school, inexplicably had a two-year old course catalog from Georgetown SFS. How it got there, who might have ordered it remain a mystery, but the fact that it was there simplified selection. Every other college or university could offer courses consistent with a target career in Foreign Service but that would require post-admission counseling to establish. Georgetown SFS catered directly to my objective and so I applied. Once mentioned, my father asked a friend in the Foreign Service what he thought of Georgetown. He replied that Georgetown was good, but Princeton or Harvard would be better. Not a flaming endorsement but sufficiently favorable to assuage any misgivings as to the school. Robert assumed I would attend the Naval Academy as he did based on no consultation with me. Probably because it would be free, whereas the $650 annual tuition at SFS was a subject of well dramatized concern, an economic disbursement possibly threatening family viability.

Location was an advantage hard to overlook. Being in the Capitol City close to international action offered opportunities remote institutions could not match. The Jesuit founder of Georgetown University, Father Healy, certainly proved prescient in deciding to place his college within the new Federal District of Columbia at the official beginning of the new United States of America in 1789. The often complicated controversial and sometimes dubious history of the Jesuit Order would require volumes without leading to anything conclusive, like the truth, which was well concealed by Vatican proscription of access to pertinent historic records. Even the Pope disbanded the Order at one point. In its post WWII version, the Jesuit Order was ruthlessly anti-Communist, hated FDR for the most part, and was relieved when finally a reliable Republican took office. It engaged a number of East European academics noted for their anti-communist past, a prominent example being Jan Karski, Polish underground activist and rabid anti-Communist who enjoyed a lucrative speaking career describing the horrors of Stalinist repression.

I had a banal mostly Methodist religious upbringing. Catholic churches felt foreign, opulent, too many statues, genuflections, too much scent, peculiar robes, beads, Saints, odd rites. Initially, Anglo-Scottish Catholics in the United States, many former Stuart partisans, settled in Colonial Maryland. Only after the Potato Famine of the 1840's, did large numbers of Irish Catholic immigrants settle in New England and New York. Descendants of the lace curtain Irish began to dominate police and fire departments, political ward heeling, and of course the Church. In New England they ranked only slightly higher than Negros. Most of the Jesuits at Georgetown were Irish. The Jesuit order was founded in 1565 by Ignatius Loyola, a military officer in the army of the Spanish King. The military Jesuit order, called the Society of Jesus, led the counter-reformation against Protestant apostasy in Europe, introducing the Baroque style to enrich the visual experience of benighted adherents. The order remained austere, plain long black robes with a Mandarin collar, often with a sword dangling at the side. The formation of a Jesuit took fourteen years, time to test his calling and learn a secular profession to be pursued 'in the real world', even as religious duties were fulfilled. Jesuits became the intellectual elite of the Church and active agents for conversion and advancement of the Catholic ethos among the common people, often wearing suits and secular duds. *Ad Maiorum Dei Gloriam* (AMDG) was their motto. Georgetown became the Western Hemisphere academic pole star of Hispanic America, a purview often overlooked by citizens of North European derivation. Sons of leading oligarchs in South America attended Georgetown College. They were obscenely rich, poised, confident and well spoken, comfortable and capable to take charge and assume leadership. They had close ties to the monarchist elite in Spain, viewing Franco's victory in the Civil War as a sign of Divine favor toward the ruling class. The traditional bond of upper clergy of the Church, selected from elite families, and State rulers reinforced their superior position among the Indian and Mestizo population, the middle class of lawyers and businessmen a consenting partner. Only after WWII did the illiterate lower clergy from the peasant population begin to oppose the abuse and exploitation of the Indian/Mestizo underclass.

My direct association with the Latin American elite was Howard Herrera, scion of a prominent Venezuelan family, beneficiaries of the oil bonanza in that country. Howard lived in a large apartment in Georgetown, had a monthly allowance of $5000, equal to the annual income of a Lieutenant in the Marine Corps, and flew to Madrid most weekends, Friday to Monday, to enjoy dances/dinners/parties with his Spanish aristocratic friends. He was portly, good looking, more Goth (blonde/pink) than Latin, as many elite Spaniards are, generous, friendly, all expressed in immaculate English. He attended classes under a specially prepared schedule that accommodated his travel and social commitments. Education was more like an indulgence for which he paid tuition and generous donations to the Order, which in turn assured him its of form of absolution, a Bachelor's degree. Jesuits and the Catholic Church at large understood the powerful and provided every accommodation required to secure and reward their favor. For example, granting to a Kennedy clan member an annulment of a 4-year marriage that produced three children is an example of how the unattainable for many is readily available for the privileged few.

My vague understanding of the life of Catholic clergy largely centered on celibacy, an unattractive obstacle to a life of service. I learned that Jesuits at Georgetown lived remarkably well, despite the vows of poverty and abstinence. Affluent parents of students often visited the campus, inviting Jesuits to gourmet dinners and chat at the Golden Peacock among other very high-end restaurants. The Jesuits were personable, capable and at times inspiring. Father Schlesinger, dean of the College, was an athletic energetic German exception to the Irish prevalence. Fun to be with, a great sense of humor. Father Fadner, melodramatic dean of the SFS, swept through the halls with black biretta, flourishing his black robes, head held back, squinting down nose, gimlet-eyed through rimless *pince nez* at students who were more amused than intimidated. He taught Russian History as though living every moment of it, striding restlessly from side to side, delivering a Shakespearian monolog in an astonishing variation of cadence tempo and volume. His stature in the Jesuit Order and the Vatican was immensely elevated as he was somehow involved with TV priest Fulton Sheen in the 1946 conversion of Clare Booth Luce, wife of ***Time/Life/Fortune*** Henry, an accomplishment in the ranks of Catholic hierarchy equivalent to winning the Congressional Medal of Honor. Father Horrigan, Plato reincarnate, taught Philosophy Ancient and Modern, calm measured in voice and manner, eyes always seemingly fixed on distant perfection, moral and intellectual. Father Bryzinski, a Polish departure from the Irish predominance, energetic, enthusiastic, believed in total passionate commitment to the work of the Lord, no anomie permitted. On the secular side of the faculty, Carroll Quigley stood out. Boston Irish, youngest PhD in Harvard history, superb public speaker, ferocious intellect, every lecture a firestorm of ideas, dramatic gestures, provocative conclusions. Polymath, advisor and lecturer at the War College, author, consultant to Congressional Committees, once known never forgotten.

But there was more to Washington than Georgetown. Theater was remarkably varied. Theater Lobby, in a large garage near Dupont

Circle, folding metal chairs along the walls, offstage for actors was in the alley adjacent, gave a start to, among many others, George C. Scott then serving his last gig in the Army. Many extremely capable actors performed *The Madwoman of Chaillot, Macbeth, Lysistrata,* scrambling to avoid the feet of onlookers who were ravished by the proximity which augmented rather than diminished the dramatic effect. National Theater was the big daddy, offering pre-Broadway productions of *Long Day's Journey into Night* and even a Carol Channing show. Arena Stage was then a start up in the upper story of a Foggy Bottom warehouse, 15-step outdoor staircase to get to the show. Much later management constructed a new ample theater in the round nearer the Capitol, now a prominent and well attended veteran venue where I saw an *Iceman Cometh* with Robert Prosky and a number of other later Hollywood actors.

What really mattered was girls, entertainment, and night life. Until 1964, all roads led to Rome. WDC was the only action in the entire region. Suburbs were being built and occupied, Reston and Seven Corners in Virginia, Tacoma Park in Maryland, but downtown WDC had everything one could want. On weekends, students from outlying colleges and even High Schools (beer drinking legal at 18) came downtown to the movie theaters and rock and roll bars. Women's colleges and nursing schools held dances open to college male talent, Visitation and a few other Catholic colleges for women among them. The only problem was well summarized by the account of a Georgetown College student. He had gone on a date with a Visitation girl, things got hot and she said: *'I'll blow you, but I'm saving my pussy for my husband.'* This perplexed me at several levels. Number one, I hadn't advanced to or even contemplated the terrain of oral sex. It may have been mentioned in connection with queers and such deviants, but not as an alternative to heterosexual coition. That a college girl in 1954 would even suggest such a possibility was extremely exciting, much less raise the matter of her pussy in such unambiguous terms. I had not heard about oral, except in connection with 'queers' and certainly not with girls. Offering oral as substitute for intercourse implied that intercourse was perfectly acceptable in general but not in her case in particular. Additionally, how many at Visitation were eager for what had been forbidden fruit? Let me at 'em. Most contacts with college girls were involuntarily aspirational, surrounded by impediments (curfews/chaperones/lack of a venue to carry out intentions).

G-girls were another matter. WDC attracted high school girls from a number of states to government clerical jobs. Pay was modest so they tended to room together, three to five per apartment. They went out on weekends together. All were looking for husbands, sometimes willing to make offers hard to refuse. They were attractive, intelligent if not formally educated to a high degree, but with the female cunning and awareness of the mating game, much like Annie in Get Your Gun, *'doing what comes naturally.'* Usually they matched up with high school boys who like themselves came to WDC from the same background for jobs, but they weren't disinclined to attracting college boys who came within target range. Their free-wheeling approach was not something I was accustomed to, perhaps others were.

My education in this matter advanced substantially on a Saturday evening with a fellow student at a bar popular with G-girls about whom we often speculated but had not yet encountered. I started a conversation with a trio of very attractive girls at a table across from us. They differed from college girls, not so much in the fundamentals, but in their more casual and flirting, coy and teasing style of conversation. Several intermediate steps were summarily disposed of, the banter and suggestive stage set in early. What made it more challenging was a pair of male students from another college, equally interested and willing to compete to obtain favor from the same three girls. To some extent it was an intercollegiate contest between two schools, as much as a personal contest between two horny males locking horns. I had for no particular reason attracted girls fairly often. I was more the seduce-compliance than overcome-resistance type, rather reticent tender and tentative at first, allowing her to step forward, take initiative emotionally. I was good looking, at least above average, but not conceited, rather the opposite, seeming to be unaware of any special advantage in appearance I might enjoy.

My opponent was not particularly good looking for which he compensated by an energetic flow of conversation, laughter, and even aggressive attitudinizing toward me. Under my seemingly unemphatic style lay a ruthless will to dominate competitors by guile and calculation beyond the normal degree available to persons like my opponent, at least in the short term. Elevator wit is all very well, but misses the occasion in which it might matter. So the contest went along for some time, he seeming to make an impression based entirely on loud assertiveness, and I checking his advantage by being more appealing and sympathetic. All the while I was thinking how I would like to annihilate this guy by indirection. The girl I was interested in was very lovely, articulate, and possibly thinking long term. My opponent had all the characteristics, and character for that matter, of a one-night-stand college buff. I looked more meditative and sincere perhaps, easier to start an equal and lasting relationship without risk of presumptuous advances. Most women once reassured are willing to express their desires. For some reason she seemed to like me and be willing to advance to a more intimate association. In the end, I defeated the homely frat boy, returned to the girl's apartment. I said I would like to take a shower. She directed me to the bathroom, past the bedroom of her room-mates, who checked me out. When I returned, my girl was in bed in a nightgown and evidently prepared for the 'worst', in fact inviting it. I had never won victory unopposed. That made it as much a surprise as a delight. No obligation or promises of further meetings on departure, entirely amicable. Does this happen every weekend? I had no idea!!! Another venue for meeting G-girls was the very large well-appointed YMCA downtown near 15th Street. Its top floor had a large rooftop 'ballroom' where dances to a small band were held under YMCA supervision. Girls wore dresses, their Sunday best, as did the male clientele. I met a beautiful girl from Virginia, employed at the Interior Department, spontaneous wholesome, to die for. I dated her as often as my means allowed, never a prurient moment, chaste and devoted love with nowhere to go. I would have married her, but I had no job, no degree, no idea what to do other than sell shirts at *Woodward & Lothrop* for minimum wage. Eventually I had to withdraw.

One advantage to living in WDC is the opportunity to see some of its famous inhabitants. I never saw Eisenhower. No regrets. I did see Truman at a Minnesota-Wisconsin football game in 1959, notable mainly for a unique event in Collegiate football history. A Minnesota player intercepted a Wisconsin pass and then inexplicably and to roars of anguish from Minnesota fans in the stadium, which he must have mistaken for approval, ran in the wrong direction and crossed the Minnesota end zone thereby scoring a touchdown for Wisconsin, the rule being that the position of the ball not the uniform of the ball carrier determines the scoring. I also saw Kennedy, Johnson, and Nixon completing my Presidential score card. In March 1963, Haile Selassi, the Emperor of Ethiopia, visited WDC on a State visit, largely a show for Cold War one-upmanship. Selassi was a Western supporter as opposed to the increasing number of Soviet-supported African governments in that tribal wracked continent. Support is a euphemism for paid-for client, but why dwell on details? Jack and the Emperor were in the back seat of a topless limousine. Jack in blue suit and Kelly green tie standing, waving, and smiling, looked like a Greek God come down to see how his worshippers were doing, beautifully tanned, large white teeth, shining abundant golden-brown hair. The inimitable youthful manner compared with Selassi, seated, dressed in a khaki tunic completely covered in medals so heavy he couldn't stay up if he stood, 81-years old, like a tobacco-brown desiccated mummy, decrepit as compared with the President next to him. I was right on the curb as they passed by, no more than fifteen feet away and no Secret Service in sight. Amazing to see. I also saw Bobby riding with Adam Clayton Powell, both creeps, Ed Murrow, as furrowed and worrisome as ever, Bob Dole in his limo, and the Chief Justice Berger riding in a horse drawn carriage at 7:30 AM on the Mall rehearsing some Supreme Court anniversary event. But the one encounter that remains like a snapshot indelible in my mind that I cannot download is a vignette from June 1958. I was crossing the square in front of Dahlgren Chapel directly behind the original Healy main building (1789). I saw five persons walking slowly toward the chapel. If I could summarize in one photo the power nexus of the United States, absent the President, it would be with this image. In order, the persons were Clare Booth Luce Ambassador to Italy elegantly tastefully dressed, Father Fadner Dean of SFS with a Cheshire grin at an additional triumph about to be confirmed, John Foster Dulles Secretary of State stooped and looking weighed down, appropriate to an international position in which showing any sign of victory or even satisfaction is impolitic and likely to arouse resentment, Henry Luce owner of *Time/Life/Fortune* Homburg-hatted and projecting total control of everything around him, and Allen Dulles Director of the CIA also Homburg-hatted, a dandy at heart, projecting prominence, perhaps deserved, in a swagger to be admired, perhaps the wink in his eye recalling the time he topped, as it were, Henry when he bedded Clare. Perhaps on no other occasion would this quintet have appeared together. And in a tenuous but arguable way it was appropriate that I, insignificant by comparison, made it a sextet. For one thing, I rented a room from Miss Fish, chaperone at Clare's coming out ball, from whom I heard my first reference to the Ambassador. Further, Henry and the Dulles brothers were sons of missionaries in China and India respectively, a territorial link in so far as I had lived in Qingdao and attended school with missionary children. The five of them were going to Dahlgren Chapel to witness John Foster junior's final vows and ordination as a Jesuit, abetted by Father Fadner who was involved obliquely Clare's conversion and in whose class I was a student. Tenuous connection I admit, but what the Hell, take what you can get. A footnote to this encounter with greatness came not long after. I was walking down a sidewalk at Dupont Circle about 5 PM when Dean Acheson, former Secretary of State, came walking toward me, an undeviating image of the endless photos and TV footage that covered his historic past, dressed in frock coat, gray striped trousers, spats, and ascot tie, the iconic moustache waxed and saucy, his look a bit downcast perhaps for being on foot in a pedestrian environment in which he was not usually to be found, much like a peacock at a wiener roast. I nodded and smiled in recognition as we passed each other but he was probably too irritated by the demeaning circumstances to reply.

Washington night life was vibrant in the 1950's. Rock and roll bars near downtown were packed every weekend, as many from suburbs as local. Beer was cheap and one could kill an evening at rather bargain rates. The bands were Blacks, the audience White and the atmosphere tawdry. Dancers were as raunchy as public display would permit, mainly college couples cutting loose. Restaurants also were inexpensive. Chez Michel had a dark sultry atmosphere of Mitteleuropean intrigue, candles at each checkered table cloth table, zither player and a cello/piano duet in gypsy garb, playing the theme from *The Third Man* and plaintiff Hungarian folk tunes, all this, coq-au-vin, and a bottle of OK burgundy for $6.95. The 823 Club located in the basement of an office building near 15th Street offered Austrian ambiance, a string quartet and a lovely receptionist to greet you after descending a 20-step staircase into an operetta setting of Stags heads on the wall, ornate beer steins and coats of arms from German Landrats and provinces. Tables grouped around an elevated stage on which the players performed mostly Strauss waltzes as waiters in tuxedos took and served dinner orders of German cuisine, hardy, sausage-driven, beer-quenched, although a fair amount of wine was also available. Well-lit and upbeat ambiance, almost cheery, more Austrian than German. One could spend an evening, meal, beer, and entertainment, for $12.00 enjoyably, even able to converse in the less noisy and therefore somewhat subdued atmosphere, perhaps more subdued than a pleasure seeking undergraduate might prefer. The Old Bavarian on 12th Street, was more *gemütlich*. Ulrich at piano and Hans with accordion played German popular songs for which Hans' slightly wheezy high pitched tenor was perfectly suited. A rectangular storefront extending deep into the room, bar to the left, tables distributed elsewhere, beer steins, laughing waitress in dirndl skirt hauling beer across the crowded and rambunctious room full of laughing and in cases singing customers. The usual German coats of arms and stag heads on the wall, rowdy enthusiastic customers with much audience participation. $6 steins of Lowenbrau light or dark, many other German brews, made an evening enjoyable. Quite apart from it all, Annelise, Ulrich's business-first wife and the person really in charge sat behind the bar intently observing the customers, calculating the take, and scheming upscale improvements. Her first was to have a velvet-covered chain barrier to entry, formal host greeting, menus, and taking each party to a table, rather than 'take whatever table is available'. To justify a rise in prices she upgraded the kitchen, not entirely noticeable given that the basic sausage-driven German cuisine was susceptible to only minimal variation much less improvement. She may also have begun phone reservations, something I never tried. Impatient with the tepid results of her innovations, she sold the OB in 1957 and bought a resort in West Virginia just over the border with WDC. Apparently it prospered and we lost our slice of Bavaria and good times forever, just an empty storefront marked *'For Rent'* remained as epitaph to Teutonic pleasures.

Movies are the National pastime. I was nuts about Jeanne Crain in *State Fair*. I thought Vincent Price was comical in his laughably scary Edgar Poe films, the first to introduce bi-colored plastic glasses in 1952 that gave the audience the appearance of three dimensions, an innovation almost immediately abandoned. We heard that foreign films were dirty but never got to see one because the American audience, other than depraved males, had no interest in paying to see them, least of all with subtitles. At drive-ins, kids wouldn't give the amount of attention required to follow the plot and the rather homely unattractive actors from France or Italy speaking an unintelligible language to no purpose, compared to the purpose at hand in the front seat. I was less xenophobic and began to attend foreign films, first at the Stanton Art Theater in Northeast Washington and later at the Capitol Hill Cinema. But the initial impulse came not from any abstract expectation of foreign enlightenment. I saw an ad in the Washington Post entertainment section for Ingmar Bergman's film *Monika*, starring Harriet Anderson, with sufficient prurient descriptive prose to make the combination of my genetic homeland and explicit sex irresistible. The Stanton movie theater was in Northeast Washington, the Black region, an American third world of risk and danger. I traveled through commercial and residential districts that felt foreign and menacing. The theater had obviously seen better days, run down, threadbare velvet seat covers, ineluctable odor of decades-long sweat and popcorn, noisy projector, the scruffy but friendly owner selling tickets, a sign of marginal financial viability. My friend and I took our seats. The film began. Story of a buxom store clerk fondled and harassed by fat homely middle-aged co-workers, yearns for better things, thinks she found *better* in a young spindly lumber yard worker with whom she runs away for a summer of fun and close up copulation. Viewer interest begins to pick up twenty minutes into the film as we see Harriet in the almost altogether revealing an exceptional endowment no hedge fund could match, and which my imagination embellished never having seen so much so clearly displayed. She gets pregnant, they have the baby, he works, she sits around the tiny apartment very bored, they squabble because he thinks she should take better care of baby, she begins to go out to night clubs for excitement and a little fun, meets another spindly guy, a night club employee, goes to his apartment, lights a cigarette, then blows smoke at the camera as it fades on her sluttish grin. In retrospect, a not very interesting film, but as a first time intro to European liberated cinema, a strong impression. Years later I bought a copy of the film and discovered that even the nudity was more a product of my fervid imagination, the only scene being one of Harriet running away from the camera nude showing her magnificent ass. The moralizing in Monika reminded me of Swedes' eminence in Hollywood from the 1930's. Greta Garbo the first, Ingrid Bergman the second. My grandmother was equivalent to a peasant 16th Century 'religious' psychotic, seeing sin and filth everywhere below the belt, ruthlessly suppressing whatever 'natural' tendencies her son and two daughters might be dealing with. When Ingrid Bergman ran off pregnant with Roberto Rossellini, the ceiling caved in, indignation and reproach from Gerda, amusement and admiration from the rest of us. Imagining that bald greasy wop screwing our lovely Aryan goddess was too disgusting and repulsive not to enjoy. On the order of Oscar Wilde's comment: *'You would need a heart of stone to read Dickens' death of Little Nelll without laughing.'* Following the Stanton caper, I regularly attended foreign films, now shown at the Capitol Hill Cinema, a more easily accessible and inviting venue. Jean Gabin, Jean Cocteau film fantasies, Gerard Philippe, Anna Magnani, Mastroiani, Kurt Jurgens, *Die Bruke,* Maria Schell. But above all, Ingmar Bergman who had become a cult favorite with the intellectual elite. Among my favorites were *Smiles of a Summer Night and Wild Strawberries,* showing many sides of Swedish emotional dysfunction, so dear to my heart and close to my family experience.

In spite of many outside distractions and diversions, students and teachers made up a substantial part of the Georgetown experience, a mixed bag as to age, origins, and cultural formation. In 1955, Jackie Kennedy attended a night class taught by Jules Davids, professor of American History, ostensibly to brush up on the subject as her husband Jack was writing his seminal thought-credential: *Profiles in Courage.* No official confirmation ensued, but Jules apparently drafted several biographies included in that work at her request, enough to make a moral if not provable claim to co-authorship. Jules was an exceptional scholar, thorough, dedicated, modest. I took his regular class in American History and later his seminar in American Diplomacy. We got along extremely well, but it nonetheless came as a surprise at my graduation ceremony to receive the Coleman Nevils Medal of Excellence in American History awarded by Jules to the student he deemed most worthy. I still have the medal, about 1.5 ounces of 18-caret gold, roughly $2200 at current exchange rate. Another pleasant surprise was an award of excellence for the highest grade ever earned in Constitutional Law, a course taught by Professor Giles, who gave me a course grade of 97%, tarnished perhaps by the fact that he had been arrested in 1950 for soliciting, a charge of homosexuality that the Dean of SFS told the court was 'intrinsically impossible'. Intrinsic or not, it wasn't a legal basis for acquittal but given the stature of the Dean and the grubby subject of the prosecution based solely on officer testimony, the judge probably felt it was in everyone's interest to bury the entire proceeding.

Our Russian teacher, Gospodin Trubskoi, could only teach a night class, otherwise and inexplicably employed during daylight hours. He was vigorous, moustached, charming, effusive and his class consisted mainly in singing Russian traditional songs. I asked to switch from French to Russian. Dean Fadner declined to accept that change because French was much more useful in the long run. Ending up with a few bars from *Очи черние* hardly a worthy substitute for ability to read Stendhal. As it happens I eventually attended the Army Language School in Monterey and got fairly fluent in my then target lingo. French-wise I was well served by Pierre Mobrey, an iconic French official in appearance, thin, pale complexion, large forehead, razor thin lips, and precise enunciation, shiny drab gabardine suit, possibly prewar. We used tapes in the language lab and advanced quite impressively in conversational ability. Our economics professor had served in the New Deal, was a nervous wreck, trembling hands, distracted look, who literally read from his book assigned to each of us for at least royalties to supplement pay, apparently composed to provide a lesson a day until end of term. If he had served at the Normandy invasion or parachuted into occupied France that might account for his PTSD affliction, but presumed desk jobs could hardly have left so drastic a mark on his nervous system.

John Waldron, our 'English' teacher, caricature of standard occupational 'literary idiosyncrasies' accrued by authors over three centuries of alcohol abuse, sartorial eclecticism, sexual aberration, and moral exhaustion. His performance conveyed an impression of unpressed suits, mismatched socks, a disheveled genius suffering from an underlying sense of the ultimate futility of human endeavor but required to soldier on. His shirts had what students called a 'Waldron collar', notably wide and abundant proportions never heretofore seen. His shuffling walk and stammering speech, the latter mimicking the former, hesitant, tentative, never quite sure whether to proceed with the initial thought or jump ship to another, or backtrack, restless movement of hands and torso, an agony of suspended animation about to burst forth once all parts of the performance coalesced, but never did. We all wondered where they found him, why they kept him.

Students were varied and incongruent, mainly because of the GI Bill that mixed veteran machine gunners with high school cannon fodder. We even had an ex Kamikaze pilot, if that isn't an oxymoron! Extreme differences in age, background, experience and temperament made for an exotic cocktail of talents and abilities, among them Jack and Harry. Jack Ellenberger and Harry Jacobs shared a basement apartment in an elegant home in Georgetown just four blocks from the campus. Jack blonde, effete slightly bucktoothed, was ebullient, sibilant, effusive, percussive, pink, loquacious, and wimpy. He looked like he had never thrown a ball in his life, much less tried or wanted to. Harry was saturnine, thick light brown hair combed straight back, hooded eyelids, teeth like Stonehenge, large head, stocky, very intent, earnest, and in some ways, imposing. Impossible to imagine him young, as if he was born wearing cordovan shoes. His father had worked with Harry Hopkins in the Roosevelt White House, which may be the upscale link to power Harry seemed to enjoy. They met in the Air Force, stationed near London. Odd that they were in the military at all, Jack being prime 4F material, and Harry presumably well enough placed to get exemption from Korean War entanglements. Be that as it may, they did serve, and attended Georgetown on the GI Bill, probably augmented financially by family contributions. Their address allowed correspondents to assume importance not otherwise corroborated. However he did it, Harry was considered to be a source of insider information on US policy and personnel and contributed articles to Foreign Affairs and other influential magazines. Perhaps editorial screening was less strict at that time than later. Off duty in London, they changed to Savile Row civilian dress and apparently crashed or insinuated themselves into upper class parties, venues, events. They were a complete mystery to me, as to ways and means. They rarely seemed excited, always composed, but on one occasion they were in considerable turmoil. Lord Whatever (I forget the name they told me) was coming to Washington and they in some way were obliged to accommodate him. How they met a Lord, how they maintained sufficiently close relations as to be relied on for accommodations which the Embassy could easily arrange was unexplained. Only one other time did I see Harry wildly excited. The main residence of their basement townhouse apartment was rented to eight High School teachers who occasionally had parties that spilled over into the back yard, visible from a clearstory window in the basement. School teachers like farmers' daughters have a reputation for public decorum and private dissipation, a reputation not belied by Jack and Harry's neighbors. A party got very raucous and Harry, curious and annoyed, looked out the clearstory window onto a scene often enacted but rarely witnessed. A teacher lying on her back, legs parted was being fucked by a Navy guy in dress whites understandably discomposed in a non-military manner, practically under Harry's nose. His excited astonished and prurient reaction recorded by Jack, who if you haven't surmised by now, disgusted and reproachful, was a flaming queer.

In 1955, Jack and I happened to land summer jobs at the Department of Health Education and Welfare, a Roosevelt boondoggle settled in a large Federal Building near the foot of Capitol Hill. I was employed (worked would be a bit of an exaggeration) in the Bureau of Indian Health, perhaps in the Health part of the Department, even though all other Indian matters were taken care of by the Bureau of Indian Affairs, Department of the Interior. Not to mock or in any way treat trivially the personnel and mission of the Bureau of Indian Health. An extremely capable nurse, Miss Aubrey, was in charge of my section, which included several other nurses, nursing being the main service provided tribes, those mostly in Arizona and New Mexico. Nurse Jenkins, diminutive, retiring assistant to Nurse Aubrey, had spent most of her career in New Mexico, mention of which State brought a look of longing for red desert sunsets and infinite black night skies sparkling with stars close enough to touch. Nurse Aubrey was plump, stocky, energetic and thoroughly principled. I admired her and helped her as much as my totally unrelated skills enabled. I came to love and care for these lovely women, committed to doing good, being honest, remembering, in the close grubby office we occupied, the deep infinite silence of the desert Southwest.

Jack was elsewhere in the maze of DHEW. We ate lunch in the Department cafeteria, a large and well-managed dining area with WPA murals on all the walls, depicting the crisis and deliverance of rural poor and industrial downtrodden by WPA and other New Deal relief programs. To conclude this duet, Harry and Jack graduated and moved to another apartment in 1956. One day Harry, suddenly without preliminary dramatic confrontation, up and left the apartment, leaving only a note: *'I've had enough'* definition of 'enough' left entirely to the imagination. He later joined the Foreign Service, was assigned to Afghanistan, quit to open a trucking business between Kandahar and Teheran, later dropped that project, returned to Washington where he also ran a trucking business, Jacob's Trucking, whose trucks I remember seeing cruising the streets. Harry was rumored to be involved with a prominent debutant when finally and improbably he was ordained a Catholic priest, ending his peripatetic incongruent lifestyle, serving at Catholic University until he died in 2010! Jack left to study Library Science at Columbia University, graduated and got a position as librarian at a prestigious law firm in Washington, where he was employed until the digital revolution pretty much automated the legal reference system, following which he returned to New York and so far as I know was under nurse's care in 2018 at 85 years of age.

Joe Nunez was a bar buddy for a time, Hispanic, small well proportioned, well-groomed in a Burberry trench coat, well-mannered, sensitive. He worked a day job at some agency, attending mainly night courses, where we met and became friends, drinking beer at the Old Bavarian, sometimes more than he could handle requiring me to carry him up to his room. He rented a top floor room in a large Georgetown townhouse occupied by a French Embassy employee, who had a magnificent collection of Picasso ceramic plates displayed across the walls of the living room. Worth a fortune today. We eventually drifted into different spheres, but in 1964 I re-encountered him. He was running an art gallery in Georgetown, partly funded by Herrera, the Venezuelan millionaire described earlier. Things did not go well, he started drinking, and eventually disappeared to wherever the desperate and failing go.

Clifford 'Ted' Reese followed a more conventional path. Son of a Major General** USAF, he graduated SFS in 1958 and pursued a similar career, retiring as a Lieutenant General*** in 1992. At Georgetown he resided in the local fraternity house, was gregarious, articulate, popular, and sociable. Very good looking, trim, well groomed, enthusiastic and extremely intelligent, he was a star in the making. He dated a student at a local Catholic College for women, once describing her in my hearing as his 'ball and chain', eventually his wife. Frank Riley, despite the name, was very French, suave, self-assured and an excellent actor, performing in Moliere at an *Alliance Francaise* production of *Tartuffe* at a Northeast High School auditorium in 1957. His wealthy aunt in Paris sustained his rather opulent lifestyle at Georgetown. He put me on to Hannah Arendt's *Origens of Totalitarianism,* of whom I became a devoted follower. Frank lives in Paris and has entirely separated from any Georgetown connections.

Kevin Robb, although a College not SFS student, became an acquaintance in connection with applications for a 1958 Fulbright Scholarship to study abroad. A generous program passed with Congressional approval to send promising students abroad, presumably to prepare for service in some capacity in international finance, business, academe, or diplomacy. About two hundred applicants submitted forms and academic recommendations. Once past the initial screening, in what form I have no idea, about twenty of us appeared individually before a final review panel of twenty-five university professors arrayed along both sides of an incredibly long conference table, who questioned and probed based on folders with information about each of us. I had applied to study in France, but surmised that Paris was just too obvious a choice, with implications of purposes perhaps more touristic than academic in view. I picked a university in Pau, near the Spanish border, presumably to study goings on in that remote region during the French Revolution. Subliminally, any professor considering my objective would be impressed more by the tedious inclement region in question and the practically unknown and likely unprepossessing provincial academic offerings of the local university, but by contrast perhaps catching a whiff of rewarding discovery in what was until now a neglected perhaps undiscovered but remarkable territory for historic investigation. Hard to claim my application was a frivolous attempt at a two-year paid vacation when I was prepared to endure the remote and unexplored territory, geographic and academic, of the Pyrenees. I was scheduled near the end of the interviews, trying to look promising with no idea what was expected. The final question came. '*Are you a WDC resident.*' The Fulbright scholarships, numerous and sought after, were offered by quota to regions and districts and only to students resident therein. Most students are itinerant, home being far from the schools they attend. I am gifted with an unconscious ability to strike at the essential solution or answer under instant pressure to provide one. I without hesitation said: '*I pay DC taxes.*' A more elaborate reply involving dates and times and other extenuations of residence would have protracted and dulled the ultimate effect. Such a monosyllabic reply appeared to settle the matter. Not that another valid resident might equally be in the running, but for some reason they selected me for the singular honor and scholarship on offer. Their first choice was Robb, but he was not a resident and so tough titty. Robb was a classics major in Georgetown College, friend of a Jesuit priest candidate who spoke Latin well. One of the truly blessed, Robb received the Dole Pineapple Scholarship, complete tuition, room and board, plus a generous expense account, to include a standing tab at the second most exclusive French restaurant in Washington! He was appropriately 'intellectual' energetic and 'spiritual', good looking, well-spoken in a combination that carried him far. After Georgetown he got a Danforth Scholarship to study classics at Yale, all the way to PhD territory, which again landed him back home in Los Angeles at University of Southern California, where he remains in Redondo Beach semi-retired to this day. He was often at Oxford with the world-renowned classics scholars who adored him, perhaps a mixed claim given that he seemed perfectly 'normal' as it were, but never married or associated with a partner inappropriate to the traditional notion of that *fach*.

Classics (Latin/Greek) are nearly extinct in High Schools and Universities but once, before the rise of science and business education, were required subjects for study in secondary school and collegiate curricula. Germany (Schliemann's excavations of Troy; Verner Jaeger) and Oxford University (excavations in Crete and *Paedea)* in England led research and instruction in this somewhat esoteric field of study. At Oxford and to some extent in Germany the *fach* attracted homosexuals charmed by Ancient Greek notions of spiritualized homosexuality. More Appollonian than Dionysian, their bias tended to obscure Priapus, Satyrs and other randy heterosexual misconduct dominant among the helots, well and explicitly portrayed in pottery art in particular. The aesthetes preferred the white marble statues (originally painted in vibrant colors) of Adonis and the 'platonic' eroticism of the eponymous philosopher himself. Bowra and other Oxford professors regularly planned rubble hikes on Greek Islands, opportunity for seducing rapt students overcome by Eros and ouzo (a Greek liquor). Early scholars claimed the icing, those who followed got the cake, contemporary scholars like Robb got the crumbs. Success as a Classics Professor required close and obsequious association with currently vetted masters of the fach. Something like Shakespeare's description of ambitious courtiers:

'Let the candied tongue lick absurd pomp and crook the
pregnant hinges of the knee where thrift may follow fawning.'

The more limited the academic following and restricted the lucrative academic appointments, the more intense the competition and courtship within an incestuous community. New scholars had to pore over insignificant newly uncovered scraps of parchment or stone engravings to fill in chronological gaps between the major discoveries of the past. Robb spent several years in Turkey rooting around various piles of Ancient Greek rubble, making more collegial contacts, and wooing superiors in the academic, notably English, hierarchy of Classical scholars with detailed articles, amply foot noted with references to work of members of the hierarchy in esoteric magazines about particular aspects of the Greek experience. All which led finally to his masterpiece, *Orality in Greek Culture,* published by Oxford University Press, 1992, the ultimate imprimatur of academic arrival, all just coasting from there. On first hearing, the term *'orality'* evokes images of dental practice or pornographic films, the word 'oral' having much wider implications not confined to the faculty of speech. By this infelicitous term Robb meant to refer to the distinct period of pre-literate analphabetic Greece when all literature was memorized and spoken, not written. The distinction hinged on the exact sequence that led to the alphabet, a prerequisite to writing, a means to convert fugitive oral to lasting print. Greek had consonants. They needed vowels. Semitic languages could leave vowels out and still be intelligible. Greek was too loquacious, complex and inflected to do without. The Phoenician language had symbols for sounds that could be adapted to serve as vowels. Problem was, people would have to get used to the range of sound each vowel represents. For example, try singing the vowels in our alphabet slowly without stop one into the other. You will get the idea. The letter 'a' can be anything from ahh to ayy. You could end up with five or more letters to distinguish all the distinct gradations the sound 'a' might otherwise represent. Too many letters, too little time. The genius of Greek was to settle on a-e-i-o-u-y and insert them between consonants to indicate the applicable sound.

Robb poked around the 'written' Greek fragments and finally found they began around 750 BC. Not that the distinction was overlooked for 2500 years, but to name it, categorize it, build an academic fence around it to keep out interlopers, and issue certificates of authenticity as a toll for disbursing the jewels therein was a major accomplishment in a field so long shopworn and down trodden as to make any innovation or novelty improbable. Passages from the introduction and credits of Robb's book are so laughable, as examples of academic toadying, back scratching and prophylactic flattery that they deserve to be sampled here. They reflect the wish to please, name every possible colleague who might present plausible counter arguments, and suck up to ultimate arbiters of Classic presumption:

'...no author who delves into as many areas of scholarship as I do here can be expert in all of them, or even many of them. He knows all too well the difference between [1] writing in his own narrow area of professional training, where he feels certain of every word, and trespassing in foreign disciplines. [2] Errors, small and perhaps large are the inevitable price of reporting on important discoveries made in fields not one's own. [3] I trust those more knowledgeable than I will not hesitate to offer corrections, and I hope they will communicate them directly to me.'

The characteristic academic sucking points enumerated: (1) Forgive my impertinence, I am fallible compared to all of you, my own claims to scholarship are modest and miniature compared to yours; (2) to err is human to forgive divine [counter argument: to err is not in your job description, to forgive is in not in mine]; (3) if you find something wrong, for Christ's sake tell me first and let ME deal with it rather than ambush me for all to see. Robb got the USC teacher of the year award based on student evaluations six times in his 30-year career. One student commented: *'He is a bit absent minded and strays from the subject, but sure knows his stuff.'* What more could you ask?

Agrippina Anderson (Aggie hereafter) lived five doors up the street from Miss Fish, but several galaxies away from her in background and experience. Bride of a member of Herbert Hoover's famine relief commission that went to Russia 1919-1921, she returned to the United States in person but unaltered in spirit. I don't know much about Mr. Anderson, who was no longer extant in 1954, but he must have been comfortably off to afford an attractive Georgetown townhouse in which Aggie could enjoy his retirement unencumbered by him. Russia is beyond the comprehension of Americans, hardly less so for Europeans. My recollection of Aggie is through the lens of later working association with Russians, learning the language, reading the literature, enjoying the music, and admiring the entire project of Russia and its peculiar destiny and outlook. Not that I was unobservant in 1954. As to person, she was Slavic but not unattractive in a heavy mascara *ochi cherniye* way. Time hardly dented her 1916 Russian wardrobe, still wearing multicolored Bakst-like dresses, long and ample, chains of colored stone necklaces, gold wristbands, and multicolored peacock feathered toque. The furnishing and appointments of her town house probably reflected exactly the internal apparatus of herself. No electric lighting. All candles, an icon in a corner of the living room with burning scented candles to animate the figure of the Virgin. Plush sofas and armchairs, heavy velvet drapes, a pervasive odor of incense. She didn't walk or talk moderately, but impulsively, dashing from place to place, her talk pulsating with hushed whispers and thrusting rich mezzo vibrato pronouncements.

Frank, a graduate student friend, was looking for a rental, I asked Miss Fish if any were available locally, she thereupon suggested that Aggie was interested, and so he set up in an upstairs bedroom in her townhouse awaiting his fate. Not an exaggerated description of life with Aggie. She was loaded financially and emotionally and eager to enjoy the good life, too long denied her for lack of friends or a male companion. In fact at no time did she speak of any association, friend, club, pot house, or *svidaniye, her modus vivendi* perhaps too exclusive or exotic to share or be shared. For a while that was an advantage. She invited me and her roommate Frank to dine. Her favorite restaurant was the Golden Peacock on Connecticut Avenue, a large mansion converted, several large rooms with three or four equally large tables for patrons. Entering the restaurant with Aggie was like entering with a large peacock in full array preceding two lackeys in tow. The head waiter was admiring and deferential, acquainted with her largesse. Aggie wore her best Scheherazade costume, multicolored, multilayered with silver fox fur around her neck, perhaps a hunting trophy, jewels, bracelets, a silvered rope belt. You could almost imagine straining Russia wolfhounds on leash drawing her forward. Frank and I were as well upholstered as our Woodies basement bargain price range would allow, at least dark blue concealed from all but close examination the deficiency of our suiting as compared with the lady in tow. Golden Peacock furnishings were Victorian reflecting the vintage of the house. Huge gilded frame portraits and Etruscan scenes, marble and carved wood, large upholstered armchairs at table, stunning white table cloth, sterling silver in ornate baroque versions, marvelous long stemmed crystal glasses in elegant forms for water, aperitif, red wine, white wine, brandy, a charming lineup of the libation itinerary at each setting encouraging, almost insisting, that every libation appropriate to each glass be ordered. The menu was beautifully calligraphic with illustrations of various fruits and garlands, varied and priceless entrees, menu prices of the *'If you have to ask you can't afford it'* kind, as JP Morgan said of his yacht. Of course the wine list was the apogee of dining, sips of Chambertin, Romanee Conti, Clos Vougeot punctuating the ambrosial concoctions that made Chef Appolite a favorite in expense account circles. I noticed with interest a family party with a beaming Jesuit dispensing his other-worldly charm and enjoying the most refined secular treats available with clear deference to his cloth but appreciation for his sanction to enjoy what any decent Middle Western Puritan would have associated with the road to perdition. Self-denial was never a Catholic obsession.

The idyll became strained in an unexpected way. Aggie was about 60-years old, a widow, and a Russian obscurantist, so my friend was surprised when the long tethered (sic) fires of Russian abandon came undone. On further consideration, she was a very well-formed lady even indicated under all that enveloping fabric. She was solid, lithe and vigorous, an indication of physical capacity not to be confined to climbing stairs or doing dishes. It began simply. When Frank returned home, she would sit on the sofa, drink (translate vodka) in hand, another on the side table. Invitation to imbibe reinforced by rising and lunging at him to take his arm and seat him willing or not. A few vodka toasts terminally impaired his capacity for homework.

After a few weeks, she began touching and caressing, eventually, when vodka had worked its magic, proposing in somewhat slurred whisper that they move to her bedroom. An impecunious student would hesitate, not refuse outright, requiring time to weigh advantages and disadvantages. In a general way, until we are financially secure if not independent, we are all for sale, have a price, can be bought. Necessity ordains this. Room and board, probably an allowance, freeing time spent in odd campus jobs to work on your thesis, at the price of only a few hump-the-hostess evenings week looked tempting. She was nearly sixty but was firm, unwrinkled and probably had a terrific body for her time and place, Russian women known generally to be physically fetching. Only problem was she wasn't an intermittent person, more all or nothing. He told me he didn't take her offer, soon moving out for calmer waters. I probably would have tried her out, at least to satisfy my curiosity, and keep the Chambertin flowing. Alas!

Practically nothing that happens in France makes sense to anyone else. A mini-revolution took place in May 1958, possibly just the habit of having one at any opportunity, preferring drama to boring elections as a way of overthrowing a government you dislike. As a result, Fulbright scholarships to France were suspended for the year. Irritating because, as usual, turmoil was mostly centered in Paris, far from Pau near the Pyrenees Mountains bordering Spain and the university to which I expected to travel for study. If given the chance I could have argued for a regional exception to the Parisian exclusion but *que faire?* If there had been a 'revolution' in Pau would all France have shut down? So in August 1958 I redirected my plans to Minneapolis and the University of Minnesota, leaving Washington after four enlightening, formative years a suitable occasion to pause and reflect on my situation in the larger context.

MINNEAPOLIS

My parents lived in a top floor condo at 4954 South Lyndale Avenue, Minneapolis. I arrived in August 1958 to attend Graduate School at the University. My father was head of the Navy/Marine ROTC, a definite comedown offered officers on their way out, but convenient to our mutual commute to University. Convenient the only advantage, as any close association was as usual unpleasant. Downstairs was the Primus family, Lee Brent Primus (Lawyer), Richard Lee Primus (21), Brent William Primus (9), and Maude Primus, mother of us all. Lee, Iowa farm boy, built a lone gun extremely lucrative practice based on his disarming country boy charm, outdated pale blue suits, Woolworth ties, cajoling country boy juries willing to award huge sums to injured peers against heartless corporate transgressors. His deep roots in the Midwestern experience during the Depression grounded him and made him a dangerous opponent in court. In the early 1930's he left home to relieve the family economic burden and hit the rails for two years, bumming around on the Northern Pacific railroad, sleeping in outdoor hobo camps, getting to the guts of America. He was strong, well built, nobody likely to mess with him. He should have had his adenoids removed, but likely realized they gave his high pitched nasal voice a milder aspirate inoffensive sound that disarmed juries and slaughtered more eloquent, well-upholstered and sophisticated attorneys. He always sounded like a slow-of-speech country lawyer aspiring to save equally modest-in-origin clients from contemptuous exploiters. Vanity drove prosperous lawyers to tailored suits and polished shoes and arguments, but Primus knew winning the Jury was what paid off, and jurors resented the slick prosperity of these upscale lawyers. The damage awards were stupendous! I once encountered a high-powered lawyer with an equally high-powered legal corporation. I mentioned I knew Lee and he was immediately impressed and said he was one of the best lawyers in the city. Lee was regularly invited to the Pillsbury family Christmas Party, and in 1958 he brought me and Richard along to the family estate on Lake Minnetonka, the mansion row of Minneapolis. Pillsbury's were unlikely to waste time on losers. Impressive!

I was enrolled in the Masters Degree program of the History Department, presumably a reinforcement of undergraduate study in the same field applicable to Foreign Service. John Bowditch, Princeton PhD, headed the division, thick curly hair, boyish, striped Rooster tie, rumpled tweeds and an abominable pipe filled with *Prince Albert* tobacco, the worst American blend. I smoked *Balkan Sobraniye* so our counseling sessions became an unpleasant olfactory contest for dominance, Balkan latafia eventually overpowering the sweetly toxic smell of Prince Albert. Professor Egbert Price, Bowditch's colleague, almost as if deliberate contrast were required, was the image of British-American in tailored Savile Row tweed three-piece suits, immaculate long staple cotton shirts, distinguished Brooks Brothers regimental striped ties, beautifully crafted oxfords, and a signet ring with a coat of arms suggesting lineage. His genteel posture and soft but insinuating voice intimidated the rather relaxed not to say sloppy dress and manner of most of the students. One exception was Adrian Crush, an unaccountably perpetual Canadian student now 34-years old, working on a PhD degree presumably to be granted soon if his thesis ever got completed. Professor Harold Deutsch had served with OSS in Europe and was an expert on German history, agreeably non-Teutonic despite the surname. I proposed as thesis for my Master's Degree *French diplomacy 1856 to 1870,* obscure, of no importance, but feasibly apt to the degree in mind. I proceeded to do research with unexpectedly good results based on three French and one German monographs printed in the 1920's. I found them in a remote region of the University Library stacks, Their check-out record showed no one had read or cared to find them in thirty years! These four monographs were critical to any originality my thesis might aspire to. Once completed and approved, Bowditch and Deutsch complimented me on the best thesis in years! Who knew?

Richard Primus became a close friend, after all he lived downstairs and rode to the University with Robert and me five days a week. Robust, uninhibited, in fact encouraged in assertive and enthusiastic adventures by Lee, who gave him a bank account, a Rolex GMT Master watch (Richard was taking flying lessons), and free use of the family Studebaker, secure in the knowledge that he would enter the firm and become a partner in Primus and Primus, Attorneys at Law. Such a rigorous and book-bound occupation seemed incongruous, Richard being as some girl described him 'effervescent', a word he liked and used for self-description from time to time. Nice looking in a frat boy way, blondish, brown eyes (his mother's) somewhat athletic, energetic and randy, easy going, enthusiastic with an ability to talk endlessly, advantage in a trial lawyer and especially in the process of seduction required for success in pursuit of the only object that interested him, pussy.

Late September 1958, Lee invited me on his annual pheasant hunt in Iowa. Lee, Richard and I roomed with a retired farmer in the town. Lee loaned me a 20-gauge shotgun, the lightest and least explosive. This was opening day, 10 AM the start, we were at the cornfields, the birds presumably unaware of the mounting mortal threat to their tranquility, so more inclined to fly away rather than run for cover through the cornrows, decidedly favorable for the shotgun toting army invading their space. We lined up on the edge of the field one row each and four rows apart. At 10 sharp we began our march, I in about the middle of the group of fourteen hunters. If a bird was flushed on the left side, it would fly low and close to top of the cornstalks, so only a second in sight of each hunter. Need to be quick and ride the bird fast. I heard shots moving down the line toward me, so I aimed at the left top side of my row, waiting for the split second when dinner would pass in front of me. I managed to hit three birds that afternoon, they dropped in front of Richard four rows to my right, the distance and time required for the mortally wounded bird to lose trajectory and drop. Lee got two. Richard didn't get any so he shot an unsuspecting passing rabbit in revenge. My reputation as hunter gatherer was secured and the nick name *'Good Shot'* bestowed by Richard in honor, envy and irritation at being the loser in this manly predatory excursion. That I provided three of five birds made the Sunday dinner ample and delicious, wild pheasant hard to beat for flavor. I noticed on the ride back to Minneapolis that there were many roadside stands selling pheasants for bragging rights for the guys who didn't get one.

Richard and I went skiing in upper Minnesota taking the train and flew in his two- seater plane to Madison for a Minnesota-Wisconsin football game, making a forced landing on the way back in a cornfield having almost run out of gas. The plane had no instrument panel, just two sticks attached to a ping-pong ball or equivalent in the fuel tank in both wings, indicating for the pilot the approximate fuel supply remaining by how high the sticks rose above the wing tanks. We had lively encounters with school teachers, students, and office girls, with one of whom he got lucky, a conclusion soon reversed when she got off his plane forward, not back toward the rear of the plane. He hadn't turned off the engine so she was hit in the face by the propeller entailing several months of insurance payouts and legal challenges even Lee, his father, had difficulty resolving.

Of longer term and more drastic effect was Richard's encounter with the love of his life, Evie Howard. They met on the train on our way back from skiing in Wisconsin in late November 1958. Evie was Jewish, her name once Horowitz, and she had her arched nose straightened to a cute button, fairly common among Jewish girls in the 1950's. Lee was a product of the German settlement in Iowa and Minnesota, a region solidly Isolationist in the 1930's and source of supporters for the

German Bund in the pre-war political turmoil of 1938-1941. Charles Lindberg as spokesman for the America First movement opposed involvement in the imminent war in Europe and had been welcomed with open arms in Germany during a visit that included a meeting with Hitler. Antisemitism was prevalent in business circles in Minneapolis, Lee no exception. This led to a long and disruptive battle of wills. Richard wanted to marry Evie, the last thing Lee wanted was Jewish grandchildren. A temporary solution came when Dick dropped out of law school in 1959 to join the Air Force fighter pilot program.

In 1959, I resumed piano study with John Templeton, an elderly gentleman who taught at the McPhail School of Music in downtown Minneapolis. The school is a conservatory that offers degrees in music. Templeton had retired from full-time teaching but gave lessons to outsiders to supplement his retirement income. The school rented piano rooms for practice. Templeton looked like T. S. Eliot in a pinker jollier version. He came from New England and had studied with Nadia Boulanger in Paris (his co student was Aaron Copeland!) the pons asinorum of classical music study in the early 20th Century and certification of Templeton's considerable talent that she would accept him as a student. As well as teaching at McPhail, he served for forty years as organist at the Episcopal Cathedral in Minneapolis, the one attended by owners of General Mills, Pillsbury, and other social and business leaders. He was the model of old school New England gentleman. He had some difficulty deciding where I would fit in the orderly scheme of musical education to which he was accustomed. I had strong facility in the left hand and enthusiasm enough to tackle most anything but obviously not enough formal technical training or mastery for much of the material I was trying to play. We settled on the Bach *Two Part Inventions* as a base line of study plus Chopin's *Polonaise in A major* as a suitably lively piece to keep up my interest. We both assumed a jolly friendly attitude once any pretense at concert level achievement was put aside. We had great times discussing music and other matters as well as trying to improve my technique. It did improve and we progressed fairly well. I had by then worked up a number of Chopin Preludes as well as *Claire de Lune, Liebestraum, the Revolutionary Etude* and other barn burners.

The McPhail concert hall was small, no more than 150 seats, but it had two Baldwin grand pianos. I would play one from time to time. Students might come in to listen waiting their turn. It was flattering to be taken for one of the full time students, and I found that playing a concert grand did more for tone, precision and musicality than anything else. I felt I had to live up to the instrument and playing the grand I heard sounds I hadn't heard before. Occasionally, Templeton and I would go to student concerts, we now irreverent friends exchanging vigorous opinions about practically everything. He would make wry remarks about the performances and we laughed after at many observations he made. My lessons ended in 1960 due mainly to lack of funds to rent a studio and pay Templeton. I regretted leaving the company of one of the true gentlemen I have known.

My father retired in 1959 and he and Alice moved to Tacoma to be with her beloved mother, Gerda. I moved into a room in a former stately home near downtown. Rooms on two floors were rented out each floor sharing a bathroom. I needed income so I eventually joined Colliers Encyclopedia sales located in the Foshay Tower Building, eponymous with a utilities tycoon in the 1930's who was indicted for fraud and I believe disposed of himself rather than face prison. The Colliers direct sales operation was an education in raw door-to-door selling. They had a conference room where about twelve salesmen gathered every afternoon to assign 'territory' for the evening's campaign. The product was Colliers illustrated encyclopedia in seventeen volumes, plus one of two add-ons, the first a 20-volume set of *The Harvard Classics,* a selection of novels, poetry, and historical essays prepared by the Dean of Harvard as a basic library for the cultivated man. The second, a bookcase, children's books, and tutorial service for the grade school or junior high school student, thereby covering the adult market and the parents with children market, all for $179 cash or monthly payments of $14.95. The salesman got $49 and the house got the rest.

Only one problem for the novice starting out. This had been going on eight years. Every summer they hired as many as forty on-vacation college students looking for jobs. They were sent out into the towns, suburbs and farm country like locusts, with some success based on boyish charm and enthusiasm. The public already was acquainted with the program, probably *ad nauseam,* and door-to-door became an agony of refusal to answer or rapid door in your face if answered. On the favorable side, there were thousands of parents with kids pursuing education and the encyclopedia with add-ons salved the parental conscience of being obliged to do something to give their kid an advantage. There were a few encouraging signs. Hank Schmidt, about 40- years old, dark hair, homely face, high-pitched voice, disarming 'country' manner was a $40,000 a year man, a combination of vigor (persuasive) and homeliness (disarming) that enabled him to wheedle his way into the heart of mothers in particular, so obviously unthreatening, personable and 'one of us' that his success was legendary. More odd, the head of the office was Bruce Carlson, 28-years old, very good looking professional suited Swede type, a graduate of the University of Minnesota Dental School and licensed dentist in the State, who made more ($50,000) selling books than drilling teeth. Other odd members of the 'team' had varying levels of success, fairly old, but still able to make a living to our general amazement.

I was teamed up with Garry Starry, a former electric utility employee who switched to Colliers to avoid the relentless 8-to-5 office grind. A kind of larger Mickey Rooney, lots of energy and bustle, a bit fat and not especially good looking, but with so much energy he could find a girl to party with. He was divorced with a daughter living with his ex In Iowa City. Our team leader and driver was Gary Turk, a fair verbal indication of his ethnic look, high cheek bones, thick glasses very precise diction, very businesslike. He drove a Mercedes diesel four door, unusual for that era but very economical, though hopelessly slow acceleration for highway driving. The group had a pep talk every afternoon before departing for the territory. 'Rock 'em' was the concluding obligatory shout given with varying levels of conviction. Within the range of candidate salesmen pessimist skeptic realist optimist delusional, pessimists would leave after the first outing, skeptics after three days, but the other categories were well represented at Colliers, I being decidedly realistic.

I was pleasantly surprised. Door to door sales are now defunct. Nobody trusts anybody and certainly will not commit funds for a fugitive pitch and promise. Those days were different. I soon was able to sell books to people I never thought would go for it. I sold a 3M engineer and his wife a set with the Harvard Classics, their newborn in a crib nearby. A couple who continued watching television while I delivered my pitch, answered my concluding question: *Is your child's education worth the daily price of a pack of cigarettes?* to which they answered 'OK'. Turk once dropped me off in a town around 6:15, and the woman in one of the yards saw me get out with my bag of materials, frowned and went inside. I made the rounds unsuccessfully, returned to the pickup spot where I started, and decided to try the woman's house for kicks. She answered, let me in. I delivered the pitch while the husband watched TV, asked the fatal question, and she said: *'OK and I want the bookcase and children's books.'* Sold and delivered by 9:30. I left. Turk was parked with the crew on the corner, I got in the car, said 'Got one', and Turk went into a *'never say die' and 'never too late'* sermon, pleased that as driver he at least made gas money off my sale. I would rank direct door-to-door selling as one of the most valuable experiences of my life. Normally we don't meet a variety of people under equally varied circumstances. We are in closed sets of school and family, neighborhood, and especially class. Poor never meet rich, rich never meet poor, educated never meet uneducated, uneducated never meet educated. Except tangentially. I learned to 'read' people, put them at ease, pace my conversation and approach, not push not pull, keep a comfortable but not slack connection, and mostly project a relaxed amiable tone. Learning to deal with anyone in general helps enormously in dealing with someone in particular.

I also met Terry Cole at Colliers, on vacation from the University of Iowa. Sandy hair, good looking, slim and fit, lots of smiles and enthusiasm personable, he was a good partner for cruising girls especially because he had a '53 Ford. We had hilarious encounters, including two girls we met in a bar. They dressed in all black, wore black lipstick and black nail polish, to go with their black hair and socks. We were so curious about their homestead we went there and found everything black including the curtains and furniture. No clue as to why this imitation Addams Family production. I met Rena Carlson at a food shop near my apartment building. I kept up with her and arranged a visit to her new digs near the University. She was sharing a room with Harriet Mether who worked for an insurance company in downtown Minneapolis. Terry and I went to the rather ancient brick building, rooms aligning a long corridor with a shared bathroom at the far end of the hall and a kitchenette at the head, opposite Harriet's room. The room was not large, but was filled with books and clothes (no closet) and a hotplate. Grimy windows were covered by grimy curtains. A queen-sized bed opposite a working fireplace. A sink at one end of the room.

Terry was immediately taken with Rena, a black-haired blue-eyed Swede, beautiful features, full body, conservatively dressed, a kind of fey disconnected aura of innocence and obliviousness, inviting the friendly humorous kidding Terry so liked to inflict on new material. Harriet was a phenomenon, like meeting Kathryn Hepburn when she was sixteen, all that potential as yet not fully unfolded or revealed. Harriet 23-years old, russet hair, short almost boyish cut, sparkling eyes, svelte not overly sexy body, nice face but not beautiful in any common sense, fascinating to look at, somewhat peaked nose, lovely bow lips, impulsive in her moves and gestures, a fullness of energy and warmth and enthusiasm that overwhelmed me and I suppose anyone else who knew her.

But her voice was the magic of all, rich, feeling, tremulous, incredible range of soft and full sound like music, pure diction and clarity, you could listen to her talk and especially read for hours, always fully engaged emotionally. Her eyes were a fascinating combination of hazel irises with small rectangles of green changing with light and feeling. We went out to a country music bar where Burl Ives was playing, we drank martinis, I kissed her, we returned to the room, chatted and then left promising a return visit the next day.

Harriet Mether

Harriet graduated from St. Olaf College in Northfield Minnesota, site of the notorious Younger brothers bank robbery in 1876, Frank and Jesse James among the gang members. Carlton College, better known and larger than St. Olaf, is in the same town. Her parents, Sven and Elsa Mether, lived in International Falls, a timber town, location of a large Finnish expatriate community. Her father had fought in the Finnish-Soviet war of 1939, inflicting a humiliating defeat on Stalin's largely demoralized troops, most of its officer corps having been liquidated in the purges of the late 1930's. They moved to Minnesota in 1940, Harriet the oldest of three daughters, commonly a position in the pecking order that imposes an unstated need to make up for not having a son, the daughter assuming many of the presumed characteristics of boys, rambunctious, hyper active assertive. Her next oldest sister was pure Scandinavian blonde, blue eyed, very poised and graceful. Her youngest looked much like Harriet but much more subdued, gentle and receding. Her mother was a knockout, beautiful, elegant, aristocratic, with an autobiography that must have inspired Harriet to emulate her expressive independent and liberated lifestyle. The mother had run off to Paris in her 20's, indulged in the Jazz Age liberation enjoyed by women for the first time, then returned and married the father, a strong, good looking, soft spoken Finn whom they all loved to distraction. I enjoyed his company, feeling a similarity to my Swedish grandfather. Swedish is the second official language in Finland and the two nations are close in economic and social characteristics.

St. Olaf tended to emphasize the German cultural heritage, rather than the French or English. Harriet read a great deal of Hofmannstahl and Rilke, admired Alma Schindler who married Mahler, Gropius, and Franz Werfel in that order and Frieda von Richthoven eventual wife of DH Lawrence for their scandalous love lives and determination to attach themselves as muse to great men of culture, a paradigm obliquely including her own mother's adventurous past. I pretty well assumed that she was following an imagined course of sexual-cultural progression, perhaps not very cultural but aspiring to the free-spirited style of female icons of the 20th Century, some higher reference required to excuse if not elevate the entirely sexual motive. Things moved along briskly. I ended up living in the room with Harriet and Rena Carlson, we on a mattress on the floor just next to the bed on which beautiful oblivious Rena reposed in a peaceful slumber, not two feet from me, as I fucked Harriet with somewhat divided attention, not being able to resist looking at Rena and half expecting her eyes to pop open to the drama unfolding literally under her nose. Sometime later Rena moved to another friend's lodgings closer to downtown, not for prurient reasons, she was oblivious to our antics.

Paul Scott lived in an apartment in an adjacent building with his black sparrow introverted and moody wife and their newborn. We became good friends, he working the night shift at a local hotel and sleeping days, so when Harriet went to work I could do coffee with Scott until he finally had to sleep. He had a junker car which he generously loaned us from time to time, first for a trip to St. Olaf to see Harriet's friends. I encountered the healthy wholesome vigorous and handsome pure Aryan students who were volunteering for Kennedy's newly established Peace Corps, world savers all. The school was immaculately Lutheran. I didn't feel equal to the level of energy and aspiration they exuded but tried to cover my deficiency in agreeable admiration for their (to me) deluded outlook for World peace. Scott had served four years in the Air Force as an MP in Vienna where he was inspired to learn and major in German studying on the GI Bill at U. Minnesota. He was a well-built guy, chain smoked, drooping eyelids, probably from chronic lack of sleep, but sanguine in his infinitely protracted march to the Bachelor Degree. His wife said little, chronically depressed or at least dispirited, both going nowhere in the immediate future, but aspiring to teach High School on his part once graduated. I have no idea what the kid had to do with this.

Harriet's sister, the blonde, came to visit, she engaged to an Air Force pilot, stunningly beautiful and entirely different from Harriet. We all slept in the room, a sheet hung up for the sister who settled on the mattress near the sink, while we rumbled on the bed. When Harriet went to work at the insurance company, I had breakfast with the sister, conversation going reasonably well for all the preposterous and irregular circumstances surrounding our situation. We three borrowed Scott's car and drove to International Falls. Harriet and I had gone to various bars and clubs and parties, met her graduate student friend who had just been hired by a General Mills partner to tutor his son during a vacation in Bermuda all expenses paid. The son arrived at a party we attended, 6 feet 5 inches tall, top hat, spats, vest, good looking, booming baritone, energetic and very overpowering presence, even at 19-years old he looked forty. Harriet often ogled alpha males who struck her fancy, mainly for their confident even dominant attitude, in the room or bar or club, so her wanderlust was unabated so far as I was concerned. I definitely lacked the spontaneity she enjoyed and probably expected. In International Falls I encountered the entire Finnish colony, vigorous, healthy obscenely attractive and energetic, her parents truly distinguished. They were members of a 'curling' club which competition we attended. A large black kind of flat bottomed bowling ball is pushed forward by using brooms to clear the way ahead and ease its advance to the finish line. Improbable diversion but they obviously played to win. At some point Harriet whispered in my ear: '*I don't want us to live together anymore*', not surprising because anticipated, but no less disappointing, I having a rather strong liking for her presence and personality, but absolutely no means or perhaps conviction that we should be together indefinitely. Perhaps to ease the parting she said: '*I will always remember you as my first*', a distinguishing biographical footnote to her later escapades perhaps to be cherished. She was fucking an Israeli student two weeks later and had left to teach Middle School in Mankato, a small town in southern Minnesota, by the time I joined the Army in June. One among many is not very consoling. First among many is somewhat better. More about Harriet later.

Applying for employment invariably ended in the question: Have you completed your military obligation? The Draft was in effect, to be resolved by one of two alternatives: 2-year enlistment in the Regular Army, or enlistment in the Army Reserve: 6-months active duty, one meeting a week, one weekend a month, and two weeks 'camp' every Summer over a total six years. I had by then got very interested in Russian, bought the Soviet Army chorus recording then popular, and took out a Russian language study book, mostly to no great result. I knew about the Army Language School, but a three-year enlistment was required to apply with no guarantee you would get the school or the language you wanted. Three years with a possible dead end was hard to agree to. I decided to do the Reserve thing, popular with professionals and presumably a more congenial form of service than the alternative.

In April I went to Ft. Snelling, home base of the 3rd Army, a lovely patch of deep green grass, a colonial style main building with large green shuttered windows, Ionic columned front portico, more like a college campus than a military installation. In an outbuilding I found a group of five sergeants playing cards. I told them I wanted to enlist, they brushed me off, directing me to the main building. If they had been receptive I might have ended up broiled in a tank. Fortune was guiding me. A civilian was in charge of administering the main office building, a very scholarly looking elder gentleman, tweeds, horn-rimmed glasses, genteel manner, very Ivy League. He inquired what sort of service unit I might be interested in. I said I would like the Army Language School Russian course if available. He said he just received no more than two days ago authorization for Reserve units to send candidates to the Army Language School. The 3rd Army was designated for European theater, Russian being their main interest. He said a language test was required, something like Esperanto to determine aptitude for dealing with tenses conjunctions and narrative in general. I took the test, usually a 2-hour deal, and finished in eighty minutes. He graded it, I tested at 98 out of 100, he immediately began the paper work and within six days I was an assigned member of the reserve unit with orders to complete Prisoner of War Interrogator training to include one year of Russian in Monterey. Seldom do pieces of one's life fall so favorably and unobstructed into one's lap.

FT. LEONARD WOOD

The second most significant experience in my life was the US Army, something I anticipated with little enthusiasm and came to love. In June 1961, with orders and tickets and funds ($87) from my Minneapolis Reserve Unit, I left Minneapolis by train to St. Louis then by bus to Fort Leonard Wood, deep in the Missouri countryside, Jesse James country. I forget exactly how I arrived, where I stayed, what procedures I endured to get situated. I had prudently got a crew cut before I left Minnesota anticipating the deflowering likely to be performed by less sensitive and esthetically challenged barbers. I remember the roll call in an open yard where barber chairs were lined up and each victim proceeded to the topiary guillotine, piles of carefully coiffed curls accumulating at the foot of the barber like the heads of aristocrats. We went through the uniform processing, our size approximately matched, tunic, trousers, fatigues, boots. We were then assigned to barracks, fourteen to a floor with bunks and a common latrine without doors for privacy. Being called a private was an ironic mockery of the new conditions of our living quarters.

A fallacy one often heard about the Army was: *Never volunteer!* Fools didn't, wise men do. The corporal in charge of getting things set up gathered the first floor recruits and asked who wanted to be squad leader. I immediately volunteered, so did George Basch. We were as expeditiously confirmed. The great misunderstanding about large organizations and those charged to manage them is that they need and must have capable and willing subordinates to run things at each level. Volunteers who relieve the next in command of tedious micro management duties are well regarded and rewarded accordingly. The span of control of one person is decidedly small. Intermediate leaders help to group the mass into manageable units rising to the top of the chain of command. If I guarantee to get my squad ship shape for inspections and keep them on point during marches and combat training that makes life infinitely easier for the sergeant. A major advantage as squad leader was I never had KP the entire time in Basic Training. Another advantage was that I had a young and good-natured bunch of recruits, two farm boys from Wisconsin strong and used to hard work and genial compliance with requirements. A good-natured kid from Arkansas, and similarly cooperative guys from Texas, Illinois, South Dakota and Louisiana. Having traveled through most of those States and been used to meeting people from all parts of the US made me comfortable with the different accents and life approaches of the recruits in question. I never pulled any *prima donna* fascist command stuff, remained supportive and cajoling rather than 'direct and obey'. Not that anyone could have got away with that approach, although William Britt in Basch's squad eventually did try.

The weekly schedule was five days field and lecture hall training, Saturday morning inspection and Saturday afternoon through Sunday liberty, leaving base not permitted for the first two weeks of Basic Training. Marching around took up much of the time, carrying an M1 rifle, a backpack on a few occasions. June-July heat and humidity were stifling. One day we had advance-under-fire training, a machine gun firing live ammunition about thirty feet over our heads as we, cradling our M1 across our elbows, crawled under barbed wire for about forty yards. As with everything military, some figured out how beat the system, three guys standing up and running to the end of the field unremarked. We had lineup for shots (typhoid, cholera, diphtheria, etc.), a brutal assault on the upper arm. It began with taking a shot record card already stamped and then proceeding to the injection lineup. Basch and I figured we could wait until the respective shot stations were filled with victims, then go to the closing line where our shot book was certified. We got that done without firing a shot as it were.

Small unit attack was especially exhausting as we ran uphill in 10-yard intervals, falling to the ground between, in 95-degree heat, dragging our M1 rifle along for the ride. Our likelihood of survival in actual combat was probably 1 in 500. Grenade drill was somewhat anticlimactic, we threw the damn thing over a wall, but the grenades were dummies. Gas mask drill was a trifle more authentic. We each went into a closed cement shed. A tear gas cartridge was activated and we had to get the mask on in four seconds, some leaving the shed choking, eyes burning, as they untimely completed the maneuver. Target range was more fun, although it was astonishing how poorly we did even at fifty yards. I got a Marksman medal for remarkably inaccurate performance, a generous disregard of military fitness, probably just to encourage the recruits already humiliated on numerous other occasions. I do remember an atavistic encounter with a 1st Lieutenant, about 5'6", slim, blonde, crew cut, Southern, high chalk-over-blackboard squeaky voice, with airborne metal pin and Ranger arch over 8th Airborne shoulder patch, a few ribbons, just back from Viet Nam among the first contingent sent there. He was what George Patton must have looked like age sixteen. We were raised on John Wayne and other Hollywood versions of battle, heroism, sacrifice and leadership. History books told us about Alexander the Great, Caesar, Napoleon. We assumed military leadership required a dominant presence, tall, formidable. I learned what charisma and will power really were about with this very short, slim, wiry Lieutenant. By the time he was through talking, we would have followed him anywhere. He commanded loyalty and respect and awe and even fanatic enthusiasm just by the intensity, conviction, certainty of his military presence. It was an experience I never expected and am grateful for. Like the German tribes who elected their leaders, this guy could make berserkers out of all of our company.

Lecture halls were like movie theaters with an elevated stage for speakers and rows of seats for recruits. The officers and noncoms who conducted our training were outstanding. Well prepared, engaging. Their greatest enemy wasn't recruit disinterest or the Viet Cong, it was the air conditioning. After marching, attacking undefended hills, and throwing dummy grenades, we had sweated and groaned through the oppressive central Missouri heat to the point that air conditioning completely demolished our unit's powers of resistance. Keeping us awake was a constant battle, *'On your feet!!!!'* a regular interruption to at least restore to consciousness the majority of attendees.

On Sunday, Basch and I teamed up to go to the Base Library, the only air-conditioned venue with comfortable seating available to us. Not that the outcome was much different than at the lecture theaters. We enjoyed wandering around the Base, looking in on various buildings and personnel. In one office we overheard a Lieutenant admonishing a black recruit to the effect that he had, if not destroyed, at least rendered inoperable a Sherman tank for which a court martial had ordered him to pay reparations. Given his current income of $85 per month, a lifetime of service would be required. This was the South and visions of the Emancipation Proclamation, Plessy vs. Ferguson, Civil rights demonstrations flashed through my mind. What could this weak soft small deferential black guy have done to inflict such damage?

When off base passes were made available, George Basch and I went to the town just off the North Base entry gate, a half-hour walk. Military bases provide a source of income and mischief wherever located. The town was overrun every weekend with recruits: movie theater, burger joints, stores with assorted junk to divert idle soldiers of low taste and no morals, the latter their real interest but suitable opportunities depressed by the Military Police who tried to keep such diversions out of sight. Women always gather in proximity to military installations, for different motives but all directly related to male desperation. One heard rumors of guys getting a $25 poke down a ravine near town, but we saw little to corroborate such claims. However, on the way back to the base we did stop in at a kind of dance bar where black girls of truly primitive Southern provenance half drunk or drugged, would say 'come out for some fun' or the like enticements, probably for the most part successful with some percentage of the base population. George and I returned to base untainted.

One weekend we went to St. Louis, stayed in a hotel and roamed the hot spots. The hotel valet took our bags to the room, greeting us as Lieutenants at the elevator and Majors at the room, pleasant ruse to arouse gratitude and obtain better tips. We had to wear uniforms, not civvies, those returned only before leaving the Fort. A bit noisy, bustling, the iconic jazz playing on speakers, bars and restaurants crowded, the Steel Arch, symbol of St. Louis as gateway to the West shining improbably in the starry moonlit night. Sunday Basch visited the son of a family friend, now teaching at Washington University, oddly the school from which TS Eliot and J *Alfred Prufrock* and *The Wasteland* emerged.

Conflict is inevitable, no planning or prevention avails. Our Platoon had a large contingent of Jews from Chicago upstairs in our barracks so fortunately nothing I had anything directly to do with. Obnoxious, egocentric, pushy arrogant, mild adjectives to describe this offensive group of semites. After the '57 victory against Egypt and *Exodus* the film extolling the Jewish settlement of Israel there was no limit to their presumption. One of them said to me during our indoctrination that Israel was his first loyalty, US second, endearing thought. The current issue arose when the Jews celebrating the Sabbath at a Friday night ceremony conducted by the base rabbi claimed exclusion from clean up duties preliminary to Saturday morning inspection, leaving the remnant crew to do all of the dirty work. 'Religious' claims presumably take priority over secular duty, fairly common Middle Eastern pickle. Much resentment and percolating anti-Semitism the result, the issue decided in their favor making it all the more a matter of injustice vs. prejudice as between the two sides. Much more significant for Platoon cohesion was the eventual downfall of our Platoon leader Jose Ramirez initially selected by the Corporal in charge of our setup. Jose was a member of the Texas National Guard, dispatched for basic training to Ft. Leonard Wood. An arch-typical Mexican, pot belly, fat brown worried face, lacking any military advantages, but a master at rifle drill, useless but decorative performance on the parade ground. IQ below 90 and scant English language skill, modest and smiling anxiously when not frowning uncertainly. We all liked him because he so obviously had no claim to command and in fact desperately needed our compliance to maintain his putative authority. But where substance is lacking form cannot indefinitely prevail. Some problem arose, he was sacked, and to everyone's surprise, more in fact chagrin it was announced to the assembled Platoon that William Britt would now be Platoon leader.

Britt was in Basch's squad, a fellow varsity man, we had a sort of class affinity over the other recruits. Britt seemed compliant with his subordination, did his part, but remained more or less aloof. Britt's

Army Colonel father was friends with the base commander, a Major General, and the general's command car was once sent to our Platoon barrack to pick up Britt for a weekend at the top of the Base canopy. No doubt that was noticed by all noncoms. Graduate of Sewanee Military Academy, Britt had ingrained habits of a career officer and gentleman, Southern style, accustomed to lead and arrogating a sense of superiority only to be revealed under favorable circumstances. Apparently he felt his sudden promotion allowed release of these generally reviled characteristics, because he started with severe strictures as to the lack of discipline, military demeanor, and alert compliance within our ranks, a message heard and pondered by all.

We were in the last two weeks of training, an overnight march and campout planned for the following week. We obtained tents and field cooking gear, shovels for tent site preparation, a backpack to augment our discomfort. The campsite was OK. Basch and I dug a shallow ditch around our tent to contain rainwater, if any, and we hammered our tent pole studs and got the thing more or less up and livable, a fun vacation type of activity one might enjoy in civilian life. We were then taken by trucks to a deep country location where each squad leader was given maps and compass and ordered to proceed to a destination three miles distant, presumed effective use of a compass critical to success. One handicap was that it was 8 PM, sun almost down, darkness in deep country total. We started out optimistically, unjustified by later events, and got totally lost, the only secure reference for where we were was a State Highway about 500 yards to the left which I figured I would follow to some happy conclusion. Unfortunately Reserve officers, including a few Captains, were bird-dogging our efforts and most ended up screaming at me and the other squad leaders for our total ineptness and lack of a sense of direction. Not singled out, simply part of a universal failure of leadership, I was spared serious consequences. Besides I was destined for a headquarters job as prisoner of war interrogator so cross-country skills were less pertinent. Official unhappiness seeks scapegoats, Britt as putative leader of the miscreant Platoon a suitable choice. No matter, within five days we received travel allowances and cash for expenses, and orders for our next encounter with Army life.

Basch and I headed for Chicago to spend our ten days of liberty pending departure for new assignments, he to Colorado and medic training, I to Baltimore for Intelligence training. His father was a physician in Vienna, George was born in 1937, the Anschluss came in 1938, and the family prudently arranged a move to Chicago, position as physician at a Jewish hospital easily arranged. They lived in a three-story brownstone near downtown, elegant neighborhood, with mature trees and prosperous residents. Very European interior, spare, expensive furnishings, cool quiet and clean, staircase to second and third floor guest room, my outrageously well- appointed quarters especially welcome after eight weeks of communal living. George owned a TR3, fun car which he was overhauling. He removed the engine and disassembled it down to the valves which he planned to have reground. He graduated from MIT as a mechanical engineer, his ability well demonstrated in this case. We drove around Chicago, hit a few bars, and met a few of his friends from MIT, including one who had just married a gorgeous redhead, astonished George and impressed me. We also met a Jewish family in an upscale walled estate, he an entrepreneur just about to start a mutual fund and later employ George in some photo equipment venture. Eventually George moved to New York as head of development for an American photo equipment manufacturer. Unfortunately, the Japanese were taking over camera production (Nikon, Yashita, etc.) and by 1970 monopolized the entire market. After five days I said farewell and boarded a train for Baltimore and Ft. Holabird.

FT. HOLABIRD

About a half hour walk to Johns Hopkins University and Athena Bar and Restaurant, and about an hour walk to the USS Constitution anchored in Baltimore harbor, Ft. Holabird was built in 1918, a number of large brick buildings embedded in the south central part of the city. Our quarters were on the second floor of a large building, hardwood floors and oddly depressing tiled communal bathroom that felt like the bathrooms in railway stations of the 1880's. Our bunks were entirely contemporary Army metal, as comfortable as such items can be expected to be. Classes were held in another building with tall latticed windows giving the feel of grade school. A remarkably well-educated faculty included an Army Major, Yale PhD Candidate in Japanese, who gave instruction on cultural distinctions internationally with special attention to Japanese variations. We had interrogator training, methods of persuasion, taught by a Chinese-descent officer who used two jars in Korea, one rattlesnake in each, on his table while the prisoner sat close and nervously glanced at the possible agents of retribution should he fail to deliver the goods. We had classes on Russian and Chinese rank and unit ribbons and badges, arms and equipment. Altogether rather interesting and diverting way to spend time, considering the alternative of Advanced Infantry, more of Basic raised to a higher level of effort, expectation and accountability.

We had weekends off, a rare treat. The classmates (appellation used to indicate the collegiate atmosphere of the school, far removed from military rigor) were exceptional mainly because the Reserve Language School training had only recently been on offer and apparently a fair number of Ivy League candidates were willing recruits to this constructive pursuit on the Army dime. Ephron Catlin, descendant of the Indian painter (he painted them), Harvard graduate and member of the Porcellan (Pigs) fraternity that blackballed FDR!, Boston Brahmin family, palled around with John Halverson, son of a high-end stationery manufacturer in Boston, graduate of Harvard Business School, a b-type male trying to appear as an a-type, constantly restless, agitated, complaining if not whining about practically everything, engaged to a horse-faced coed from Barnard College (which may explain his disposition). Nick Vontsolos from Ohio University, Greek immigrant family, intending to get a PhD in Russian, with whom I paired up to go to the Greek Athena taverna every weekend and listen to bouzouki music and drink beer. Leroy Elsing a High School teacher from Minneapolis, quiet reflective *echt* German looking, and Montgomery, feisty tending to querulous, got into a squabble when Leroy returning to bunk very late inadvertently sat on Montgomery who immediately took offense at what he interpreted to be a homosexual advance which led to a physical tussle and ended with an agreement to a wrestling match to settle a dispute that in an earlier century would have ended in a duel at dawn with seconds. The contest took place at some suitable location unknown to me in which Elsing soundly pressed Montgomery, a victory quietly welcomed by the rest of us, Montgomery being an unpleasantly hostile sort none of us cared to be around.

Nick was engaged to the daughter of an International Cash Register executive, she soon to meet him, travel to Monterey and marry there. So he wasn't available for dances held at the Nurses School of Johns Hopkins. Askew from Tennessee agreed to partner with me in this quest for civilized diversion. He was from a prominent old south Nashville family possibly connected to the State's ultimate hero Andrew Jackson. At the dance I met Ann Harding, a quiet gentle nursing student, and we managed to keep company on off hours. Her parents lived in Dundalk not too far from the Fort so I was able to visit her at home on weekends, enjoy home cooking and other fringe benefits of domestic life. We were in love, the kind of love that transients, destined to move on, imagine will last, very spiritual, not much sex, at first.

Survival, a basically defensive approach to life, requires cunning. Friday afternoon the Staff Sergeant in charge of our paperwork distributed tickets and travel funds for our move to Army Language School in Monterey California. Leroy Elsing along with most of the group got Greyhound tickets, a 5-day, 2500-mile grind in sweltering heat across the entire United States. Catlin was driving so he and three others took off on a not much better drive Saturday morning. Vontsolos drove with his fiancée the entire distance, which provided a kind of pre-honeymoon to their marriage a week later in Monterey. Which left me without ticket, orders, or plans. Here is where the cunning comes in. I said nothing about my stranded situation on Friday, deciding to wait to the last minute to inform the sergeant, on the chance of getting more favorable accommodations. My last night with Anne was atypically intense. She arranged with a friend to use her apartment. We had takeout and then as parting lovers began to kiss and hug, one thing leading to another until she was on the floor, I was removing her blouse and skirt, panties and bra, with a rather pent up store of mutual erotic anticipation. After much crying and kissing we parted, agreeing that she should visit California during the summer 1962 two-week break at Army Language School. We would write each other devotedly, which we did. I then returned to the empty sleeping quarters and waited until Saturday morning to bring the sergeant the bad news. He was surprised, as expected, and annoyed, as expected, but not vindictive, as expected. Just one person presented less of a problem and expense as compared to a dozen or more. He rambled on a bit about how to deal with the oversight. Fortunately in his position he had authority to disburse travel funds and buy tickets. When he grumbled about having to contact United Airlines I knew a very favorable outcome was in view. They could get me on a Sunday flight to San Francisco and a connecting flight to Monterey. $85 travel money came out of his ready cash, all signed for by me to make it legal. Travel east to west had the immense advantage of going with the Sun, meaning that if I left at 10 AM from Baltimore International, I would arrive in San Francisco around 1:30 PM, in time for a leisurely local flight to Monterey leaving at 3 PM, arriving 3:35 PM, and a leisurely cab ride to ALS.

ARMY LANGUAGE SCHOOL

In 1961, Monterey, where I attended the Army Language School, Russian 12-month course, was not bad duty considering that Advanced Infantry was the likely alternative. Cannery Row made famous by local author

John Steinbeck was still partly operating, Monterey was still a fishing village, none of the concrete that now replaces the original sandy beach and very few tourists, most of whom preferred Carmel. Carmel never changes, it's written in the City Code. I met Joan Baez in the Carmel Record Shop in December 1961, at the time she was having an affair with a girlfriend and just before her famous liaison with Bob Dylan. Henry Miller lived in Big Sur, where we visited the original Nepenthe bar/restaurant, a Miller and other hipster hangout. On weekends we went to San Francisco and the Broadway progressive jazz bars, where I ran into people from Minneapolis I knew at U. Minnesota, interesting times, nothing the same now.

I arrived nearly a week ahead of schedule which perplexed the resident staff sergeant, who improvised and feigned annoyance at such a break in the established orderly process that presented difficulties and required special rather than routine handling. I got a bunk in the prospective Russian class barracks and settled in. With no other students, no class assignments, and no barrack supervisors available, the sergeant more or less ignored me, much to my satisfaction, requiring nothing if I would only take care of myself. Agreed! I wandered around Monterey, ate at restaurants downtown and checked out the beach and the pier with its restaurants and gift shops but very subdued and practically no tourists. By Thursday, other tenants arrived and former tenants returned from the summer break. Henry Bosch, great grandson of the founder of the German auto electronics firm, since relocated to Chicago, looked much like a German emcee in the film *Cabaret* of the 1920's. Short, thin, unathletic, Teutonically neat, who as scion of a major industrial company, well acknowledged and accounted for, got extended leave every weekend, but where he went and what he did remained a mystery. We had a New York Jew, son of one of the founders of the E. J. Korvettes (Eight Jewish Korean Vets) chain of stores, first to acquire cheap-labor produced goods from Japan and market them in the States. His every other word was fuck, he was energetic, chutzpah personified, impulsive, and for some reason married a Chinese waitress he meet downtown.

Henry Hess, son of one of the owners of Hess Oil, drove a TR3 every weekend all over California, unconstrained by the military management, aware of his rather prominent connection. Richard Burbank, recent graduate of Philip-Exeter Academy, descendant of the famous horticulturalist, at 18-years was engaged and did marry within the first three months of class. The son of an Exxon executive and graduate of a New England Prep School was a natural party animal, played piano by ear extremely well, was a horny skirt chaser who married while at ALS. He invited his prep school buddy, son of actor Ray Milland, to stay in the barracks one weekend. The budding Hollywood star was 6'5", loud, reckless, and mostly out of control. Tell Schreiber son of a Hollywood studio executive, got parts in the local Monterey Theater Group acting on weekends. Tall, blonde, amiable, good looking, he was involved with a prosperous Carmel matron and a number of actresses encountered at the theater. His son by a New York Jewish lady much later became a film actor, starring with Angelina Jolie in Salt as the traitorous Secret Service villain. The son of a major furniture manufacturing firm in Pennsylvania also attended the Russian course. A graduate of the Yale acting school who wanted to be an opera baritone, apparently irresistible to Madam Balaxh my B-class teacher, visited her every weekend in what seemed an improbable conjunction of talents and passion. The list of characters and connections could be extended indefinitely. Pierre Berce, very Jean Gabin in look and manner, eventually married a waitress at a downtown restaurant, apparently a fruitful occupation for ladies in search of male partners.

The teachers were equally unusual. General Vlasov deserted the Soviet Army and organized anti-Soviet Russian prisoners into a regiment that fought with the Germans on the Eastern Front. A very sweet guy, handsome, quiet, modest, grey-haired, how he got to Monterey is a complete mystery given the price Stalin would have paid to grab him. Madame Karpov, large fat bouncy Jewish lady in bright flowery dresses, enthusiastic, always called on me when the supervisors visited her class to see how things were going. For some reason I could manage to speak a lot of Russian to suggest great progress was being made under her tutelage. I had artistic pretensions, especially portraits, and tried to draw some of the teachers during class, not especially easy for an amateur given their frequent movement, with two elderly exceptions shown here, one of

whom, Mr. Asimov, probably narcoleptic, often suddenly dropped off in class. Classes were ranked A B C D E G (F too deflating to use). A-class was academic and linguistically inclined under Madame Krasny, B-class under Madame Balaxh emphasized conversation, the others did whatever they could manage, students distributed to class based on test performance and an oral exam. I was in B-class and graduated #7 out of 56. Madame Orlov, a blonde gorgeous buxom around 30-years old sultry teacher spoke in a smoky furry mezzo, the personification of Slavic seduction, but entirely contrary to her arch and off-putting conduct and behavior. We listened to audio tapes to improve our ear for Russian. Whenever she was on the entire class groaned with admiration but no matter what happened she would say dismissively *Nichivo!* Mr. Govorov lived in Pacific Grove in a dark candle-lit tenebrous setting of icons and booze, a confirmed alchoholic, he would drink a tumbler full of white wine to start the day.

Carmel was a 20-minute bus ride from the base, a jewel of cute shops, expensive summer homes and a stunning white sand beach as if some Hollywood producer had designed the entire set, entirely protected by strict zoning laws. Hollywood was well represented, the lovely Jean Arthur retired in seclusion, Kim Novak withdrawn from tinsel town and married to her veterinarian, much later Clint Eastwood, mayor for a year, multimillionaires from film and oil and who knows what. Now overrun with tourists abetted by highways and a booming economy. In the era before 1965, Carmel was a quiet, secluded unspoiled town. One of our ALS Mandarin language students, son of a psychiatrist in Baltimore, rented a small house in Carmel, an address with cachet on the East Coast. He sent manuscripts of stories and excerpts from a novel he was working on to publishers mostly in New York who, cartographically savvy and prudent as to emerging talent or proximity thereto, returned them with equal regularity, replete with compliments regarding literary promise and developing style, *please do call again once the work is nearer completion*. With a car, a house, and an expense account that supported a modest coterie of friends, admirers and opportunists, he held court in Carmel every weekend. I couldn't stand him.

I was shopping in the Carmel record store in December 1961, rifling through their 33-rpm record collection when Joan Baez showed up beside me as I selected her latest recording. 'That's a terrible record', she smiled. She was having a lesbian affair with her girlfriend at the time and soon after began the Dylan gig. '*Marry me*' I said, to myself.

Nick married and rented a house just off base. His lovely energetic temperamental wife was fun to be with, although she could explode without warning, slamming doors, screaming epithets. I liked her, she liked me. They had adequate support from the Cash Register end of the family, but nonetheless she took a job at a senior facility caring for the indigent remnants of our elder population, including bathing their unsightly bodies, a remarkably penitent occupation for a very secular and spirited girl, worthy of Mother Teresa.

The base clubhouse was a Victorian two-story, language library on the first floor, seven rooms on the second floor each with an upright piano and a record player. I used to practice piano and listen to classical records with the Yale baritone, Nick and other aesthetes. A large central drawing room, setting for the annual Monterey Peninsula bridge tournament, had a half dozen leather sofas and chairs, including a Baldwin grand which I played occasionally as other students read or chatted. I was complemented on my *Claire de Lune* by a professional pianist who somehow turned up at ALS. He also played to an appreciative audience. Piano raised or more likely confirmed the superior tone and education of the current student body, always deferring respectfully to talent in the more difficult forms in which it is manifested. One of the most talented guys I have met, Peter Bell, was a graduate of Swarthmore, consummate dancer, piano player, whatever. His sister was a Vogue model, and he later went to work for IBM, he at all times a completely placid even indifferent participant in his own perfection, never a trace of emotion or reaction of any kind.

B class was second from the end.

The ALS Russian chorus had achieved national attention in the 1950's, director Yuri Kalinsky gaining favorable mention even by the Army Chief of Staff for its accomplished renderings of Russian and Soviet patriotic and religious songs. He went on national tours with the chorus gaining praise for mastering such an impossible language and musical style. Large numbers of students were diverted from classes to a road show that contributed little to national defense. Eventually this PR gig was curtailed, and returned to base. To end up being able to sing *Очи Черние* but not be able to interrogate prospective Soviet *ryadavoi* was not in the national interest or a worthy expenditure of taxpayer dollars. Yuri nonetheless auditioned all the students and assigned, with or without any ability to sing two notes, each of us to a bass/baritone/tenor section of the chorus. I ended up in the baritone section, did benefit somewhat in improving my pronunciation, but otherwise left culturally indifferent to the entire enterprise. I did enjoy singing *Podmoskoviye Vechera* however.

Catlin had a red VW bug so he and Harrington and I occasionally ventured to outlying areas in search of girls. The Cannery had one outstanding folk music bar hangout for folk singers and guitar improvisers who volunteered their talent as part of the general camaraderie. Catlin and I went there one Saturday night when a group of coeds turned up from Mills College, a women's college in Oakland. After several volunteer performances and impelled by the possibility of attracting the favor of the coeds, Catlin and I volunteered to sing some Russian songs, *Kalinka, Polushka pole, Podmoskovniye Vechera,* our greatest hits. Generous, in part enthusiastic, applause greeted our effort, and apparently created a favorable impression, especially one coed taken with Catlin. He later dated her a few times, ending with *'There is nothing I would rather do than go to bed with you, but I want to be a virgin until I marry.'* A kind of tribute to his animal magnetism considered from a certain point of view. We also went to **Nepenthe**, the original one not the current tourist travesty that has replaced it, with some local girls, very sweet and charming but decidedly unequal to the academic standards we represented. Fun but not repeated. Harrington and I took a trip to Tahoe casinos in his car, interesting but ultimately tiresome playground of mostly Hollywood weekenders. I saw one of them lose $2000 and give the dealer (well built, young, personable) a $200 tip.

I had corresponded devotedly with Ann, sending poems of doubtful merit but great conviction, one using oceanic metaphors, sea foam, Poseidon whipping his dolphin-drawn sea chariot through the waves, coffers of pirate treasures of gold and jewels buried in infinite sands of the bottomless sea. A metaphorical bridge created by memory and imagination to reconstruct and reinforce the experience now long past of the person I loved when sitting in twilight and dark on Baltimore public park grass, holding caressing and murmuring vows and aspirations. We planned for her to come to Monterey for a passionate and nuptual reunion. The week arrived, summer two-week break began, and I waited at the Monterey airport for her flight. The plane landed, the deplaning steps were in place, the door opened, Ann walked out and down the stairs, and I realized I had not the slighted interest in her or our projected two week adventure. But what can one do but fake it. We got on a bus headed for Seattle to 'visit the folks', stopped in San Francisco to see a Chinese nurse schoolmate, got to Seattle where she stayed with Gerda and I with my parents, Alice as ever inebriated and Robert the tin soldier looking like the weight of creation bore down on him. We survived, returned to Monterey, I made a perfunctory play for her private parts, she was unwilling, I was disinclined to persist, we parted at the airport, and she returned to Baltimore.

I left Fort Ord late in October 1962. The discharge office gave me $86 for a return bus ticket to Minneapolis, location of my reserve unit, and $80 cash for expenses. I had no intention of returning to Minneapolis. I got a ride to St. Louis with Ephron Catlin in his red Bug, got a bus to Chicago to visit my basic training pal George Basch, newly wed with a blonde nurse he met during his medic training near Denver, then got the B&O to Washington, arriving with $145 and no prospects. I never saw Catlin or Harrington again.

WASHINGTON

I arrived in Washington November 1, 1962, wearing my Specialist-4 patch and Green Army uniform, preferring the anonymity, even invisibility, a uniform provides, a form of invisibility much like H. G. Wells short story in which witnesses to a crime completely overlooked the postman perpetrator, uniforms so common and unremarkable as to pass unnoticed. I had located the Army Navy Airmen Hostel close in northeast sponsored by churches in the Washington area. $28 a week, bunk bed in shared quarters (only one other guy in my bunk room), common shower, breakfast and dinner daily, special turkey dinner with mashed potatoes, cranberry sauce, and fresh coffee served Sunday by lovely High School girls from vicinity churches volunteering to help 'our boys in uniform'. Those dinners were more satisfying than any later wine/dine extravagances in more prosperous circumstances. I figured I could afford to stay there for at least a month until prospects emerged.

I went to a Federal employment office in search of such prospects. A fat unattractive but dedicated lady of about 35-years inquired about my interests and skills, a laughable concept in my case, Russian being in demand about as much as hair braiders. I said I would like something that required Russian language, so totally unexpected as to excite her interest. There is a mistaken myth that bureaucrats are lazy and indifferent. They are often tenacious in the face of impossible odds, and she was fortunately especially so. She told me to come back in three days. She would seek and find if it killed her.

I required provisional income and answered an ad for seasonal sales people at Woodward and Lothrup (Woodies) department store on 12th Street. I applied took the training and was hired. It was fun helping shoppers select ties, shirts, belts, cologne and ringing up sales. My experience in direct sales at Colliers in Minneapolis prepared me for the variety and perplexity of customers who welcomed amiable assistance. Time passed quickly with so many holiday shoppers to assist. Fred worked as salesman in the men's section, blonde, FBI crew cut, eager and optimistic manner, surprising since the job had no prospects whatever. He was married, two kids, and a Mormon, which is where any ambition he had must have been directed. I mention him because 20 years later during a business trip from California, my then residence, I saw Fred in the same men's section, unchanged in dress, manner and form, as optimistic as ever.

I returned to the employment agency as appointed. The lady informed me that the Aerospace Technology Division of the Library of Congress, adjunct of the DOD Defense Intelligence Agency, had positions open for Russian capable candidates. I complemented her on her remarkable find and arranged to visit the Library and interview with Walter Counts the person in charge of hiring. The Library of Congress was established by Thomas Jefferson who donated his considerable personal collection to get things started, the purpose of the Library being to provide expert reference material to Members of Congress in support of their legislative duties. Now an imposing late Victorian marble and granite pile occupying an entire city block opposite the Capitol, four stories above and two below ground, a vast array of bookshelves in the storage areas and a somewhat smaller but equally vast reference card collection in dozens of card catalog shelves tracking every significant book and publication over 160 years. A large reading room with an amphitheater of encircling desks provided scholars a place to read the material brought by book searchers from the maze of shelves hidden within the innards of the Library. Offices were distributed along the perimeter of the Library, the Congressional Research Service, the Poet Laureate, the Prints and

Photos Division, a Music Reference Section, where I once saw Julian Brendel looking over a pile of Mozart manuscripts in preparation for his definitive recordings of the Master's piano sonatas.

The Aerospace Technology Division (ATD) occupied a 40x25-yard rectangle within the 'stacks' as the book shelving area was called. I took an inside elevator to the third floor, turned left into the Division workspace past a striking amply endowed jet black lady of about 25-years with silver nail polish and silver lipstick, yellow-red-green flowered dress, looking like Big Mama at a Yoruba food fair, and met Counts, an abrupt contrast in ethnic context. Selling books I chanced to meet so many different types that I became a quick estimator of what I confronted. Counts was socially retarded, uncomfortable in encounter, awkward in conversation, seeking refuge in formality of manner and inexpressive explanation of the position and duties. I had already learned that I had to place the interviewer at ease, he often more annoyed, terrified or uncomfortable than I was. We got along because Counts had served in the Army in Korea and was familiar with the Army Language School. He asked me a question in badly accented Russian and I replied quickly in unaccented Russian, probably an obligation on his part to verify to some extent the skill presumed essential to employment. He quickly decided I would do and began the vetting process. Within ten days I was told to report to work December 17, a most welcome Christmas present since I was down to $85!

On the appointed date I turned up in Count's office, first door on the left entering the Division area. We shook hands and he said: *'Let's introduce you to the staff.'* Private offices for section directors, with doors and windows, were located on the outer perimeter of the Division area. Other employees had desks partitioned within the large central area. The workforce was divided into Americans and Russian/East Europeans. We entered an area of four desks, one empty for me, where John Jordan Jr., Eric Powell, and Bill Crumb were as welcoming as initial concern as to who would be invading the space would allow. We all relaxed in amiable chat once we realized we shared an outlook on our common employment and our prospective solidarity in face of it. I was not going to disrupt the established pattern of office life. We, American and foreign, were all displaced persons thrown up by chance and misadventure on the beach of ATD employment, no one considering this as a desired and foreseen career destination, simply a means of survival.

John Jordan Jr. was a case in point. He graduated Haverford College, a noted Quaker institution in Pennsylvania. His classmates claimed he would 'go far', 'most likely to succeed' with no practical achievements to support such claims. He was tall, lanky, an unruly cowlick of brownish blonde hair falling irrepressibly over his eyes inducing as frequent a signature head toss to clear his view. A receding chin, pale blue rabbit eyes, prominent nose, a bit like John Updike, impatient manner, frequent choppy dismissive laugh, and an unsettled manner complete the picture. At 29-years he was approaching the sell-by date of youthful expectation soon to enter the flatland of opportunity foregone. His classmates had by now acquired advanced degrees and begun academic careers or were otherwise at the third or fourth rung of the ladder of success. At 29-years, John was becoming desperate.

Bill Crumb was from Charleston West Virginia, a University of Michigan graduate, younger brother of George Crumb the emerging major American composer of exotic sound-scapes and artful piano scores. Bill's father was clarinetist with the Charleston Symphony Orchestra, the mother cellist, and Bill played flute as an avocation, music talent spread equally if not in equal degree within the family. Bill, the more modest of the four, had an equable personality, liked to be liked, and never sought to stand out or be noticed. We became friends and attended George's concerts at the Smithsonian and other venues, he spending at least half the time plucking strings under the piano hood with occasional more recognizable keyboard intervals.

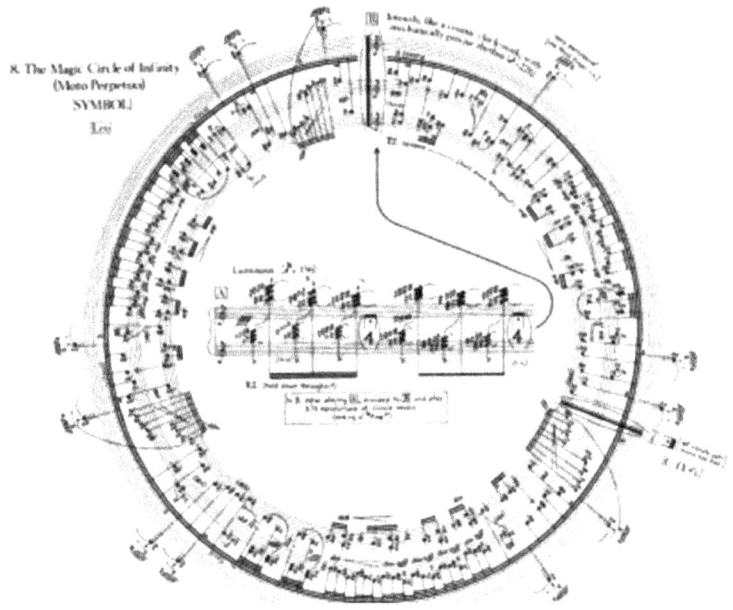

Eric Swenson was a veteran, family man, three kids, a source of desperation and frequent comment. Blonde, crew cut, black thick-rimmed glasses, cheap suit, nervous, even anxious, manner, his serious doubts about the long-term prospects of ATD and concerns about financial jeopardy for himself prompted him to issue applications for employment in several directions.

Counts also introduced me to Dan Pyle, occupying an adjoining cubicle. Surroundings totally subject to the control of the occupant eventually come to manifest the character of the proprietor, in Dan's case irretrievable disorder. Effete was the word come immediately to mind, a total defenseless weakness as though the slightest impact would floor him. He was equable, articulate, amusing and engaging, enjoyed irony and wit and was well read so that references did not fly past him. His large glasses continually slid down his nose provoking a signature push back that emphasized the impression that books and reading were his most favorite pastimes. He was disheveled, wrinkled cords, jacket, shirt, a tie hanging forlornly from his neck, more like a noose foreboding ruin. Three nearly empty Styrofoam coffee cups, papers and books stacked on the floor, desk strewn with manuscripts, Russian journals, several dictionaries perched precariously on a makeshift shelf, appropriate to his personal look of abandoned effort to manage even the inert objects surrounding him much less himself.

A more interesting American worked in the Chemistry section. Bradley Cooper was a light mulatto, large handsome head, well built, pigeon toed and near sighted, peering intently as if Othello spotting Desdemona in a secluded doorway, although bad eyesight not jealous fury accounted for the appearance of sharp scrutiny. He played flute in a dance combo at a Black hotel in Northeast Washington four nights a week. He learned Russian at Army Language School. He had no Negro accent, his father was a conductor on Northern Pacific Railroad based in Denver.

During coffee break in the basement cafeteria I met Linda Mondragon, employed in some obscure section of the LOC, a friend, perhaps more, of John Jordan Jr. An alert black sparrow, quick head swivels, as though perched on some tree limb observing the passing scene, stationary, unsuited to brisk activity. Black hair, large limpid brown eyes, attractive in a Mantilla/Jalousie, rose-over-left ear, Spanish kind of way, somewhat plump, pale, she had the aura of post-revolutionary melancholy, all titles privilege and property gone with the wind, only memories and nostalgia for better days remaining. Her mother married a Spanish diplomat who later was killed in the Civil War, leaving a home in Northwest Washington and a pension of exiguous but livable provision. I once took her to dine at an upscale restaurant near Dupont Circle where autobiographical reminiscences revealed she had been proposed to by a Naval Academy graduate but declined to marry on the sensible opinion that she would not be able to support the highly competitive spousal agenda of an aspiring young officer. She and Jordan shared the aura, perhaps pretense, of aristocratic derivation fallen into exiguous circumstances, no support or infrastructure to fence them from plebian contemporaries. Their sell-by dates long past, the future uncertain.

I met other female staff members over the first few days. Judy Pence, small, pockmarked, attractive in an acetic way, pointy nose, precise, quiet-spoken, a fairly good flute player (but no Rampal according to Bill Crumb), she looked much like Julie Harris, whose major role was Emily Dickenson, the size-5 genius of the Bean State. Lynn Mandana, tall, well built, attractive, wanted to acquire a more intellectual formation to offset the corporal advantages with which she was so amply endowed, attracting the attention of males she had concluded were unprepossessing and definitely not for the long term. Judy, Lynn and another girl planned a trip to Mexico, discussed at length and anticipated with existential intensity. It occurred to me that prosperous American and European countries had ID-countries (in the Freudian sense) they favored for vacation relief from rationality, clocks, 9-to-5 schedules, conformity, order, discipline. For England it was Italy or Spain, for Germany it was Greece. For the United States in the 40's and 50's it was Mexico, think *Night of the Iguana, Puerta Vallerta, The Wild Bunch, South of the Border Down Mexico Way*. I tried to encapsulate the overall impression in a poem:

Yucatan, etc.

Cortez, De Mille are gone
It's now the locus
Of postgraduate honeymoons,
Urban fugues, a minor literary genre.

Knowledge and ejection predispose us
To technological parody--
Antique busses, burros, plumbing, pyramids
As if nothing ever caught on.

130

There is no CHRONOLOGY, the pace and mores
Are too counterproductive--
Poster Indians pee along the road,
The women never dust.

We like the Sartrean-Spanish askewness--
Bugs, sex, dysentery, moonlight--
As if, though settled with us,
The Fates vacation here.

Close quarters, frequent encounters and relatively light workloads led to distractions, including a sexual quadrangle involving Bradley, Jordan, Judy and Linda. Judy played flute and joined Bradley in practice sessions. John smitten by Judy's wistful asceticism invited her to dinners. Linda, withdrawn on her perch of Quixote-like elevation of spirit and soul, was suddenly plunged earthward in sexual competition with Judy for Jordan. Bonded by flute and music to Judy, Bradley had an advantage only shared skill can provide. Jordan, mostly adrift, enjoyed the novelty of pursuit. Judy, whose specialist appeal confined her prospects to a comparatively small group of potential suitors (as in '*sell when you can you're not for all markets*'), enjoyed the unaccustomed attention and subtly nursed illusions and encouraged advances as appropriate without divulging a preference for one over the other, that might end up losing both. Such mini dramas occur often, and end similarly, usually when the principal party departs suddenly for unforeseen greener pastures. Judy did just that and all returned to their former preoccupations.

Boris Bohun-Chundiev, an ATD employee, announced his departure to become a guru for Harvard's Dr. Timothy Leary's LSD transformation movement, mainly of American coeds, offering opportunities for seduction never before so easily obtained. He planned an itinerary of Midwestern universities, organizing group sessions of about ten students each, inducting them into the communal experience of taking the drug in a presumably safe and supportive environment. Intelligent, edgy,

26-year old Belorussian, full of himself, Bohun bequeathed to me his basement apartment in a townhouse at 132 North Carolina Avenue, just three blocks from the LOC. Dream location! His landlord, Leon, New York Jew, retired WDC HS teacher, the shuffling, cynical embodiment of the Nazi caricature, agreed to the transfer without enthusiasm. Since the last time he was enthusiastic was VE-Day1945 his depressive mood did not signify disapproval or reluctance, just disillusion in general. To wrap up the Bohun epic, he visited Leon in summer of 1965. I had married Renee Engel and was having dinner with Leon and his wife when Bohun showed up with a mature plump red-head. He took one look at Renee, probably the most beautiful girl in creation, blue eyes, lovely face, ravishing body, and clearly was transfixed. His dream of sexual adventure collapsed into a pleasant but unappealing red-head age 32-years.

In April 1963, we were authorized to go to Pennsylvania Avenue near the White House to form a cluster of acclaiming enthusiastic citizens welcoming the Emperor Haile Selassi of Ethiopia, our only ally in a Continent turning increasingly red. I was about one-hundred yards from the White House and directly on the curb with an unimpeded view of His Majesty and of course Jack Kennedy as the open limousine passed fifteen feet in front of me. In-person views of notables seen frequently on television are usually anticlimactic. The ordinary man or woman erodes the romantic illusion sustained only by distance and fame. Although celebrities standout, they seldom knock your socks off. Kennedy was another thing altogether. I have never seen before or since a more beautiful man. Not in any queer or degenerate sense. He looked like a Greek God just turning up to say hello to his devotees. Tanned, blue suit, white shirt, Kelly green tie, flashing white teeth, golden brown hair, vigorous gestures and waves, standing in the back of the open limousine, no Secret Service in sight, juxtaposed with Haile in peaked Army hat, khaki military tunic with epaulettes, literally covered with medals such that he likely would fall over if he attempted to stand, parched tobacco brown complexion, frozen mummy face of 85-years, seated and oblivious of all that was going on around him, including our amazing President. Indelible!

A decade of violence, disorder, confusion and war began in 1963. The Civil Rights movement of the past decade culminated in the March on Washington that summer. I rode my bike to the Mall which was crammed as far as one could see. The March gathered 'delegations' from the South and North, a merger of Black sharecroppers and college students, plus a mixed bag of the curious the idealistic and the drugged. White coeds holding hands with Black boys, speeches at every corner of the Mall, the ultimate MLK *'I have a dream'*, Joan Baez sang *We Shall Overcome*, Dylan sang a tribute song to martyr Emmett Till, *Only a Pawn in Their Game*, but no one seemed to be listening.

The **1963 March on Washington** was a one-day celebration, so peaceful and inspiring that organizers decided to hold a week-long follow-up in July 1964, **Resurrection City**, optimistically presuming it would be even more kumbaya and brotherly loving. The Resurrection City of tents and song fests all over the Mall began well enough. Police lined the perimeter of the Mall but left the inside to participants without risk of drug enforcement, no other infractions expected. Tents were set up, songs and chants ensued, all well and good until about 11 PM. Then screams and shouts for help began to punctuate the peace-loving melodies, coeds with torn blouses and terrified faces ran to the perimeter for police intervention, white male college students ran up with bloody faces and torn clothes. The police remained facing outward, took no notice of their distress, resolutely following instructions not to provoke participants. Cops are from the labor class, they hate college students almost as a genetic trait. Nightly rape and pillage by squads of Blacks raiding each tent, taking money if not virginity in the bargain. During the day ceremonies continued in the kumbaya vein, inspiring an Assistant Secretary of Agriculture to join the fellowship, only to be assaulted by a baseball bat, losing an eye and severely damaging his suit. Baseball bats became the weapon of choice of the ghetto gangs that drifted out of Northeast Washington to check the action during the 'City' and during riots in 1965 through 1968. After three days, federal officials summarily closed the 'City' and sent ambulances, garbage trucks, sanitation workers and mounted police to clear out the debris, human and material that made the Mall look like landfill. You hear about the 1963 March to this day. You hear nothing about the 1964 Resurrection City, for good reason.

John Jordan Jr., a generous guy, loaned me his Cinelli Italian racing bike which introduced an era of cycling in my life. Reynolds 451 aluminum light strong frame and Campagnola crank and gears made Cinelli one of the leading racing bikes for the Tour de France and other competitions in Europe. Over the next ten years I rode every weekend all over Washington, as far as Annapolis Maryland and Great Falls West Virginia, Mt. Vernon and throughout the Virginia hinterland. I rode early weekdays to Redskin Stadium and became as fit as I have ever been. Aerobic lean good color and reasonably strong considering I was a bit of a recluse and aesthete. I had played football in Fallbrook so I wasn't a complete loser. All which contributed to engaging what really matters, women. Although the structural character of the pursuit is conventional and much the same in all cases, the specific variations in persons, circumstances, emotional expression, physical charms, and eventual outcomes are infinite and different for everyone. Dance venues were fairly numerous, providing occasions to meet and evaluate. One such dance led to an experience I had read about but never encountered. I met Anna Dubrovski, a girl of Polish descent from New York who worked at the State Department. Ethnicity does influence affinity. I have no problem with Celtic or Germanic or Chinese. I have little affinity for Latin or Japanese, but I have no affinity at all for Slavic, Russian or Polish. So it was astonishing that quite beyond any control or even volition, I was attracted to her like a magnet. She was very realistic, energetic, not formally educated to any great degree, working as a secretary, complaining how queer-ridden State was, who 'shook their asses at each other'. We arranged dates walking around parks, sitting on blankets. I would hold her and kiss her and suddenly be overcome with a powerful inner upsurge of desire to the point that my head spun and I would nearly lose consciousness. This apparently happened to her as well! Obviously too good to be true much less to pass up. She invited me to have dinner at her apartment. Very charming and fun, I joked and complimented her, she laughed and responded. We sat on the sofa. I began the kiss and petting which became so imperative that I had her skirt and blouse off, she was spread ready for me, when she cried '*Don't make me pregnant!*' I had purchased the requisite condoms and sheathed my instrument which relieved any further objection. We then fucked like our lives depended on it. We were both exhausted and satisfied, a not invariably common experience no matter how much people claim otherwise. It was too wild to last at the same level of intensity, and it didn't. But I am grateful to her for the only truly intoxicating sexual delirium of my life.

I met Victoria Alperowitz in the LOC cafeteria, she doing research in Chinese her main subject of study. Exchange of encouraging glances motivated me to join her over coffee. We got along well and she invited me to her apartment for drinks, with one caveat. She was divorced and had a daughter, which might discourage interest. I said no matter. She had been married to Gar Alperowitz, currently teaching American History, his career based on revisionist politically fashionable denigration of past national policies and Presidents. His big strike in the academic gold mine was to argue that Truman's decision to bomb Japan was unnecessary, a criminal act of genocide, not a necessary alternative to land invasion. The Japs were ready to surrender! Disproved by captured documents but a claim that had very tenuous support from the vast array of Japanese documents available after the war that included much wishful thinking but had nothing to do with the Emperor's decisions. I turned up at her apartment to find one of her friends, a New York Jewess, exceptionally loud and abrasive and her daughter an equally annoying combination of insolence and importunity. After experiences with Jews from Chicago during basic training I acquired a strain of anti-Semitism not directed at Jews in general, but at some, and rarely, Jews in particular. A complete bust from which I withdrew as gracefully as possible, the final inducement being the Jewess' diatribe about Goldwater the likely Republican candidate in the 1964 election.

Closer to home, ATD had hired a Ukrainian girl, Vera, full but shapely body, large tits, and a yielding look about her that excited erections in practically every male who encountered her, including yours truly. I invited her for dinner, she accepted. We were on my sofa bed, I stroked her breasts, she undid a few buttons on her blouse and then said: 'You can do the rest.' I did, including her skirt, bra and panties leaving her luscious body to full display and my perusal. She fucked willingly and enthusiastically which led to regular encounters over coming weeks. Fugitive sex can sustain fugitive relationships for a period of time. The question is, when will either the sex or the ability to sustain the intervals of conversation play out first. We had virtually nothing in common, no inspiring interests to share, no sense of common heritage to lean on. Things became difficult, I could hardly retain interest and she began to look forlorn. About this time her figure showed signs of new development, now unmistakable. A number of Russian employees began to eye me aggressively: Was Bowen the culprit? Would he make her an honest woman? She apparently told them the truth: she was pregnant when she arrived. Very decent of her not to try an alternative explanation very definitely not in my favor. She soon left for relatives in California to come to term and terms with her condition and I was much relieved.

Mary Ann Snavely worked in the Prints and Photos Division, a fairly recent addition to the LOC roster. Erich Dienst, a German from Berlin, had contributed his rather large collection of art prints and photos to establish the Division collection and to more or less bribe the selection committee to choose him as its head. They did and he came to Washington, only to be sorely disappointed at the meager space and accommodations provided, hardly enough to house his Prussian ego much less the apposite prints and photos themselves. His Jewish assistant director, Yuri Finkel, pretty much ran the workaday business of the Division, cataloging entries, writing for and publishing the monthly annotated listing of new acquisitions including essays about special items and parts of the overall collection, all this while Erich sulked in his private windowed office, decorated with valuable prints and furnishings from the fatherland.

He provided his staff with a welcome source of amusement at his expense about a year before. The division hired a summer student assistant named Andreas Vonkolonos, majoring in art history at Dartmouth College. Instinctively compelled by some Teutonic gene to defer to anything beginning in 'von', he came to attention and clicked his heels upon meeting Andreas, who was startled, perplexed but not displeased at this display of deference. Similar genuflection occurred on all occasions when they met, not often but not infrequent either. Only after Andreas returned to Dartmouth in September did Erich learn that von was a common prefix in Greek patronymics, not an indication of title or noble birth. Erich's disillusion deepened after that contretemps, Yuri's optimism correspondingly flew skyward.

Mary Ann had an apartment not far from mine. We dated and dined and attended parties and dances. She seemed to be quite taken with me, I did like her, we got along well. She graduated Wellesley College, her parents lived in Maryland. A classmate came to visit her, very talky and smart and inclined to imbibe whatever was on offer, eyeing me suspiciously as to intentions. I was vulnerable. Mary Ann was a perfect college girl, educated good family, and so on. I was excessively horny and sometimes got her partly undressed and myself entirely undressed on one occasion when I walked her the three blocks to her apartment wearing only a raincoat and a hard on. On another occasion we were in bed nude, she was holding my engorged penis and I was saying: *'Put it in Mary, put it in.'* If she had we probably would have married, the bond of fugitive pleasure motivating a long-term commitment to repeat at will. She didn't based on the *'saving myself for my husband'* rationale, perfectly reasonable although at that time in our history a man really didn't care if the girl he marries is virgin. A sense of sexual reciprocity prevailed and besides, a little experience may improve performance. She moved to Berkeley to take a degree in Library Science, met a business major from Pittsburg who proposed, wrote me about it, I answered best of luck, and about seven years later I saw her at a shopping mall in Maryland with her mother walking a little girl about four years old.

Steady income and a place to stay liberated tendencies long curtailed. I am a clothes horse, even at 5-years old exhibiting a liking of flamboyant or exotic dress, cowboy outfits with boots, holster and six gun, hat and lasso. I once did a Tarzan outfit with rubber tree leaves tucked into a string belt. I began looking at Garfinkels, the upscale social register go-to place for things sartorial where I bought a grey tweed three piece suit and a Pierre Cardin sport coat. Lewis and Thomas Saltz was an Anglo fashion purveyor where I bought a brown tweed suit with bellows back and sewn belted *ceinture.* I bought Wright jodhpurs and wingtips. Then I had to find suitable places to display these acquisitions.

The LOC had poetry readings, among the more prominent was W. H. Auden, friend of the Poet Laureate Steven Spender. Auden, massively wrinkled almost topographic face, prompting the suggestion that he should be spread out so we can see what he looks like, a charming speaker and reader. Vosnesensky, during a thaw in relations, gave us a taste (mostly sour pickle) of the declamatory pub-style poetry popular in the Soviet Union. A bit too bombastic for the LOC. Howard Nemerov from Bennington College soon to be a significant part of my life (the college not the poet), and Denise Levertov with her obscure dark and brooding observations in verse among many others.

In September we were told a new editor, Zina Pisarko, was coming to the Division. I first saw her at the LOC cafeteria buffet and went up to introduce myself. Unusual. A bit like Eleanor Roosevelt, hair in an untidy bun, pug noise, full lips, long dress with a rope belt, glasses, lithe strong looking body, bright smile and taunting eyes, definitely appealing to IQ types, not to the general. Graduate of Bryn Mawr, adjacent to Haverford, she had the sparkle, perhaps endemic to the college, that its most famous graduate Katherine Hepburn displayed so well on screen, the direct confident look that said 'try me if you dare', all the more provocative inasmuch as she had none of the physical attractions normally associated with female confidence. Pale skin, flat chested, the standard T&A evaluation in negative territory. Which confirmed my belief that IQ is the most aphrodisiac characteristic, to which more tangible assets can be subordinated in the overall evaluation. Looking at her my first impulse was to fuck her hard and long, her nolo me tangere and 'try me' look combining to arouse a primitive lust to possess and ravish. Incredible in someone so outwardly unappealing.

Zina in 2016, much as she looked in 1964

Zina emerged from a colony of Ukrainian expats settled on farms in Connecticut with its Orthodox Church as community focus. She majored in Russian at Bryn Mawr, an expedient choice given how close the languages are, providing her a cachet in knowing well that then exotic language with the curious alphabet and political timeliness. It left time for other pursuits, one of which was Philip Musgrove contemporary with her at Haverford. They had graduated in 1962, Philip went to Princeton for a Masters in Economics and she came to the LOC awaiting his assignment to Brookings Institution. Zina and I got along well, my ability to ramble on about practically any subject with amusing and instructive comment held her attention. We had both seen a British film based on a play called *A Taste of Honey*, story of a British girl getting involved with a West Indian Negro. She felt there was something awry in the film but couldn't quite put her finger on it. I said the problem was the dialog was too efficacious, which defined exactly the problem which she had until then been unable to articulate. I mention this as an example of how intellectual acuity can influence and inspire attraction, as I said IQ is sexy. She was more willing to spend time on long walks with me throughout the city, ranging to Georgetown and Dumbarton Oaks Park, Connecticut Avenue plus the National Gallery and other hot spots. However, any carnal advances were abruptly rebuffed, not that I pursued with great conviction. Zina did have a sour petulant side, saying once: *'I want to be old and spoiled'*.

The East European staff of ATD was much like a transplanted miniature of that region's geo/demographic, cultural, and religious contests over the last 300 years. Russians were dominant, resented by all, but especially the Poles and Czechs. The oldest was a gentleman about 90-years old, very short, lean with a white Toscanini moustache, bow tie, natty tweed three-piece suit, graduate of the Imperial Academy of Astronomy in 1898. In deference to his extreme age, he was allowed a half-hour nap after lunch. Knyaz Volkonsky, whose family figured prominently in Tolstoy's *War and Peace*, was prominent in the Russian expat community centered in New Jersey. His great aunt had converted to Catholicism and moved to Rome in the mid-19th Century, her home Casa Volkonsky now serving as UK Embassy. Knyaz Volkonsky moved there after the Soviets took over Russia and after WWII emigrated to the United States. He was truly the image of a Russian aristocrat: sleek white hair combed straight back, sharp black eyes, small ruby mouth, charming smile and laugh, gracious manners and flawless English. A bit irregular in dress, sometimes a tie used as a belt, mixed colors and non-matching socks but in every respect a nobleman.

Quite unlike small recessive Knyaz Cantecuzene (Knyaz translates more like Count than Prince given the very large number of them in Imperial Russia) with his rumpled Goodwill mismatched coat and pants, no tie, un-shined shoes, and puzzled look oddly resembling the French actor Alain Delon. His grandmother was the daughter of President U.S. Grant. In 1880, she married the then prosperous and socially prominent Knyaz Cantecuzene, on duty in Washington implementing the Alaska Purchase with Secretary of State Hamilton Fish. The family lost their estates to the Russian revolution, and through a circuitous route the current Knyaz ended up in the United States where he enjoyed citizenship through his grandmother. The amusing part was that he received an invitation to a Nixon Prayer Breakfast, his name on a Republican notables list based on his connection with President Grant, although no personal distinction or political leverage would motivate such an honor. He went. White House staffers and Secret Service, according to him, seemed perplexed as to why he, *deguiser en mendiant,* should be there and what to do with him. He felt much the same.

Others were from Soviet disruptions and purges of the thirties, many from the WWII generation. We had an ex-fighter pilot who hooked up with a blockhouse Russian lady who had also been a fighter pilot! Gospodin Nartsissov, a Himmler look alike, was a noted poet and cultivator of roses. Dimitri Vvedensky, a metallurgy expert with whom I worked and befriended. He moved to Czechoslovakia in the 1930's and worked at Skoda steel works. Jews of all nationalities were followed with contempt and fear of their invariable talent for rising in place. Andre Valiunus was the only Balt, from Latvia, whose landlord family supported the Germans in 1941 and withdrew with them to exile in 1945. He somehow got a commission in the US Army, wore his uniform with double bars of Captain once a month for a Reserve meeting after work.

A clever jewish Pole was a personnel analyst of the Soviet Academy of Sciences, noting changes, disappearances, reappearances of scientists in that community, possible signs of purges, emerging leaders, changing areas of emphasis in Soviet research. The head of the Russian staff was a product of the Soviet regime and Soviet scientific academies. He was an efficient and ruthless administrator with a velvet-glove Peter Lorie voice and a steel fist. Once we had a very minor dispute with Nartsissov. The administrator invited us to a formal meeting in his office. N appeared before us, head down, contrite, and confessed he was wrong (to our amazed embarrassment since the matter was so minor), a very Stalin purge thing to do. Confession, self-abnegation, punishment is a deep seated tradition of the Russian Orthodox Church, easily redesigned and appropriated by the Stalinist State.,

I bought a Volvo 122-S two-door, black sedan. Swedish ancestry and assumed superiority of Swedish engineering made me overlook far better appointed Ford/Chrysler/GM alternatives. Price $2200. The Volvo had no a-c, no sunroof. It had a school bus type gear shift with black knob rising up from the floor, much like the Camp Pendleton school bus that took us to Fallbrook HS. One advantage, bucket seats much more comfortable than a bench seat across the front. It drove well but did not have power steering. Main point was it provided mobility.

November 23rd, 1963. Every American then extant remembers what he or she was doing at the time they heard about the assassination of Jack Kennedy. Thanksgiving weekend was consumed with sorrow, loss, ceremony and poignant scenes of Jackie and John placing flowers on the casket in the Capitol rotunda, the empty saddle horse led up Pennsylvania Avenue by the color guard, seen by thousands of curbside onlookers to say nothing of millions worldwide. I heard about the killing when returning from a picnic lunch with a ravishing blonde employee who had suggested her husband was unsatisfactory, a clue that sparked dishonorable intentions ultimately unfulfilled. Kennedy's timing was perfect, Camelot was preserved as a Golden Age, and Lyndon Johnson took all the blame, for the most part deserved, for the domestic riots and military disaster in Viet Nam that consumed the rest of the decade.

Early December I saw Bobby Kennedy riding with Adam Clayton Powell, black congressman from Harlem, probably colluding on the prospective campaign for Senate. Jack nostalgia was a winning tide to surf in, his Shakespeare quote, *'cut him up into little stars'* pretty much brought a tear to every eye. Bobby was a creep but the back story on him and the Kennedy's had not been revealed or widely publicized as yet. Jackie remained the tragic heroine until her unfortunate marriage to Onassis in 1968. I met Jackie Kennedy early on a Saturday morning in January 1964 at the Saville Book Store in Georgetown. A black sedan was idling in front but I thought nothing of it. I entered the store and there she was talking to the current proprietor about hiring an au pair girl from Guatemala. Always startling to see a prominent person suddenly before you. I dissembled my surprise and briefly joined the conversation before heading to the foreign language section upstairs. Jackie was identical to the TV and media photo coverage. About 5'10", bouffant hairdo, wide face, large brown wondering eyes, full novocaine-numb lips and speech and MM drawl, as though troubled forming consonants, large foursquare figure, frozen unyielding smile. She looked more manikin than real, and I wondered how Jack could stand to spend much time with her. Of course he didn't. She would often show up at breakfast with a handful of hairpins to drop on his plate in silent rebuke or perhaps not that strong a word applies. She knew what to expect and got ample reward from Joe to accommodate his son's sexual *seitensprungs.*

Saville Book Store was a Georgetown icon run by a plump loud bisexual reject from a prominent wealthy family whose father gave him $10 million just to disappear. The store was well stocked with fine editions on all subjects worth reading about, including a French+ section run by an elegant French matron upstairs. All the Pleiade editions, leather bound classics in English literature, the very latest high end history and social commentary, all in beautiful oak bookcases, leather club chairs here and there, and a staff of one comely female usually no later than 27, and a soft bottomed boy no later than 23 who earned salary plus free room and board in onsite accommodations whose location remained a mystery at least to me. The store was in fact a large townhouse with floors above the book establishment with likely staircase access to all concerned should the proprietor wish it. At some point the proprietor after nearly 15 years in the business sold the store to a great grandson of Charles Darwin of *Origin of the Species* fame, a British queen in the Oscar Wilde tradition, very articulate, lisping, knowledgeably on many subjects, effete and perpetually horny, which must have kept his 'partner' very busy in as much as he basically ran the store and accommodated Darwin III with bilateral skill. Unfortunately, Darwin III was killed in an automobile accident in Vermont in 1967 and the store was purchased by a bookstore franchise hoping to set up other franchise stores US-wide capitalizing on the cachet of the original. Much as Banana Republic, whose original store in San Francisco I was among the first to patronize in the mid-1980's, was sold to a franchise and became the slick operation it is today.

When it happens it is always a shock, a pleasant and overwhelming surprise, despite years of anticipation, expectation, imagined scenes of the encounter, rough sketches of the party in question, criteria informally itemizing the range of acceptable variation. A routine Monday in February, coffee break in the cafeteria, Crumb, me, Pyle got our coffee and went to the 'ATD table'. On the same LOC deck but opposite ATD there was a Chinese research Division of about five employees working for CIA. Occasionally they joined our table, today a familiar Chinese translator and a new girl, Renee Lynn Engel. As the Bard said, *Who 'ere loved true who loved not at first sight?* When you have grown fond of an abstract, potential daydream it is at first unsettling to finally encounter the real present and in-person lady that will end that enchanted yearning and bring you home to roost. She later confided that she had exactly the same reaction I did, our mutual astonishment and wonder probably intensifying the encounter. We dated and connected and she returned to Bennington College to complete her junior year. Much more about her later.

Renee Lynn Engel

1964 was an election year, Viet Nam was heating up, civil rights were heating up, political and social fever rampant. Johnson and Hubert Humphrey leading the Democrat ticket, Barry Goldwater and a nonentity the Republican. Senator Dirkson of Illinois led off the pro-Barry nomination, reminding me of Ralph Baumgartner of Chicago days. Barry accepted the nomination: *Extremism in the cause of liberty is no vice, moderation in the cause of freedom is no virtue.* Handsome despite the thick black-rimmed glasses, articulate, and doomed. Johnson won. He then proceeded with the Gulf of Tonkin deception and got us into ten more years of pointless war. The Great Society which would raise Blacks from oppression, poverty and ignorance, all on display at Resurrection City that summer. The Imperial Capitol was under construction. New granite piles to accommodate Education, Health and Human Services, Transportation, Energy, Housing and Urban Development, Smithsonian, Congress, CIA, and other tangible forms of nanny State supervision and control. Add thousands of new bureaucrats and their need for housing and logistics. Of more immediate impact was the WDC Metro system, an underground *Nibelheim,* plywood boards covering streets where excavation was under way. Total disruption of street travel in downtown Washington isolating and terminating the city as the focus of regional entertainment and diversion.

In May1964, Zina Pisarko went to Mr. Counts and demanded an immediate promotion. He temporized, explaining that promotion required certain forms, procedures, seniority and so on, to which she said: *'I quit'* left the building and was not heard of or seen again, except by me. A few weeks after she left, she and Philip attended a party given by a LOC coworker. Philip's father was a Gulf Oil executive who traveled frequently to South America, Philip sometimes accompanying him and of course fluent in Spanish. Philip was going to serve as Brookings expert in the economics of health care policy in South America. We met and he apparently thought I was trying to poach on his territory (Zina not South America). We got into a surrogate discussion about whether political reform should precede economic reform, I supporting the former. I also doubted that health care reform would work unless some population control were in place.

Zina and Philip married in summer of 1964. She characteristically demurred, crying and complaining, refusing to come out of the dressing room or wherever the bride prepares to legitimize her prospective deflowering. Philip in a final act of appropriation went to her. She asked him: *'Why do you want to marry me?'* He answered: *'Lust'.* She laughed, found the answer adequate, and completed the 'til death do us part' bit. She had a daughter in 1965. In 1966 they moved to South America. It was hard to imagine Zina as a *hausfrau* doing dishes, changing diapers, shopping at market, and cooking dinner, especially in South America where she didn't speak Spanish and probably had no intention of accommodating to local customs. Perhaps the main factor in their divorce in 1977 had more to do with Latin standards of female beauty. Within their group of college graduate colleagues they would associate with in the United States she fit in without difficulty. In South America standards for women are rigorously physical, face, body, movement all calculated around a sexual standard of beauty. Zina would stand out like a cactus among orchids, in hopeless contrast to the groomed, made-up, and fit women of the affluent social groups with which Philip associated professionally. Language and culture completely alien to anything the Ukrainians in Connecticut could prepare her for. To draw the story to its conclusion, after the divorce, Zina and her daughter moved back to their Northwest Washington house, very elegant, and Philip paid their expenses. Years later the daughter worked with him at Brookings. In 1988 he married an Argentine lady, very much up to the Latin standard of beauty and they had two daughters. She divorced Philip in 2002. He drowned in a fishing accident off the coast of Buenos Aires in 2010, Zina died in 2018. Probably happily old and spoiled as she foretold.

Renee came to WDC and a summer job, hair dyed bright blonde, in some break-out move from her customary conformist approach to life. As a consequence, male students from local colleges circled the prey, sensing an opportunity often offered by more adventuresome Bennington ladies, noted for their Bohemian artistic pretensions. Renee didn't actually 'do it' but certainly signaled the possibility. We parted on good terms when she returned to college in late August, but no major commitment was made.

I met, in what manner I have completely forgotten, Helen Randolph of the distinguished Randolph family of Richmond Virginia directly related to Thomas Jefferson, Martha Washington the Lees, and numerous First Family connections. She was lovely, beautiful face, complexion, light brown hair, great body, graceful manner, soft voice, no trace of privilege or superiority, gentle green eyes, looking tenderly and even lovingly at me across the table in her apartment where she prepared and served the dinner she so graciously invited me to. Her roommate and friends were going to a Johnson victory party, which indicated Helen was well acquainted with the political class in WDC. With her background that would be expected. I was in a state of calculation and amazement. Assuming I could pull it off, I would be marrying into one of the preeminent families in the South with concomitant business and political connections of a very significant level. What would take three generations of major planning, success and incredible talent, energy and effort to achieve on one's own, I could leapfrog to in one marital gesture. All through the main course I was trying to ignite the fire, persuade myself, but she was unfortunately so bland and passive I couldn't even raise a sexual flag. We parted never to meet again, the kind of theoretical opportunity foregone that could torment one in later less favorable circumstances. Fortunately I had found what really matters and in February 1965 I took steps to get it.

Skiing is an especially strong indicator of male virility, daring, and appeal. To see one slalom down slope in an elegant swoosh is enough to win the heart and whatever ever else is on offer of most females. Experience had shown me I have no aptitude for speed, skis largely an impediment to grace and control rather than otherwise. Richard Primus and I had once gone on a ski trip to Wisconsin. I started badly, fell down backward, had a hell of a time trying to get enough purchase in the soft deep snow to turn over and get up. I almost dislocated my shoulder (it is still susceptible) and at best could snowplow my way downward toward the chalet, fireplace and hot cocoa. I had acquired the equipment, skis, poles, gloves, fancy jacket, boots and elastic pants, but had to admit this was a role for which I was miscast. On the slopes, action separates the men from the boys. Before the fire in the chalet drinking eggnog with brandy, face red and eyes bright, all men are equal where no challenge to dissembled achievement can immediately be made. The showcasing potential of the ski costume is sufficient off-slope.

I wrote Renee that I would like to take a ski strip to New England and if possible meet her at some place of her choosing. She was on 'Spring Break' and at home. She said I could stay at her grandmother's house, a room on the third floor vacant and available, plus Athol was more or less central to a number of ski areas. A list would be forthcoming. So on February 10, I began the drive north. New England is a very mixed bag. The magazines and legend describe the fall foliage, the maple syrup, the charming colonial churches with white steeples, red brick and latticed green-shuttered windows, the pleasantly tart apples, the crisp winter air in bright blue sky, and so forth. They ignore the dreary industrial residue of brick factories, grim barn-like houses, the slush for seven months and the bitter cold damp climate, much like Northern England. Athol was a factory town, unprepossessing, undistinguished, uncharming, driving through slush and snow plowed up along the street. Starett Tools was the economic driver, a still successful company not forced to leave New England and head south. The actor Bill Starett, a Hollywood star in the Thirties, was a scion the family.

Turning up at the house of your intended (but as yet not confirmed) is a very risky proposition. Of course they were aware of my existence and knew the date of my arrival, but as a totally unexpected intervention in their routine I was anticipated widely differently by members of the family. The mother, Winifred Engel, was excited. Renee had never brought home much less acquired a suitor of such imminent potential. A local guy, Bruce, attending Dartmouth very nearly got her. He invited Renee for a prom weekend at the college but had to cancel upon the fortunate (for me) death of his grandfather. A choice between dead grandfather and living angel would pose no problem for me. Bird in hand as it were, but I am atypical in that I have no sentimental ties to family. Build up to the Dartmouth excursion implied a proposal at the end, now foregone. Her grandparents, Luther and Mabel Daniels, were curious. Any disruption, especially one that got Donald upset, was welcome entertainment. Her brothers were away at college and had no particular opinion or role to play in the forthcoming drama. The big problem was her father, Donald, already parted with his older daughter, not at all pleased at the threat of parting with his favorite. He and Renee were close, too close. Renee played down any suggestion that this was anything but a ski trip. At times I wasn't sure myself what I was up to.

The mother is a good indicator of the long-term viability of the daughter. Fat forebodes long- term disappointment. I drove into the courtyard, went to the kitchen door, knocked and awaited with some trepidation the first encounter. Winifred opened the door and my wildest dreams were immediately exceeded. She was a knockout. Beautiful face, complexion, stunning body, warm welcoming personality, effusive, I would have run off with her right then and there. Some internal appraiser pushed the affirmative button and I was prepared to make the move on Renee, maybe somehow I could get them both. Renee was a very modest girl, no flash or attempt at provocative dress or demeanor, but as with most women she was subconsciously savvy about the great game, what it takes to soften up the prey, how to entice without appearing calculating. Whereas she normally wore a skirt and blouse, during the visit she wore tight ski pants, a garment sanctioned by the sport to which it was deemed appropriate, both men and women requiring streamlined clothing when descending the slopes at speed. It just happens that such a garment has other advantages for the girl in that she can display, albeit upholstered, her assets in pretty much full detail. I wanted to take the mother and rape the daughter, a perfect basis for a lasting relationship.

I next met grandfather Luther Daniels, instant recognition between us, two bad boys about to enjoy a delightful week tormenting Donald and smoking up the house. He looked mischievous and made no effort to conceal it. I bummed a cigarette off him and instantly won him over, a fellow smoker with what other collusive bad habits to come? Mabel was dotty after a fall two years before rendered her inhibitory faculties incapable leading to remarks of incredible, embarrassing, and profane candor, enough to burn the ears of the party line at the summer cabin on the local pond where Luther and Mabel spent the months of May through September. Her calls to 188 Highland Avenue were heard by members of the party line with amusement and sometimes shock that such a traditional matron of 67-years could have acquired the vocabulary of a drunken sailor.

I made a token effort at skiing, managed to take the chairlift to the summit, calculated my best route for returning undamaged to the chalet, proceeded to snowplow my way down the periphery of the ski run, get to the parking lot and ditch the equipment for a more agreeable pursuit. Thereafter I made no pretense of skiing. Renee and I drove all over the region, dined in burger joints, talked and laughed and pretty much bonded. She walked me back to her grandmother's house and to my room where we kissed and fondled but didn't do it. I didn't want to until we were firmly committed which happened the day before my departure. I was seated in the dining room in Donald's favorite chair, Renee on my lap. I said I think we should get married, she said yes, we agreed that she should complete her senior year but we would meet and write often. I left and according to Winifred, Renee told her *'He wasn't here to ski!'* I ordered a subscription to the New Yorker as a thank you gift for their hospitality. Donald would at least enjoy the cartoons.

One advantage to separation is that letters were necessary, providing a record of correspondents' thoughts and feelings. I detest phone calls. In letters one can formulate one's statements precisely, nothing depends on the mood and presence of mind of the moment as with phone calls. Plus, phone calls become desultory since ending them is perplexing for both parties. When does the ardent lover decide enough is enough to the satisfaction of both? A phone call has to die, correspondence lives. However, the disadvantages of constant letter writing are obvious. How many times in how many ways can you say *'I love you'*, or whatever else prompts the correspondence to begin with? What else do you write about that either amuses or informs or shares something so you don't come across as deficient in invention and imagination? Women forget nothing. They may postpone punishing deficiency in the groom, just to get him to the alter. But vengeance is only postponed, not foregone, and sooner or later he will pay. I wrote three or four letters every week for fourteen weeks, a considerable demand on my ability to entertain and interest, but managed. If I could fool Renee, I could fool anybody.

We were married in Old First Church in Old Bennington, gathered 1765. Robert Frost is buried in the backyard cemetery, his epitaph: *'I had a lover's quarrel with the World.'* I at once began devising my own. In another plot in the cemetery the deceased had two sculpted Moet Chandon champagne bottles wrought in stone for his gravestone, clearly a form of gallows humor surprising at first, later understandable in the pious traditions of Puritan New England where final departure absolves one of accountability to the society at large. Renee's brothers Paul and Mark, parents Don and Wini, and some classmates witnessed the event. The minister said: *'Do you Christopher **Brown** take Renee Lynn Engel…'* which both Renee and I agreed invalidated the whole caper should we at any time in future change our minds. We departed Bennington for a three-day honeymoon at Rehobeth Beach Delaware, where Renee got sunburned and I improved my tan, then returned to my 'efficiency' apartment in the basement of a townhouse at 132 North Carolina in Washington and the usual delights and challenges of first days of life in common. 'Efficiency' is euphemistic. Adequate for one person, my apartment was a challenge for two. It had a small bathroom, a small kitchen, a small dining table area, a small living room, which required a small roll out bed and daily rearrangements of the small living space. In one of her letters Renee had said that the apartment couldn't be too small since she wanted us to be as close together as possible. I believe she qualified that statement after a few months of 'smallness' at 132 North Carolina.

Marriage is basically the merger of two alien cultures to form a new civilization with its unique 'language', customs, stuff, habits, standards, likes, dislikes and points of view. If lucky both conjoin, become a union to the point that even thoughts are shared without being expressed. Life together acquires texture and subtle coloring, becomes richer in implication and reference, comparisons and judgments, experiences good and bad, creating an ambiance of care, memories and feeling, the greatest moments just lying in bed together reading before the peaceful sharing of close and loving sleep.

Renee was the most elegant and beautiful person I have known. No one came close at any gathering or event, her natural glowing loveliness just eclipsed the competition. But her clothes were awful! Raised in the bleak, wet, cold greydom of austere New England, where any 'flashiness' was excoriated, grey-brown-black, loose-bulky-inelegant, pretty much defined the aesthetic spectrum. The great sartorial turnaround came in February 1966 during the Washington's Birthday sales. She needed a new overcoat, so we went to Woodies to check out the remnant stock. She found a grey drab Army blanket of a coat, size 10, but cheap. I found a coat, size 8, made in France that was discounted substantially but still more expensive than all the others. It was light-brown tweed, form fitted to the waist then flared in a pleated skirt, lapels elegantly rounded like petals. She looked like a *Parisienne* model the minute she put it on. She had sticker shock, but I insisted and we never looked back.

We also made innovations in our wining and dining. I have two prejudices which few share and fewer understand. Eating is not dining. Dining requires good food, candles, and wine. Since neither of us was raised that way it was an adjustment for her that I had already made. Wine was not imbibed regularly outside California, excepting high end income and class brackets, until the 1970's when Americans gradually acquired the taste. We got into the wine and candles bit quickly since we took to the relaxing and gracious dinners we enjoyed. Once we sat down to

dinner we didn't get up, period. No phone calls, no door bells, no nothing interfered with our leisurely enjoyment of dinner. Worse, among the modest uptight muddle classes wine was a somewhat sinister alcoholic insinuation tending to undermine wholesome milk-fed Americans. Too Italian and worse French. Even worse, wine was pretentious, an undemocratic claim to superior manners, not something the wholesome *'this Bud's for you'* community could tolerate. The pretense spilled over into the shops like Plain Old Pearson's Liquors on Wisconsin Avenue just north of Georgetown where an elderly gentleman in beret counseled the novice wino on selection and varietals. Much elaborate prose and approximations of French facial and hand gestures to reinforce the esoteric nature of this domain. Fortunately, the good stuff was still affordable so we did try Clos Vougeot, Talbot and other premium wines. Eventually we settled on Beaulieu Vineyard Pinot Noir and Almaden Brut Champagne, both California vineyards, which we had delivered by the case every month by Lacey from Central Liquors in downtown Washington. No berets or wine-speak but they had the best price and free delivery, an unbeatable combination. We got to be good friends with Lacey. We had to because he had to lug the stuff up two flights to our third floor apartment landing, sans tipping.

A most important change in our diet was to drop sugar, salt and fat and become vegetarian. Somewhere in the late 50's early 60's, American agriculture became an industrial rather than family-farm economy, mass production replacing the modest organic and flavorful results of small farm production. Feed lots, growth hormones, pesticide-driven thousand acre cropland, thousands of chickens and turkeys cooped rather than free-range, strawberries other fruit without flavor, chicken/ beef/pork tasting like wet dog, mass-produced bake products like Sarah Lee tasting like straw. I was inspired to change by Alik Montmorency a LOC groupie for Liberty Lobby, a right wing lobby group. Alik a descendant of a French aristocratic family that fled during the Revolution to Russia and 150 years later from Russia to the West. He was the healthiest guy I have ever met, total vegetarian, often commenting that *cadaverins* emitted by cattle during slaughter tainted the meat and made it unhealthy to eat, etc. etc.

Vegetarian in the 1960's was associated with long-haired nuts in robes and sandals beachcombing in Santa Barbara or joining Hari Krishna compounds. Most vegetarian cookbooks, what there were, presented endless ways to preserve the illusion of a meat entrée, to create meat substitutes. Nut and soy combinations cooked to resemble pot roast or chicken strips. The point is not to approximate the meat but to replace it. With experimenting we got to the basic Mediterranean diet of pasta with cheese and fresh vegetables and huge salads which we followed thereafter. Today, the basic food groups--sugar fat salt alcohol tobacco--once defended as virtually part of the Constitution and American Way of Life, are now universally disparaged as the cause of most health defects. In California they are practically illegal, as businessmen lunches are now austerely vegetarian and lean cuisine, and the upper income class has almost to a person abandoned the once staples of American success: dessert, smoking, and the pre-prandial martini.

While Renee and I were pulling ourselves together, America was pulling apart: enforced school integration, bussing, Viet Nam casualties, draft resistance, burning draft cards, moving to Canada, civil rights demonstrations, antiwar demonstrations, riots in major cities including Washington, George Wallace and Southern resistance. During the Washington riots 1966-1969, Police cars regrouped on North Carolina Avenue, shattered windows, dented fenders, police looking harassed and fearful, unable to believe the rioting and vandalism, partly by well-paid black federal bureaucrats.

The conflicts were varied. The Civil War between North and South never ended, just extended to school bussing, integration, and Southern resistance. The Supreme Court ruling in Plessy vs. Ferguson 1896, that separate but equal was legal, established segregation as a sanctioned policy. D. W. Griffith's film *Birth of a Nation* given a White House viewing by Virginian Woodrow Wilson (he segregated the armed services and bureaucracy) marked the triumph of 'The Cause' and apogee of KKK in the 1924 parade down Pennsylvania Avenue. The KKK was headquartered in Indiana, indicating the north/south division in Ohio, Indiana and Illinois, where the southern part of those States had been settled by Southerners moving to jobs and prosperity in the North. In 1970, National Guardsmen fired on anti-war student demonstrators at Kent State University in Ohio, indicating a second division in US society, between college-educated and high-school educated, the latter filling the ranks of the armed services and police departments, who despised the privileged White college students who mocked and despised the religion and patriotism of the blue collar class.

Women's Lib evoked another division between college-educated women and high-school educated women. The movement for equal opportunity for women enforced through Consent Decrees that drove equal hiring and promotion favored mainly the college educated professionals competing directly with male counterparts, not the high-school educated secretaries, clerks and technicians accustomed to subordination to male bosses (for singles always a prospect for marriage) who sided with the men whose dominion over the workplace was challenged.

In addition to regional, class, and sex divisions, the Environmental Movement driven by Rachel Carson's *Silent Spring* 1962 was an urban white collar attack on traditional management practices of mining, forestry, farming and industrial businesses now constrained by Threatened and Endangered Species Act, National Environmental Policy Act, Clean Air Act, Clean Water Act and other laws and regulations. The assassinations of Martin Luther King and Bobby Kennedy led to violence and chaos at the Democratic convention in Chicago in 1968 and continued riots, burning, and pillage in all major cities with the implausible result, a reaction election of the least likely candidate, Richard Nixon, to the White House.

This provided the public context of our last years in Washington. In 1967 Renee inquired about accommodations available in the large apartment building at 101 North Carolina Avenue. Miss Goldie, building manager, said a tenant on the third floor of the townhouse adjoining had just declared her intention to move. Renee looked, called me to come over immediately, I did and we signed up. Miss Goldie was a very fat pleasant jewish lady of about 60-years, confronted with the unpleasant task of climbing three stories to show the apartment, an effort she would take any excuse to avoid. She even dropped the two-month deposit just to induce us to sign. The top floor had a picture window view of the Capitol, free firewood for a delightful prefab fireplace, all for about $78 a month. Our next caper was to furnish the place beginning with a dining table.

Renee loved Bennington College because she could discover and develop new interests, among them drawing and painting. The College employed major contemporary artists, such as Paul Feely, Jules Olitski, and David Smith, whose work was shown periodically at major New York galleries. My interest was entirely ad hoc, having no training in drawing or painting. At Georgetown I began to frequent the National Gallery of Art gallery and learn the repertoire of European and American painting, old master, middle masters, and young masters. Renoir's *'Girl with Watering Can'* was my first favorite, my taste to improve muchly over the next decade. At Army Language School I drew sketches of teachers and latterly charcoal drawings of no distinction. Renee introduced me to contemporary art and we visited galleries public and commercial in Washington and New York that included Motherwell, Johns, and many minimalists and color field painters. In 1972, we attended a life-drawing workshop in Alexandria Virginia. Each three-hour session had a nude model. We drew and painted without instruction. The models were a droll and very mixed bag. Stewart arrived wearing only a raincoat. How he managed to travel from Washington to Alexandria by bus remained a minor mystery. Bruce was a dark, hairy, bearded fellow, fairly good looking with a large penis he managed to thrust into a prominent position in every pose. Lucy, a very prim, pretty girl, liked to wear broad-brimmed hats. She generously displayed her pussy in every possible position including one leg thrust over the arm of a chair the other spread wantonly to the side. She had nice breasts and her dark hair and eyebrows made drawing her easy. The best model was a redhead dancer with a stunningly

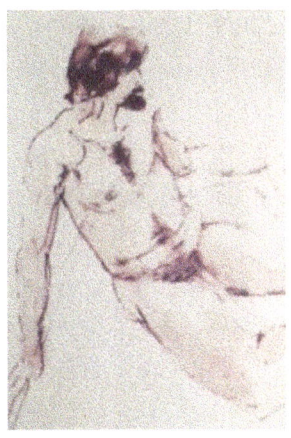  

fit body and marvelous poise, such that her head was always alert and directed the rest of her body. Another model had abundant dark-red hair, a very large beard, very pale and thin with strong bone structure. His eyes were dark brown and he looked in many ways like a religious figure, perhaps a Russian mystic or Christian devout. Through a bit of luck, a fellow member of the session photographed us. The photo is reversed (I am not left handed) but you get the idea.

Bennington College remained a major source of activities, the local chapter of the Alumni Association particularly active, given its central location in the Nation's Capitol, the wife of the Norwegian Ambassador, for example, among the alumna who hosted events. Bennington enrolled its first class in 1932, not especially good timing given the Depression and turmoil of the time. John Dewey helped organize and develop curriculum, to include heavy doses of the Arts/Dance/Theater/Writing. Martha Graham, Merce Cunningham, Jose Limon, and even Betty Ford the future President's wife taught or attended. The faculty over time included Shirley Jackson, Bernard Malamud, W.H. Auden, Mary Oliver, Theodore Roethke. Carol Channing and Alan Arkin were graduates, along with Jasmine Kahn, daughter of Rita Hayworth and the Aga Khan. The faculty was closely tied to New York and the contemporary art-theater-literary scene. Given all the artsy-fartsy, the college had neglected endowment and from 1960 on faced financial challenges. During the period we were in Washington several college presidents came and went under not entirely admirable circumstances. The chair of the Washington Alumni Association required mainly a large house in which to host meetings, visiting faculty and social events. There was no pretense at 'leadership', the College arranged whatever events seemed appropriate.

Denice Rzewski Bredt held this ambiguous honor, presiding over a lovely Northwest Washington home with very large living room, enclosed porches, big yard, classic 1920's quality design and build. Her husband, Jim Bredt, Harvard PhD physicist, worked at NASA, amply funding his wife's hobby and social climb. She was homely, plump, restless, intellectually shallow but probably intelligent enough, a daughter and son both in college, freeing her for the idleness she required others to fill. She came from one of those high IQ, quirky, Polish families unique to the race.

Her brother, Frederic Anthony Rzewski, composer and pianist, attended Philips Academy, Harvard and Princeton where he studied with Randall Thompson and Roger Sessions. A prolific composer and brilliant pianist, now teaching in Belgium, his *The People United Will Never Be Defeated*, a 2-hour piano solo diatribe against capitalism and

American imperialism, was performed at the Bicentennial Celebrations in 1976, clearly a counter-intuitive commemoration of the event but reflecting his 'communist' bias and the social/political themes that inform his works including on the Attica State Prison riots in 1972, the American bombing of Libya in 1986, and even *'The Price of Oil'.* A sort of classical music Woodie Guthrie, sharing themes and attitudes and in fact close friends.

1975   *2018*

Her father wanted Denice to rise so he sent her to Wellesley for about three months. She had a nervous breakdown, ran off, was missing for about three weeks, became the subject of a region-wide search and newspaper coverage (moving from front to back page over the three weeks). Once found, the father had her examined to be sure she was 'intact', and transferred her to Bennington for part of a year. She soon after married Bredt and was safely disposed of. Jim was a physics PhD candidate at the time, and after graduating worked in Industry for a few years then transferred to NASA.

Bennington grads were generally well placed and Washington was an easy and desirable venue for outsiders from New York and elsewhere to turn up. Denice's short-term association with Bennington of course meant she had no friends from the college and hardly spent enough time there to acquire its mystique. She hosted lunches and evening get-togethers for visiting faculty. She and Renee got together for gallery visits. We had no special social cachet but we had class, looked good, and were available. About the best she could do. I liked Jim. He was an autodidact, studied everything all the time, something Denice had no interest in. She constantly tormented him about not 'getting ahead' or 'getting promoted' at work, her idle mind so restless she eventually decided to sell the elegant Northwest Washington house and buy a fixer-upper townhouse several blocks from the Shoreham Hotel on Connecticut Avenue.

Buying a house. Jack Kennedy called Washington D.C. a place of Northern charm and Southern efficiency. He probably didn't originate that statement, but someone had to get the credit so it might as well be him. The Washington he described was destroyed in the 1960's, partly by his administration, more so by the Johnson administration, and mostly by the METRO construction, which lasted nearly ten years and left Washington a desert while the suburbs flourished. Washington is now a city of hustlers without a core in all homophonic senses of the word. Everyone is desperately craven for status since there is no money to speak of (government salaries are at best derisory compared to corporate) despite the extravagance and waste. Real money is in San Francisco, New York, Los Angeles, Dallas and so on. All you can get in Washington is the illusion of 'prestige' and 'status', both relatively unimportant outside the Beltway. But I digress.

In 1974, we had lived in apartments for nine years. We had traveled and enjoyed ourselves without the burden of a mortgage and home maintenance. But the 1974 trip to France was disappointing and we began to realize we were lagging in the upscale housing market. A price we thought unimaginable two years before looked a bargain in retrospect. Money was to be made, the mortgage paid itself in equity appreciation, and women Renee met at the Western Market planted the seed, or introduced the worm, of doubt. Two in particular, Monique and

Candy, both married to successful bureaucrats, were in the real estate market in a big way. They joined two other couples in buying small apartment buildings on Capitol Hill. They of course already owned or were buying their own townhouses. Monique was the daughter of the French military attaché. She had married a defense analyst at the Pentagon, a former student of Henry Kissinger at Harvard, which may have helped under the Nixon administration. Monique and her husband had very pale complexion with acne scars. Both were quite nice to know but I wouldn't want to live with either. The status virus was virulent in their case. He was angling for a job in Belgium at NATO headquarters, something she badly wanted so she could be closer to France and her parents who were returning home soon.

I liked Monique. She was eager, restless, amiable (too restless to be called friendly) and seemed to take to us. I would sit next to her at restaurants during the large party gatherings they favored. I was getting rather fond of her and maybe John, the husband, was getting irritated, a possible reason she was so agreeable to me. She seemed to go out of her way to pay attention to me and Renee, but of course we were dedicated Francophiles. She gave a dinner party, which included a Hungarian immigrant I knew from LOC. He was renovating a rundown townhouse with his female 'partner'. He served as foreman of the Watergate Grand Jury and got two years leave with pay to carry out that civic responsibility. All were in houses, we were not. It just made a move to buy more imperative.

Monique and Candy had opened an organic food shop near the Eastern Market on 8th Street. Eastern Market was a half-block enclosed structure where 'farmers' sold their goods in stalls every day but Monday, The 'Sesame Seed' natural food store did great business in that location. I had to admire Monique's entrepreneurship, although her restlessness probably derived from less admirable motives. She had unsatisfied ambition, for what one never really knew. A Dominican au pair girl lived in and took care of the two children, so she wasn't likely predisposed to be only a full time mother.

Candy Barth was cute. She married a jewish economics professor at U Wisconsin whom she studied under as it were. He subsequently moved to Department of Commerce and then to the World Bank, checking investment projects in Kuwait among other Arab States. His father was an established news man at the Washington Post so they were comfortably off. Barth's father gave them $10,000 for a down payment on their very large townhouse on Stanton Park. Candy had the perpetual 'come on' look that reminded me of Aunt Jenny, to whom men gravitated like flies to honey. Candy worked part time selling real estate, half of it spent warding off passes from male clients. As a flash forward, when John didn't get the 'big job' in Brussels, he and Monique divorced. She took the young daughter and newborn and returned to France with her parents, and John got a job on a Congressional Committee staff and bought a Porsche.

Washington has three main areas. *Area 1,* the Northwest, long established as the premiere upper class White area, was affluent and settled. Housing in Kalorama, Georgetown, north to Chevy Chase was expensive, there was little speculation because turnover was microscopic, owners tended to stay for decades. Prices kept rising, but the owners were in no need of speculative gains. *Area 2,* the Northeast, is the Black area, some middle class but mostly under class. Before desegregation the areas were totally separate. Anything east of 11th Street was Black, which meant that Woodward & Lothrop on 12th Street was White while Hechts on 10th Street was Black. *Area 3,* Southeast and Capitol Hill, is the grey area. Once it had been a lower middle class White neighborhood. J. Edgar Hoover grew up about six blocks from our apartment at North Carolina Avenue. After WWII, Whites who lived on Capitol Hill and environs sold and moved to new suburban housing projects in Tacoma Park Maryland or Arlington and Alexandria Virginia. When I was at Georgetown a student invited me and a friend to his home on Capitol

Hill, probably not far from the one we bought on 14th Street SE twenty years later. Small, cramped, rather depressing place, which he assured us his family was selling to move to ampler housing in the suburbs. Eventually Capitol Hill became part of Area 2, the Black ghetto. The Congressional office buildings, the Supreme Court, the Capitol and the Library of Congress were of course entirely protected and exempted from the demographic decay raging in surrounding residential neighborhoods.

Eisenhower attempted to starve the federal agencies and Congress blocked attempts to create new ones much less build new megaliths to make them permanent. The agencies grew but were accommodated in temporary wooden buildings built for New Deal and WWII expansion under emergencies economic and military. Both considered temporary by Republicans. So the illusion of stasis was maintained and seemed to be the case. Washington was small, interesting, complicated, in some ways a sick place. All this was blown apart under the Imperial Presidencies of Kennedy and Johnson and the 10-year METRO construction. Until the debacle of the 1960's, everyone from all over the city and suburban areas came downtown for entertainment on weekends. College students, bureaucrats, everyone. All this collapsed as streets were dug up, piles of mud and construction materials made getting to and through Washington nearly impossible and certainly undesirable. Restaurants, bars, and other entertainment locales one by one moved out. New cement and glass buildings were constructed to house new and additions to old agencies. The boom brought thousands of new employees. Most of the influx was drawn to the more familiar conditions of suburbs. Only the intrepid, at first, 'pioneered' on the Hill by buying a more or less rundown townhouse and renovating. One by one, houses that had been abandoned by Whites in the 40's and 50's were being reclaimed.

Renewal by individual buyers began as close to the major Hill offices as possible and affordable. But soon real estate business speculators and realtors decided they could buy a block of large well-built rundown houses at reasonable prices, renovate them, and make a lot of money. Several buyers, each encouraging and reinforcing the other, would move into somewhat remoter parts of the Hill with the understanding that all the properties would go sky high in a very few years, This was the situation into which Renee and I entered with our rather meager financial assets. The question was, *How far out can you go, how much intervening unpleasantness can you tolerate, for the amount of money you have to invest?* The market determined that for you. We first went to Marie Antoinette Realtors on Pennsylvania Avenue and 4th Street. This is where we met Alice Ogden Bellis then a student and Protestant student advisor at Catholic University where she was studying Aramaic in the Divinity School. She worked part time at Marie's as real estate agent. She didn't have a car, somewhat unusual handicap for an agent in such a peripatetic occupation. We drove her! We got along well because the last thing she wanted to do was sell real estate, and whether she made money or not didn't matter much since her husband Douglass Bellis had a well-paid position on the House Office of Legislative Counsel staff. As her name suggests, Marie Antoinette had regal standards for houses and clients, disinclined to cater to the exiguous or not well placed. Her listings were mostly close-in large well-restored three-story town homes of ample cubic footage and elegant appointments. We soon fled to Kramer Realtors in the speculative pits ten blocks farther down Pennsylvania Avenue from the established precincts of the Capitol and LOC.

We 'worked with' John Khanke. He was patient but irritable, inevitable result of working with indecisive clients one has to keep coming without a clear path to success and commissions. He wore rimless glasses, was deadly earnest most of the time, looked like what I thought Kafka should have looked like, a *mitteleuropa* intellectual. We looked and looked. We saw very nice homes (at least they were in 1895) that were Black slum houses and needed practically everything vital replaced. One was supposed to pay $50,000 for the wreck and then spend the rest of one's natural life but more exactly every weekend and weekday evenings on amelioration and purchase of needed fixtures. Khanke was. Why not me? I had no desire to live in the middle of plaster piles, unworkable electric outlets, desperately banging trickling pipes, rusted bathtubs, and pee smell in the hallways. No amount of 'equity appreciation' seemed worth it.

Khanke did have the ability and instinct, without which success in sales is impossible, of knowing when to make the decision to buy for the client once a critical mass of house hunting has taken place. This is the key to success in the business because most people are so horrified at the prospect of buying the overpriced junk they look at and would never decide on their own. So he decided for us, after a fashion. We looked at 545 14th Street SE and sort of liked it. Two-story, two bedrooms up plus bathroom and enclosed rear porch, bay windows up and down. Living room dining room combo and kitchen downstairs and enclosed back porch. It had a four-step walk up above street level to the front door which was painted red. It had an 8 1/2-foot high ceiling basement that was clean and in which we could play ping pong (basements are rare on Capitol Hill, especially really useable ones). It had refurbished floors and everything was clean if not new and ready to roll. It was small, I mean SMALL, about 13-feet wide throughout. It had a fireplace in the KITCHEN!!!! Khanke said we could install a prefab fireplace in the living room. Where? How? We would lose half the square footage running a chimney from the first floor through the second floor front room to the roof. So why didn't the developer do that? It was obvious, there would be very little living room left. Anyway, they were asking $55,000, Khanke said offer $50,000. Renee was weary of looking and liked the house so we nodded assent. The seller said OK and we were in.

We did install a very neat corner prefab fireplace upstairs, similar to the one at 101 North Carolina Avenue, which took up only about half of a rather negligible closet in the upstairs front room. Khanke said that was a mistake: *If you ever want to sell the place you need a fireplace downstairs.'* His first mistaken judgment. The fireplace made the upstairs sitting room (we didn't use it for a bedroom) delightful and much more useful than a fireplace downstairs would have been. The room had a bay window that overlooked the crown branches of a large oak tree, providing leafy splendor and dramatic tossing branches to view. Everyone who visited agreed. The small bedroom next after the upstairs front room was for sleeping. Why waste the front upstairs room with its bay window and view of the tall oak tree on a bed? I built quatrefoil wood screen covers for the radiators throughout the house. Water heated radiators are absolutely the best form of heating I have ever seen: silent, totally effective. A radiator under each window heated the entire house in five minutes without the suffocating forced blowing dry hot air that is the common alternative. I also designed a rather large bookcase cum shelving complex that separated the living room from the dining area. Altogether a very charming pleasing house, just

very small, and again I mean small. We could sit on the enclosed back porch at night, have tea, and look at the trees and grass in the back yard that abuts the dead-end alley that had no traffic with the occasional exception of a hot-footed fugitive running from sirens and shouts coming from a block away. But the nightlife was out there and we were cozy and unobservable in the dark of our glassed-in porch and fenced back yard.

When we were arranging to sell and move to California in June 1977, we contacted Khanke. Typically he said the house would sell at about $60,000. He was going out of town for about ten days but would talk details with us when he returned. We couldn't wait and called Beau Bogen Realtors. Beau came right over with all his agents, looked the place over, and said: *'We'll put it on the market for $75,000 and it will sell in five days for $72,500.'* The mark of a pro is his ability to predict outcomes in his field of specialization. Beau was exactly on the money and time. There was great interest in the house, lots of buyer traffic. It sold to a woman who worked for Blue Cross, traveled a great deal, wanted a basement for her photography hobby, and needed access to METRO to get to National Airport. The newly opened METRO stop a block away on Pennsylvania Avenue plus the basement and overall ideal size of the house fitted her needs precisely. It sold within six days! Close enough. Kramer at Kramer Realtors called about two days after the sale to tell me Khanke would be back the following Monday and would come by to discuss the sale. I told him that wouldn't be necessary because the house sold two days ago. Kramer nearly choked. Khanke did call. He asked how much it sold for. I told him $72,500. He said: *That's too much.* Has a real estate agent ever before said anything so absurd? He seemed to resent the sale altogether. I may have said '*Sorry*'. If I did, I certainly said it ironically.

Frank O'Gorman moved into the apartment below ours. Jews and Irish make the best politicians and Frank was no exception. Plump, personable, energetic, sociable, shock of white hair, ruddy complexion, he looked formidable and accessible in the best Honey Fitz tradition. He was administrative assistant to Congressman Hardy from Pennsylvania, working the ropes in Congress and back home to insure success in both. He was married, six kids, all daughters, a statistical improbability to which he bowed humbly but without much consequence since he spent most of his time in Washington while the wife minded the store. He also followed the Kennedy tradition, acquiring at one point a female

Hill employee live-in old enough to be her father, to reverse the standard observation. He was a guy you liked instantly, no pretense no barriers. I got the impression he had served in the Air Corps during WWII, or maybe it was just his frequent mention of the film *Decision at Dawn* that made it seem a personal experience. He had lived in New York, frequented the Village and heard Jussi Bjorling in his cups singing at a favorite Village pub. Which led to his very significant contribution to our happiness, opera. He had opera recordings he offered Renee. *La Boheme, Tosca, Butterfly.* She became addicted and so did I.

The early 70's were a time of thaw in Soviet-American relations. Nixon prevented a Sino-Soviet War and the rise of China tempered Soviet aggressive attitudes toward the US. A KGB agent, known and admitted, was assigned to Capitol Hill to get acquainted with the politicos and promote better relations. Yuri Volkov, 25-years old, looked like a New England prep school tutor, immaculate dark blue Brooks Brothers suit, white shirt, regimental tie, totally without accent idiomatic English, very Anglo looking, not a bit Slavic, and personable. Frank had him over for chat and booze and I joined them from time to time. I remember Frank played Sinatra's *My Way,* which brought tears to Frank's eyes (an autobiographical narcissistic rant if ever there was one) and acclamation from Yuri. Frank later told us that Yuri tried to 'turn him', the FBI told Frank to play along, and Frank became a vector for misinformation, regularly planted in the crotch of a tree branch in the park at the end of our block, an improbable but amusing spy ring plot of little use to the Soviets I am sure.

Given Frank's generous prompting and our newly acquired love of opera, we subscribed to Washington Opera productions and joined the WO Society, a membership support group that had access to lectures, meetings with singers, behind-the-curtain life. Ian Strasvogel became director in 1972, an imaginative and brilliant impresario. Coincidentally, I had met the son of one of supporting families that helped established the WO in 1956. Spaulding was a classmate of John

Jordan at Haverford who got his PhD in Latin American History and was beginning a successful academic career, also acquiring a toothsome girl bride *en route*. The Latin American thing carried over to the opera in that WO premiered works by Ginastera, *Bomarzo, Lucrezia Bogia, and Beatrice Cenci,* which we attended. Strasvogel's triumph came in 1973 with *Incoronazione di Poppea* by Monteverdi circa 1630. Noelle Rogers, of fabulous 38-25-36 vocal and mammary distinction, ill-concealed in a see-through gauze costume, shook the opera world. She returned in the repeat performance by popular demand the following year, and later appeared in *Thais* as the seductress of the quivering novitiate, seen from the side with binoculars in sizzling focus by me. Although the Philippine soprano Evelyn Mandac in *Thais* two years later was more foxy sexy and overpowering just by her slithering eroticism. Jose Carreras in Donizetti's *Lucia di Lamermoor* and Frederica von Stade in Rossini's *Barbiere* and *Ritorno d'Ulisse in Patria* by Monteverdi were among the many delightful productions.

In 1975, George London took over as Director and with his extensive connections brought in many major performers, including Nicolai Gedda. George was quite taken with Renee, we had many delightful chats with him. I remember an opera fundraiser at the Cosmos Club where he was plying wealthy donors when he broke away and waved enthusiastically at us, we waving back, much to the perplexed and annoyed looks of the donors who wondered who these nobodies were distracting the Director from their lucrative company. On another occasion he invited Sherrill Milnes for a master class as a benefit for WO Society members. George had lost his voice to a vocal-chord infection but was a dedicated teacher and promoter of emerging singers. We deeply regretted his incapacitating heart attack age 57 in 1977. He died in 1985 age 64! We traveled to the Metropolitan Opera in New York a few times, first in 1972 to see Tosca with Franco Corelli, James Levine conducting for the first time. We later saw Othello, Karl Bohm conducting, James McCracken as Othello and Sherrill Milnes as Iago.

Martin Douglass Bellis and Alice Ogden Bellis, our one time real estate guide, lived in a small townhouse on 7th Street SE. He was a legislative counsel at the eponymous Congessional Office of Legislative Counsel staffed with a dozen lawyers subject to erosive advancement by seniority with only rare fortuitous leaps ahead. Doug graduated Cornell (Classical Latin/Greek major) in New York and Duke Law School (JUD magna cum laude) in North Carolina, where he met Alice Ogden, an undergraduate majoring in Divinity, admission of which to other students met with repressed laughter or astonishment, trying to imagine the divinity to which such a course of study might apply. An anachronistic choice due perhaps to her father's avocation as active member of their Presbyterian church, provoking a sibling competition for spiritual eminence and paternal preference between Alice and her younger sister. The latter chose psychology as a profession, Alice a ministerial vocation.

Doug affected a Bohemian indifference to conventions (sandals, jeans, tee shirts) largely to disarm the otherwise paralyzing effect of his superior intellect on the coed cohort, always a target for male disport. He played the ukelele, sang his favorite 'Earth Angel', a tale of teen love and loss in a car crash, the favorite lethal instrument of fated love in the 50's. Alice was uptight in the sense of sincere, dedicated, totally without a sense of humor or 'street smarts'. In addition to her degree studies and Protestant student counseling at Catholic University, she served as assistant minister in a Presbyterian Church in Falls Church Virginia, 'falls' perhaps an omen. The pastor, Reverend Winston Crowe, once invited her to give the main Sunday sermon just to advance her skill in that direction but didn't follow up the initial invitation. Too many parishioners left the Church heads shaking, faces perplexed, to risk undermining the lucrative attendance that made the institution such a plum. Her objectivity, neutrality, trace of relativism regarding the Savior was not what was needed or wanted. Affirmation and aspiration the rule. Plum the operative term.

Alice had heard whispers suggesting possible straying from the true path by Reverend Crowe. Long counseling sessions with female communicants behind closed doors. Frequent and inexplicable presence of 25-year old Miss Adele Funk at all hours of the day and night. Doug thought Crowe was 'fishy' the first time he met him. In support of Alice he attended night Bible classes and Sunday sermons and even joined the choir to get an inside track on church operations. Sure enough, Alice oblivious of all around her, Crowe absconded with $2,250,000 in church funds and the pneumatic Miss Funk, never to be seen much less apprehended again. Alice missed all clues, hints, *sub rosa* warnings, and physical signs--lipstick smear on his collar, a spent condom at the bottom of the waste basket, untucked-in blouse as Miss Funk left his office.

We exchanged dinners for a short time. We always were on time with adequate provisions, usually prawns in champagne sauce and cheese *souflee* with chocolate *mouse* dessert, champagne by the glassful. Bellis' were less predictable. Usually some key ingredient missing from the erratically stocked fridge. We opted for restaurant excursions thereafter. Doug, an ardent Federalist, had a suit circa 1778 made up including buckle shoes, frilled shirt, stockings, and a tri-corn hat for inclement weather, looking a bit like Ben Franklin across the dining table. He had mastered Latin and Ancient Greek, but he excelled in the most esoteric and convoluted language of all, *Legalese*. His career breakout as counsel to Congress came in 1974 when he drafted the Articles of Impeachment for the Nixon trial, the desk at which they were drafted in his living room having special place at all their gatherings. Furnishings were all 18th Century English Chippendale, Persian rugs, Revere silverware, walnut bookcases with complete sets in green and blue wrappers of the Oxford Greek and Latin classics. He commissioned two portraits hung on the wall behind the head of the dining table, one of himself holding a copy of Blackstone's Comments on the Laws of England and one of Alice holding Pilgrim's Progress. A Russian émigrée painter somehow acquired a political clientele, attesting more to the abysmal ignorance of the clients' knowledge of art, the results more embalming than enlivening, since great portraits always give the impression that the subject is actively looking at the viewer not just an inanimate assemblage of pigment.

Douglass memorized the US Code and intended by his own admission to revise it. I told him that the difference between Russia and America (and England) is that everything is forbidden that is not expressly permitted in Russia, and everything is permitted that is not expressly forbidden in America. He suggested he would impose the Russian principle upon the Anglo-American legal tradition. His job required him to turn the whims and follies of Members of Congress into formal legislation, in legal format, language and ambiguity. He wrote a *Guide to Legislation* which was praised publicly and ignored privately. It involved a labyrinthine search of precedents, infinite use of qualifying phrases (heretofore, in consequence of which, *ex post facto*) and other legalese strewn across the path of later interpreters as to make progress toward clarity impossible, and by the way to provide an infinite source of employment for lawyers (hence the praise).

Doug was an example of thorough specialization and immersion in his *fach*. He also made some claim to being a poet, and once sent me a bound copy of his verse, a blind spot many talented people have of esteeming a personal sideline far above its market value. A great deal of 'love and caring' and Hallmark Card devotion presumably directed at Alice. I sent him a satirical punch at specialization just to stimulate further debate.

Descent

The Engram in our genes has found
The descent from trees
And opposing thumb empirically sound,
But being pragmatic denies Kultur
An Imprimatur.
Nothing subtle works
Is Nature's theme.
Though guile improve Aesop's fox
And men are warned by dream,
That still saves the paradox:
Success and failure are narrow views,
Rigorously pursued.

In 1976, Alice graduated from Catholic University with an MA in Divinity and was hired as an instructor by Howard University, the Black college. (She is still there!) Both she and Doug were avid liberals, dedicated to Black equality and improvement, even to the point of sending their daughters Margaret (born 1980) and Elizabeth (born 1983) to the local public grade school and high school, closely monitored and supported financially by like-minded liberal parents to pay for and insist upon academic supplements, internal and external, to the school staff curriculum, that would maintain high standards of educational study while allowing them the virtue signaling of sending their kids to all black schools. Jimmy Carter had done the same with his daughter to validate the integration of WDC schools instead of sending them to Sidwell Friends prep school, the preferred alternative of nearly all politicos.

Over time Alice, embedded in an all-Black Divinity faculty, and writing and studying about early Christianity, including visits to Ethiopia to review 500-year old Christian manuscripts, imposed African intrusions onto the Colonial oasis so assiduously cultivated by Doug. In 1987, they moved to a large (5 bedrooms, 3 baths) townhouse near Stanton Park. She bought African masks, spears and voodoo drums prominently displayed in the Federalist entryway, African fertility sculptures placed on Chippendale end tables and fireplace mantle in the living room, gave Afrocentric parties for Howard students and colleagues, rolling back the Persian rug to dance to loud rap and chunky Black rock music rattling the window panes to 2 AM.

After Renee and I moved to the San Francisco Bay area we corresponded and they visited once in 1987. Over time their Xmas letters conveyed information about their jobs and family. Elizabeth graduated University of Chicago and Harvard Law and worked for a New York law firm. Margaret graduated Georgetown Law and worked for an Atlanta law firm. Both married with children. Douglass became a chief legislative counsel, Alice was promoted and recognized for her book: *Helpmates Harlots and Heroines*, a review of biblical heroines targeted at a secular audience. Christmas letters are catch up, a summary of the year's adventures, mishaps, hopefully achievements. I used them to provide a diary of annual events and my observations of the passing scene. Alice was literal, descriptive, no critique, analysis, opinions complicated her detailed account of events. She gave birth to Margaret in 1980, which she described in anatomical detail, down to the last suture and clamp. Equally detailed was her account of painting her house and replacing kitchen fixtures, like watching paint dry to read. An amusing excerpt from a 1995 message shows her absorbed attention to detail on matters I, if I bothered to mention, probably would not have described in such detail.

As we write this letter, there are a few injuries, but none of us is out for the count. Margaret has bunions, which makes dancing on point more difficult. Surgery would take care of the problem but would sideline her from dancing for several months, so she's putting up with it. Doug is just about over a problem that began as a pain in the heel, probably resulting from insufficiently supportive gym shoes and a change in exercise routine with a return to squash playing. Hobbling around to favor the heel led to a strain in one of the tendons or ligaments in his knee. That kept him from playing squash for a few weeks. It's slowly getting better. However, during his time off from squash and leg exercise, he worked harder on his bench press. While doing that he strained his wrists not wearing wrist bands, so he has had to lighten up a bit to give his wrists time to heal. Elizabeth has a knee condition called (phonetically) Osgood Schlatter. Her muscle tissue is not growing as fast in one leg as her bone, creating a painful bump just below her knee where the tendon that the thigh muscle to the bone pulls on the bone and slowing her down in her gymnastics. We recently visited a pediatric orthopedic specialist who told her to take a month off to let the bone heal. Alice is seemingly injury free at the moment. A slight twinge in the knee from running more miles than perhaps she should have recently seems to have been taken care of by the simple expedient of a knee brace from the local drugstore. Margaret is now wearing a Jones Jog in her mouth which is supposed to open up some space for her teeth in preparation for braces.

Alice was my introduction to the massive religion industry. Most early colleges in New England were founded to train ministers for the flock. Divinity faculties remain to this day, though greatly diminished by the triumph of secularism. Yale Divinity School, a prime supplier of talent to the Presbyterians, was the alma mater of the head of the Ecumenical Library in Berkeley, a multi-denominational Library of Congress of sorts for all Protestant denominations. We met him in connection with SF Opera, a nervous wreck, unappeasable fidgit, hyper Alpha male, who in fact died of a heart attack two years after we met him. Given Alice's publishing record I decided to visit the library and look up her books. A truly astonishing three-story building packed with books on every Bible chapter and verse *ad nauseam* in what must be 70-miles of shelves over hundreds of metal shelves. Hers were there, timidly pressed between large tomes dealing with Ecclesiastes on the left and Song of Solomon on the right. This is a closed guild, no intruders, monitored by vetted apostles, mutually admiring and validating in a hierarchy of proselytes accountable only to themselves.

Doug and Alice were devoted even fanatic parents, driving Margaret and Elizabeth to gymnastics, ballet, cello and violin lessons with Washington Symphony Orchestra musicians, special classes, in one case Calculus for Margaret at George Washington University, frequent recitals, the girls participating as onstage extras in professional performances. Alice ran, swam, danced, biked, Doug squashed, bench pressed. Both once biked eighty miles out to a resort in West Virginia and back for a weekend of fun, did 10-mile runs every week, sometimes three miles a day after work. Work also kept them busy. Doug was for a time connected via the State Department to respond to requests for legislative advice in Romania, Slovakia, Ukraine, and South Korea, involving trips and setting up legislative counsel shops in their various Parliaments. A distinction of sorts, but also one suspects a relief for those in charge from his rather conceited presence. He had reached through seniority the #3 position. Alice attended religious academic conferences, lectured on homosexuality in biblical literature. I had read about such a conference in San Francisco in summer 1999, and in my Xmas letter *said I thought I saw you at Union Square last Summer,* a fabrication just to see if it produced a reaction. She guiltily replied she was there but so busy had no time to make contact.

In 1998, the Bellis' moved to a smaller house on 7th Street, across the street from where they started in 1972. Margaret was at Duke, Elizabeth was headed to University of Chicago (age 16). No constant duty to care and educate left Alice and Doug alone together. All seemed favorable with the Bellis clan, until the early 2000's. I had mentally speculated on the African intrusions and their effect on Douglass, but assumed he was a docile participant in this primitive eruption. In a 2002 Xmas letter Doug announced that the *'candle of our love had extinguished'* still doggedly following his antique romantic poetic bent. They divorced that year.

I don't believe in divorce. Marriage is the start of a pocket civilization with its own language, customs, traditions, all gradually acquired and reinforced over years. A symbiosis of body mind spirit and soul. The texture and depth more complex and deeper with every new event, setback, boon, or achievement. Or at least I thought so. In fact, divorce after the 'kids are gone' is as likely as not. My sister, Renee's sister, several couples we knew, all divorced once the parental stage passed. Although I could intuit sources of their conflict, Doug and Alice, like most couples we knew, were so unmarketable (as in Shakespeare's *Sell when you can you're not for all markets)* after years together that I assumed they could not find anyone else to tolerate them, making divorce impracticable or too wearisome to attempt. Assumption is the fount of misapprehension. Alice continued to write, whereas Doug returned my 2013 Xmas message unopened with US Congress stamp: *Return to Sender.* In a 2000 Xmas letter he had included a hand written invitation: *If you are back this way--please visit. You could make a sentimental journey to 14th Street! Let us know enough in advance and maybe we could get opera tickets--- Doug.* He had never before sounded so warm and inviting, certainly 'please' was not a term he often used! In retrospect I feel guilty. I let him down, ignored his underlying appeal for support and counsel in face of the breakdown of their marriage and impending divorce. I should have gone back for a visit, but his generally unsentimental approach to everything seemed to impede a more intuitive understanding of what he meant. I feel I failed him as a friend.

Alice subsequently remarried a member of the Arms Control Commission who got interested in St. Augustine, writing an endlessly footnoted biography about his conversion to Christianity which he argued was the result of impotence, a nicely contemporary, even Freudian, interpretation of Early Christian motivation. Our Xmas correspondence continued. In 2019 she wrote to tell me Doug had died, result of a failed heart transplant! Rather shocking since he had such a biceptual obsession with fitness. Most interesting was to learn that Doug, a few months before his death, had married the mother of one of his daughter's husband, creating an interesting definitional challenge, what is his relationship--father/step father/misstep father? Alice and Doug had so intertwined their rights to succession of pensions and property that to marry just before dying left a legal knot to untie, probably intentional in order to remain a thorn in all sides *post mortem.* The Washington Post obituary was written by his new wife, including a complete list of mourning friends, survivors, children, and so on, but no mention whatever of Alice Ogden Bellis. No further editions of the Bellis saga to be forthcoming. *Vale!*

The 1960's-era was tumultuous and game changing, beginning with the election of John Kennedy and ending with the impeachment of Richard Nixon. Two paradigms of American social contrasts, the ersatz Irish Aristocrat and the uptight petit bourgeois Quaker Anglo descendant of Thomas Cornell (also an ancestor of Ezra Cornell founder of Cornell University, and Jimmy Carter and Bill Gates!). Jack lived large, encouraged by his buccaneer father Joe, formed during Joe's stint as Ambassador to England by close association with the English aristocracy (his sister Kathleen married William Cavendish Marquess of Hartington) into a liberal articulate free-loving live style.

Poor Richard (literally it appears) raised in a no liquor no smoking no dancing moral straight jacket of emotional and sexual repression converted into a willful and vengeful ambition to succeed. He drove the family truck four hours to Los Angeles from Whittier to buy vegetables for the family grocery store, a moral tale worthy of George's apple tree. He was offered a tuition grant to Harvard but had to remain in Whittier to help the family run the store while his mother cared for his sick brother. You can imagine the sublimated anger he must have felt. Dick graduated summa cum laude from Whittier College and got a full scholarship to Duke Law where he graduated in 1937. He married Pat Nixon in 1940, was commissioned in the Navy in 1942 and was discharged in 1946 rank Commander. Elected to Congress in 1947, he joined the House Un-American Activities Committee and was elected to the Senate in 1950. Jack and Dick were the bread of the Lyndon Johnson (1963-1969) sandwich which destroyed the economy, upheaved the society, undermined law and order, killed 55,000 boys in Viet Nam, and entrenched the drug culture. All three served in the Navy in WWII, Jack as a torpedo boat hero, Lyndon as a phony Navy Cross winner given his Congressional background and friendship with FDR, and Nixon who received several commendations for service rendered.

The 1963 March, 1966-1968 urban race riots, assassinations of Jack, MLK, Bobby Kennedy, 1968 Chicago convention riots, antiwar demonstrations all had direct repercussions on life in the Capitol. But nothing like the METRO construction and agency buildup. Except for riots in Northeast Washington and the police regroup area on North Carolina Avenue, life went on rather peacefully like in the eye of the cyclone. Of course, there were social and familial contests between supporters of either side of the ongoing saga. Renee's mother inclined to surrogate retargeting of her domestic frustrations launched a steady and bitter invective against Sam Erwin the Dem Senator in charge of the Nixon impeachment. Better Erwin than Donald. The decline from Jackie and fashion designer Oleg Cassini to Lady Bird, Linda Bird and all the birds was precipitous, the Chad Mitchell Trio producing a satirical song commemorating the birds. As body bags piled up and live TV coverage of combat in Viet Nam brought war into the homes of the suckers who were sending cannon fodder and tax dollars to keep the disaster going, the aura of Executive wisdom and virtue dispelled. Muddle class aversion to the real time effects of integration and the War on Poverty drove them to the suburbs for protection and immunity, social contracts were in bankruptcy on every turn. Joany Phony Baez with her '*girls say yes to boys who say no*' and Hanoi Jane Fonda visiting the Viet Cong and trashing America got students to protest nationwide.

181

Poor Hubert Humphrey smiled his way to oblivion or rather to Nixon in 1968 in one of the amazing comebacks in US political history. A guy nobody liked finally won the White House. He got the Jewish Metternich, Henry Kissinger, to negotiate a truce in Viet Nam, open the door to China, and restrain Russia from invading the later. If not great, Nixon was a well above-average President. He signed the National Environmental Policy Act in 1969 that made environmental assessments a part of all federal projects that might affect the environment and established the Environmental Protection Agency. He signed the Clean Water Act, the Clean Air Act, the Endangered Species Act, the Act linking increases in Federal pensions to the cost of living index. He left the gold standard. He signed the Equal Opportunity Act authorizing 'affirmative action' to increase 'representation' of minorities in hiring practices. In effect he established the financial, environmental and social structure of the last quarter of the 20th Century. But…. He was *petit bourgeois*, the low end of the muddle class, closest to the blue collar class just below. They live in dread of falling out of the muddle class, losing white collar status. They are insecure as is the muddle class in that they have no permanent economic or social status. All can be lost in an instant. The petit bourgeois are most at risk and often are the support of right wing radical political movements, as in Germany with the Nazis. In the US, J. Edgar Hoover is the prime example. Nixon also envied the sexual libertines Jack Kennedy and Lyndon Johnson. White House leaks before the 1972 election made Nixon paranoid, irrational, so he directed illegal searches of the Democrat National Committee headquarters in Watergate. Beginning of the end.

Getting to California: We traveled to Minneapolis for Christmas in 1976--a gamble, a hope, a possibility. Maybe Alice would be 'better', Robert tolerable, Linda and Dick Hume getting along. We had misgivings but it was worth a chance. Living on Capitol Hill in the frontier 14th Street area meant you had to have a strategy for every departure. We took it to extremes, devising subterfuges to deceive prospective burglars. We packed our suitcases, put them in black trash bags, ducked out the back door, down the alley out to Pennsylvania Avenue, took the bus, transferred to the airport bus, and sat relieved on the way to National Airport. Renee asked what time it was. I said 1:45 PM. She decomposed. *The plane takes off at 2 PM!!!* How this happened is stupid but simple. Instead of targeting a time to be at the airport we talked in terms of how much time we had left. For some reason I estimated a takeoff at least one hour later than the actual one. So, all reassurances that we had plenty of time left were entirely wrong. We arrived at the airport around 2:20 PM in a panic, went to Northwest Airlines, explained the situation. They reassured us that there was no problem, they would put us on the next flight at 4:30 PM. Since the flight time was about 1 1/2 hour, everyone in Minneapolis was on the way to the airport to greet us. We asked Northwest to leave a message for them that we missed the 2 PM but would arrive on the 4:30 PM flight.

Timing figured in two seminal events in my life: the first, Army Reserve authority to assign recruits to Army Language School, a matter of 2 days; the second, a matter of 2 ½ hours. We got on the 4:30 PM flight, settled in. I casually looked around. Bill Hamilton, someone I knew at the Agriculture Department (a colleague of Edgar A. Poe III, descendant of EAP himself), happened to be in a seat four rows ahead of us. There were two vacant seats next to him. We went to say hello after takeoff. Bill's sister had called him around noon and told her husband had been shot to death in a barroom brawl early that morning. She lived in Montana near Billings and Bill got the earliest flight he could. Exact circumstances were unknown, perhaps even to her, so the tantalizing possibilities remained matters for speculation. I was rather impressed. Such a cliché demise, a last remnant of legendary Western methods of settling interpersonal disputes was exciting to consider. How many identical scenes in how many movies, good and bad, had one seen? Was Bill's sister wrapped in a shawl outside the barroom swinging doors waiting for her impecunious and perhaps mildly alcoholic husband to give up the poker game and return home? Were there dancehall girls promoting consumption beyond the capacity of customers to handle? What about the bartender? Did he attempt to intervene, call the Sheriff, break the bad mood with a joke? Were there musicians banging out dancehall tunes on a battered tuneless piano? Such images kept circling around and around. As a matter of taste we didn't pursue speculation about circumstances audibly. Eventually conversation got round to jobs and I expressed interest in transferring. With Renee there to charm him and me to acquaint him with my job interest, we left him in Minneapolis well informed about our situation. He apparently got to like us and we parted on very amiable terms, although we didn't hear from him for nearly five months.

Back in Washington, we spent several months looking at houses in Virginia and Maryland. Fredericksburg Virginia was as far south as we looked, Columbia Maryland as far east. Mostly new construction, isolated, poor logistics, high prices. We had the feeling we would be stranded in any of the housing projects and neighborhoods we saw. Why leave a centrally located house on Capitol Hill? Besides, the METRO a block and a half away was nearing completion, an enormous asset for the neighborhood. So it was with some surprise that late in June, Bill Hamilton called me and said there was a position at the Forest Service Regional Office in the San Francisco that might be of interest. I tried to sound calm, interested but not too eager, much less desperate. I had by then gained quite a good reputation among the working members of my organization as my estimation fell with the management of the section I happened to be in. Such disparity is common in bureaucracy, where managers in rather marginal positions are especially irritated by staffers who take initiative in serving the rest of the organization. To make the obscure and uninteresting details of bureaucratic infighting short, I had a portfolio that some thought was impressive, and fortunately that included the San Francisco office of the Forest Service. I was also helped by my branch chief, a capable but desperate chain-smoking guy who knew the people in San Francisco and had the grace to recommend me. I calmly told Bill I would call my wife and then call San Francisco right back. I called Renee and rather indifferently said that I could get a job in San Francisco if we wanted to go. Once she peeled herself off the kitchen ceiling, a coherent affirmation came through followed by '*Whoopie*'. I called San Francisco, accepted the offer, and was told all expenses including costs for selling the house and buying a new one would be paid but I should make no moves in that direction until officially notified so the costs can be paid by the Forest Service.

As expected, misfortune gains friends and sympathy (however *schadenfreude* it may be). Bounty, a windfall, unexpected good fortune loses friends and exposes a number of flaws (mostly envy) in relationships one hitherto thought were amiable, even close. The Sesame girls were livid with envy that we punks got a plum assignment to San Francisco, a city that enjoys a mythic reputation everywhere, whereas they were still struggling to break out of Washington vicariously through their husbands' career moves. Denice Bredt even went so far as to say: *You don't deserve it!* What a Pal! Realtors, prospective buyers of the house straggling through almost came to attention when told we were leaving for a new assignment in San Francisco, the prospect invariably conceived in idyllic terms and presumed to indicate hidden powers, authority or favor.

We had considered taking an opera vacation in San Francisco in 1975 and 1976, but my impressions of the city dating from Army days in Monterey were not at all favorable. In the early 1960's the city was grubby, two story, queer ridden in a degenerate way. None of the renovation that came along from about 1965 on had begun. But all this enthusiasm for Baghdad by the Bay began to convert me to its favor. So between June 10 and September 12 we lined up our ducks for the move. When I received official authorization to incur moving expenses in July, we checked realtors and listed with Beau Bogen. He sold the house within a week, to be occupied after closing was completed within six weeks. We arranged for air tickets, and Don and Winifred agreed to drive the Chevy Impala to California, making a cross-country vacation out of the opportunity, including a visit to Graceland!

Where you think you are genuinely liked good fortune arouses envy rather than good wishes, though congratulations (the civility of envy) are also on offer. Curiously, where you know you are disliked, at least in the bureaucratic snake pit, good fortune and imminent departure (mutually favorable) arouses a mild amicability as though a burden soon to be lifted can be tolerated, even indulged. I began to get along with everyone with whom I had been, shall we say, distant, at work. They even gave a farewell luncheon, albeit awkward because the predominant feeling was relief not regret at my departure. Since I was never going to look back, I became insufferably agreeable, talkative, amusing. I loved thinking how I would never see these clowns again.

Did someone up there take care of me? California turned out to be a mixed bag with respect to Renee's health. It wasn't paradise but I never thought it was. It has provided wonderful opportunities so I have no complaints. I wouldn't have survived in Washington, I thrived in California, at work and in my interests. I think Renee did too. If he sent me Renee in 1964, he sent us to California in 1977. I keep thinking both were part of a beneficent plan. Why not?

CALIFORNIA

A nice neighborhood to have bad habits.

Raymond Chandler captured the aura, David Hockney the light, Roy Orbison's *California Blue* the tone. Except for Napa wine country, Northern California is more Oregon, Sierras Colorado, Southeast Arizona, Valley Iowa. Real California is westside of the Coast range, San Francisco-Monterey north, Santa Barbara-Beverley Hills central, Laguna Beach-San Diego south, a 600-mile door sill to blue-green infinity, the Pacific Ocean. If you are more than thirty minutes from sand, surf and barking seals, you are not in the California of dreams, yearning, illusion, gently baking summer sun, palm trees, white sand (Carmel), sea gulls, calamari, fantasy (Hearst Castle/Disneyland), Apple, Pixar, and MGM. Hearing the word California, Americans conjure palms, sand, bronzed surfers, coast cypress highways, Golden Gate, Packard convertibles, movie stars, thong beaches, sunset dining, the pet rock. Monterey jazz, SF Opera, LA Symphony, *parfum d'eucalyptus,* salt-tang ocean breezes, fresh-baked sourdough, bouquet of Petit Syrah. And the girls, heart stabbing beauty, seen at a distance, too far to reach, too lovely to grasp, the metaphor for yearning pursuit of soul's Shangri-La. *California*!

But let's get real. Renee and I arrived in San Francisco September 14, 1977 and signed for our house at 4125 Fruitvale Avenue in Oakland on Halloween. Perhaps an apt juxtaposition since every house purchase combines equal parts terror and travesty. That I was less than enchanted showed in my pallor. Renee had been accusing me rightly of considering remaining in the furnished apartment on Greenwich Street in the Marina that the marvelous Irish manager of the Lombard Street Motel rented us '*as long as we wanted*' for $200 a month with free parking! He adored

Renee. He was also a member of IRA's Sinn Fein and participated in hanging effigies of Prince Charles, then visiting San Francisco, from every lamp post in the downtown area. We missed seeing Beverly Sills in *Turandot,* every performance sold out on the chance the Prince would turn up, which he did at one of five, 3200 capacity house fans delighted, the others not so much. We also just missed Jose Carreras and Teresa Stratus, onstage and offstage lovers, in a torrid *La Boheme,* but did manage *Die Walkure* and *Aida,* a Wagner-Verdi showdown.

For nearly a month we had dined out, gone to operas, walked around the Marina, taken in the glorious city that if not in its Golden Age, certainly was enjoying the twilight of a Silver one. Restaurants in the Cannery were especially wonderful, one being Le Cassoulet with French provincial décor and excellent food. At Pergola, an Italian restaurant near Washington Square, the waiters were more interested in listening to the football game in the kitchen where the radio drowned out *Come Back to Sorrento* in the dining room. An occasional disappointment didn't dent the charm of San Francisco, all, 44-years later, gone with the wind.

We looked at apartments in San Francisco and were particularly depressed by one in the Castro, one bedroom, one bath, with a view of the grey cement wall of a neighboring office building for $50,000. We looked extensively in Oakland and finally found a reasonable prospect owned by a Mormon couple about to retire and return to their Holy Land (Utah). He sold Aladdin bottled water, not a particularly distinguished occupation, but was equivalent to an Eagle Scout in the Mormon lay hierarchy enjoying Sunday status to assuage his weekday blue collar humiliation. He reminded me of the 20-year+ career salesman at Woodward & Lothrop mens section, enjoying an equally surrogate career in the Mormon hierarchy. The Fruitvale area was a bit seedy because most of the owners were elderly, a class overly reverenced in America. For the most part they have no taste, do not take care of their properties, live on the cheap, are lazy fat petulant and self-indulgent. As they died off, the shabby deteriorated homes were sold off by inheritors to yuppy couples who invested in improvements over time, we hoped. The first requirement after we moved in was to sort out the logistics of daily life. Our house, though spacious and provided with a series of rooms and cubby holes, suffered from the embedded bad taste and economies imposed by the impecunious Mormon occupants over nearly twenty years. Gilt wall paper in one room, Grand Central Station lavatory green paint in the bathrooms and basement, tacky linoleum in the Kitchen, and wall-to-wall carpet throughout. Much editing was required over several years.

California was disappointing to look at. A dry brown monotonous landscape relieved only by the Bay and Ocean. There had been a 5-year drought, to which my arrival signaled an end, appropriate for an Aquarian. But our principal landscape was cultural and our North Star was the San Francisco Opera House (SFO). We gauged everything according to how long or how easy it would be to get there. Had we not, we could have lived anywhere in the Bay Area. But had we not, we would have had no appreciation for what the city still had to offer in addition to SFO, namely restaurants, theater, museums and most notably Pippin Pocket Opera, which we attended in 1978 for the first time.

Donald Pippin had just begun performing opera at the original Old Spaghetti Factory (OSF) in an area off the main dining room, a small bandstand, folding chairs and footstools for the audience separated from the diners only by a red-white checked curtain. OSF was Italian North Beach at its most authentic, a great barn-like building (once serving the purpose of its name before conversion) within a residential enclave that attracted hundreds of diners, a casual style of good heart-warming Italian food and 'family' style service in the best sense of that corrupted adjective. It ended in 1979, so few remain to remember one of SF's most iconic establishments. The name survives as a franchise but any resemblance is purely coincidental. Pippin called his company

Pocket Opera. Handel operas were his specialty, sung in Italian with intervals of comment by Donald on the convoluted plots and complicated deceptions, disguises, and emotional entanglements of the largely mythical characters. His comments were as amusing as helpful for the audience in following the operas. He translated operas of other composers in his inimitable style, translations now widely used for opera productions nationwide. We went to several Pocket Opera performances our first season, including Pippin's first translation, *Un Giorno di Regno* (King for a Day), Verdi's only comedy. Sitting on footstools and folding chairs in the garlic-and-tomato paste scented atmosphere of OSF was a unique delight never to be recovered. SF Opera also was remarkably accessible. Opera Fair every fall for about five years included Pavarotti and Domingo, pre-inflation. We stood ten feet away from Luciano as he sang *Nessun Dorma*. Domingo was even closer when he played piano and sang *Zarzuela*. We met Giorgio Tozzi and the great great Cesare Siepi. More about the opera later.

The real challenge was settling into and establishing turf in the new job. I have described the *freudenschade* and *schadenfreude* commonly associated with departing an old job. The feelings and complications of entering a new one are more intense and treacherous, largely because in the former case things come to an end, in the latter you face a new beginning. All offices are hierarchies of sorts and the interests of any level are usually entirely opposed to those of the level above and below and are opposed in different ways for different reasons. This applies to individuals at each level as well. Generally, the intensity of interest and concern increases or decreases with the distance from the person exciting the attention, namely the newcomer. All this by way of introducing the snake pit that was the Public Affairs Office of the California Regional Office of the US Forest Service in 1977. The director was Jane Westenberger, a capable, formerly quite attractive, never married but definitely not maiden busty ex school teacher sexpot from Southern California who joined the Forest Service when they started public school conservation education programs in the 1960's. She was a swinger, had been involved with a few

Rangers and others but had toned down her proclivity to escapade in order to get the position she held. The Regional Forester, Doug Leisz, was a strikingly handsome rugged, wiry, white-haired, blue-eyed, ideal forester type adored by everyone in the Region. Jane made sure he had nothing to complain about her.

Bob Tribble was Jack of all trades since the Public Affairs staff was small. His main skill and interest was filmmaking but he had a hand in media contacts, publications, and so on. French mother American Indian father, good looking, well built with a John Wayne slur and swagger, he was pure cheesecake with lots of attitude. I had a great deal of experience with emotional complexes and early recognized his erratic personality through the pattern he established. He was agreeable up to about 2 PM, when his meds wore off and he began to deteriorate and start brow beating the two members of his group, Bill Powers a firefighter who liked to write and Sedge Thompson. Bill wrote an amusing article, *Asparagus,* published in American Airlines flight magazine, but no more account of him was available after he left in June 1978. Sedge later became a successful public radio show host (West Coast Weekend at KQED and West Coast Live at KKHI) based on an unbeatable formula of offering free public air time to every act, author and show passing through the city in need of publicity, an endless supply of willing, eager and grateful entertainment for his weekly two-hour show. When he started with a DJ show at KQED in 1978, he followed a suggestion of mine and played *Incoronazione di Poppea* by Monteverdi in its entirety for one of his 2-hour shows. I had no idea my influence would carry that far. But that was later. In 1977, Sedge was dealing with media calls about the most extensive and damaging fire season in California history.

The rhetoric surrounding fire reporting is almost ludicrous in its simplicity, banality and redundancy, but it always seems to attract rapt attention wherever fires get out of control, especially in multimillion dollar residential areas of Southern California. I reported on and did media interviews regarding wildfires for many years so I know the drill.

In 1977, it seemed quite impressive and original to me as a newcomer from the soggy fireproof East.

I never rely on immediate associates to define the terms of my employment. I always take the broadest possible look at the organization and become acquainted with everyone I can possibly find within as short a time as possible. I did just that my first two weeks at 630 Sansome Street, my occupational home for the next 20 years! Within ten workdays I had introduced myself to every staff and in particular, every clerk of every staff. This had a disarming and perhaps alarming effect on Westenberger and others in the Public Affairs Staff. I seemed to be known before they had a chance to tell someone on another staff about my arrival. I also had the technique of talking about what interested the other staff members, mainly their own job and interests. So I came across as intelligent, interested and willing to help. Most staffs avoid contact and certainly don't go out of their way to 'help' other staffs. Creating an impression of being 'swamped' with work requires diligent and unrelenting effort to impress bosses and avoid colleagues' claims on one's time. I met people who had worked in the Regional Office for fifteen years and didn't know people from other staffs I had just made it a point to meet. Such insularity provides opportunity to an inquisitive type like me. Plus it was my job to know what they were doing and include it in our Public Affairs communications. Unassailable!

No one with whom a new arrival may present even the slightest competition welcomes the newcomer despite the effusive jargon characteristic of such introductions. This was the case with Bob Tribble, whose paranoia was difficult to repress at the best of times. I actually liked Tribble even though I had a good idea of what to expect. Unlike many people, I am very difficult to impress or impose upon. I don't show my hand until necessary but I don't hesitate when the time comes. Tribble hosted a welcoming party at his home. It was very nicely done and Tribble and his wife gave Renee and me a royal welcome, knives kept in the kitchen drawer for the moment. Other members of the staff having no great liking for Tribble's hysterics seemed genuinely glad to see me. John Wicker, one of my staff members, was especially friendly and helpful and I responded in kind. After the welcoming party he invited Renee and me to his house, more like estate, in Ross, the most expensive real estate in the entire San Francisco Bay Area. A swimming pool directly below the living room floor for one thing, which could be exposed by retracting the floor, but how and where the floor went was unclear to me. The house had been custom built with all the ill-conceived and ill-coordinated eccentricities and dysfunctional personal preferences typical of such attempts to personalize a residence. Much better to stick with tried and true designs, but *l'argent fait tout.* John's wife was Swedish, friend of Swedish soprano Birget Neilson appearing at this time at SF Opera, so we had a bit in common, plus I am half Swedish, not usually a recommendation to fellow Swedes, but we do instinctively understand our common personality traits and emotional complexities. John had two teenage sons over whom he expended much worry and as little money as possible. He had worked in government for nearly twenty years while waiting to receive an inheritance from his wealthy New England manufacturing family, some $33 million from an estate of $100 million, evenly divided between him and his two sisters. He invariably dressed in sport shirt and jeans, a capable and personable guy of 55-years. He drove an enormous Mercedes sedan and as indicated lived in the most expensive neighborhood in the Bay Area. His mother passed away in 1978 and he soon retired amply provided for.

On my third day at work, Wicker took me aside and told me that my secretary Eunice was alcoholic. I had spotted that the first time I was introduced to her and told him so. He seemed to be impressed by my perspicacity, nothing unusual for anyone who has been around alcoholics for any length of time. All the signs were there but I wasn't going to make anything of it. Enough had been made already. The agency had sent her to clinics to dry out and to shrinks to get at the problem. Alcoholism had been defined as a disease, not a character flaw, by the AMA, so greater care and rehabilitation services were available at

Agency expense, up to a point. That point had been reached in Eunice's case. Her timed departures to the rest room for a snort of vodka were no mystery to me. Stumbling on her feet and frequent typing errors led to polite insistence that she retire, which she did within a year.

Such tolerance was characteristic of the Forest Service in California. The management followed the practice of giving you a job loosely defined and then left you to figure out how to do it. Initiative not supervision was the rule, especially in public affairs about which the foresters were wary, uninformed and in some respects suspicious. Public criticism by Sierra Club, Audubon Society, Wilderness Society, Wild & Scenic Rivers Society and so on meant that they needed someone to deal with the criticism in order to smooth the path for forest managers. My kind of briar patch! Major federal agencies that manage public lands are Bureau of Land Management, National Park Service, and Fish and Wildlife Service of the Department of the Interior, US Forest Service-Department of Agriculture, and the Pentagon for all military bases. States have their own park system and regulate forestry practices on private forest lands. For those of you who reside in the urban East Coast corridor Washington-New York-Boston, these public lands are of little interest and even littler significance. There are national forests, national parks and wildlife refuges here and there, and in the South extensive National Forests provide pine, hickory, oak, maple and other tree resources for Louisville Slugger baseball bats, dining tables, plywood, hickory walking sticks and other timber products for local timber, wood products and furniture industries. In the Far West, public land is a major source of mining, recreation, timber, water supply, and grazing. Federal land makes up 45% of California, 85% of Nevada, 52% of Oregon, 29% of Washington. National Forests make up one in five acres of California, 20% of the State land base. Timber sold by competitive bidding is the major resource provided by the National Forests, timber industry making up roughly 10% of the economy in Washington, 30% in Oregon, and less 1% in California. Therein lies the problem. 97% of Californians want recreation and resource preservation, less than 3%

depend on agriculture, timber harvest and grazing for a living. Until 1960, the latter had no interference. As a result of Rachel Carson's *Silent Spring* in 1962, and environmental group lawsuits and challenges to clear cutting and over-grazing, the entire nation and most of California became environmentally conscious and conscientious. Fighting a losing battle for timber was the background for National Forests in California from 1977 to 1998, my time in the Forest Service.

Through 1978, I introduced several projects that helped other staffs gain public recognition. My specialty was to explain and promote the large number of agency programs which affected many sectors of the economy as well as recreation available to the general public on the National Forests. Letters of appreciation poured in from corporations, the mining industry, ranchers, wilderness guides, environmental groups and the general public. Even better, favorable internal comment came from national forests and other staffs in the Regional Office. Most organizations don't care what the public thinks, they do care what people within the organization think. I became an asset. That gave me protection!

I was hired in 1977 more or less by mail order to head up issues management with emphasis on speech writing for the Regional Forester, policy statements, public printed information and the like. I found an Agency in conflict, much of it funded by timber sales but many employees angry and opposed to timber practices that were destroying wildlife habitat and the environment. Perhaps because Wilderness was a direct threat to timber lands, little had been done to inform the public about this part of National Forest management. I also observed that nothing had been done to explain much of anything about the extremely interesting and significant management activities of the Forest Service in California. I decided to do a series of publications to accomplish just that, leading off with a brochure on Wilderness. I was surprised to learn that nothing on this subject had been done, since wilderness was the canary in the mine shaft for all environmentalists and most of the general public in California. Protecting and designating Wilderness areas was a leading public issue nationwide and perhaps for that reason no publications had been issued because there was tremendous resistance from timber and range staffs to designating more land as wilderness. Why promote and advertise a land use you basically oppose? This gave me a golden opportunity although I didn't realize it until it was published. *Wilderness on the National Forests in California* was published in October 1978. I received an astonishing amount of mail. Retirees who had worked for years in recreation acclaimed the style and the fact that we had *'finally done something about National Forest Wilderness.'* Public affairs people praised the 'jargon free' prose, effective layout and photo and graphic illustrations. Wilderness groups sent letters to the Chief and Regional Forester commending the publication, requesting copies for distribution to their supporters, and expressing hope that this publication would introduce a new era reflecting environmental values in forest management. A back country travel guide came in to request several hundred copies for distribution to his clients because: *'It is the best introduction to and preparation for wild land travel I have read.'* A prominent manufacturer of hiking boots wanted to place a copy in every box of boots! All this for someone who had never camped out except in the Army one night or ever visited a National Forest. What imagination and ingenuity can do!

In short, it was a smash hit with the public and within the Agency. We submitted it to the annual federal publications competition, where awards for best of category were presented at a banquet by one of the media assistants to the President, usually someone working in the White House. In April 1979, they announced that Wilderness had won first prize, in effect naming it the best federal brochure issued in 1978. This is an oxymoron to most taxpayers, any brochure issued by the government by definition a waste of money, bad writing and confusing information on average. But even conceding that, the sheer number of brochures issued by every department, branch, staff, agency, field office station, unit and office makes the distinction of 'best' at least unusual.

The Region hadn't won a prize in its entire 62-years existence. They were ecstatic and immediately authorized my travel to receive the prize first week in June.

The award ceremony took place Wednesday over a noon luncheon, Ray Jenkins from the Executive Office of the President smiled energetically through the presentations. What turned out to be the most important part of the ceremony for me was the photograph taken as my award was presented. A professional photographer in front of the stand took this picture, copies of which were sent to me. It was the best photo of me ever taken. I was smiling a Kennedy smile and Jenkins was also smiling, as though we were both immensely amused by some private observations between old buddies. I looked very LA cool in dark sport coat and tie, fit and handsome for me. If I ever took a knockout PR photo, that was it. My photo appeared on the front page of the Department newsletter, and more modestly, since I was the one to decide, on the awards back page of the Regional newsletter distributed to more than 5000 employees in California as well as to hundreds of State local offices. My presence in the agency and the results of my presence were obviously well promulgated, and the photo virtually ruined the marriage of our film maker guru Bob Tribble, whose wife monitored his career advancement or lack thereof as closely as her period. Unfortunately for them, I had placed on the same back page a photo of Tribble receiving an award for work done on a

Ranger District. He looking fat, slovenly complacent. Juxtaposing trim, glamorous Chris at a National ceremony receiving an award presented by a White House representative with tubby swaggering Tribble handed a framed document at a grubby field office was more than she could bear and immediately put him on a strict diet.

The greatest personal benefit of all this was that I was authorized to attend the national public affairs conference in October 1979 held at the Sheraton Hotel located just above Dupont Circle, and three blocks from Denice and Jim Bredt's townhouse. Renee and I had comfortable accommodations and the central location easily accessible by METRO allowed her to visit friends during the day while I listened to Tom Peters and other futurist gurus expound. It was a ball, since we also rented a car, which made possible theater visits to Arena Stage, sampling of interesting restaurants in the city, and evening travel to friends.

Denice and Jim Bredt showed slides of their trip to Greece, which were unimpressive because of his poor photography. She was as always incredulous and jealous of our frequent travel and obvious luck in transferring to California. She as ever was badgering Jim about his failure to advance in NASA, a pressure expressed by arbitrary moves such as to this undistinguished town house from an elegant NW Washington home. Within a few years she probably ground him down to the point that whatever ailment he got could kill him. Renee and I were invariably shocked at how little help this plump, homely, Polish frau gave her diminutive, rimless bespectacled physicist husband. She aspired to social distinction that was certainly beyond their personal reach, although higher position might have provided more official opportunity. Jim's failure to attain higher office simply aggravated her restlessness and disaffection which led to sordid revelations during our next trip to Washington in 1985. Their mini psychodrama reinforced our now definite preference for California over Washington, great place to visit but no way to live. California was liberating. We realized that Washington was like living in a room without open windows or fresh air, a stifling stagnant atmosphere of narrow views and careerism to no meaningful purpose, a competition for meager gains enduring constant envy and dissatisfaction. California was open windows, optimism and space.

My sister Linda's daughter Heather, age 15, visited us in 1979. She arrived at SF airport where I was waiting uncertain of what to expect. Linda and Alice, our mother, were worried because Heather had left Minneapolis in silent despair. Her first trip away from home! She came down the ramp looking down. I asked about her luggage and she handed me her receipt. No comment. We walked to the baggage pick up, got to the car, '72 Chevy, and headed across San Mateo Bridge. I tried to make conversation but she was resolutely silent. We drove to Kaiser Permanente where Renee had just gone for her first cardiac appointment with Dr. Ohm. We saw Renee waiting at the curb. She got in and we went home. Perhaps Renee's incomparable charm finally made the difference. We got home and suddenly Heather started talking, hardly stopping for the entire visit. Linda *et al.* called obviously expecting to have to arrange a return trip post haste. Instead we were all jolly and put Heather on the phone. She was laughing and talking and wouldn't hear of returning. Over the week, Renee and Heather went shopping in San Francisco. One weekend we saw Offenbach's operetta *La Perichole* at Spring Opera, a comic ballet satire shocked Heather but was hilarious. We then had dinner at *La Mere Duchene* across the street, an authentic French provincial restaurant now long gone. La Mere couldn't get over Heather, a petite blue-eyed blonde who looked as much French as anything. She kept showing up at our table asking if everything was all right. We had *Peche Melba,* fired up at the table. Everyone in the restaurant was looking at us. Heather had never seen anything like it. A magic trip for all of us.

Unlike most people I met, I never had a 'career'. I was unsuited and perhaps not endowed to specialize, pursue a particular profession 24/7 for thirty years. Living a *l'improviste* had disadvantages, never having a corps of associates to populate my social life. I never went to lunch with coworkers if I could avoid it, needing respite from occupational congestion and conversational subject matter. It had advantages. I have always placed avocations first, and devoted all my free time to their pursuit. Mainly opera, theater, art, more or less in that order. Central to this was SF Opera and the Merola Opera Training program of SFO. We of course were season subscribers. We found out about Merola through the program guide made available for each opera performance. Merola was astonishing as was the entire management and public access SF Opera provided devoted opera buffs. Kurt Herbert Adler, who succeeded Gaetano Merola, first General Director of SFO, made this all possible.

A little history of opera in San Francisco is in order. Only 1/10 of 1 percent of Americans (or anywhere else) knows, cares or is curious about opera. Before television radio and movies, it was actually immensely popular. After a fire department, city council, and police force, San Francisco established an opera house. Gaetano Merola was a member of the San Carlo traveling opera company whose lead soprano 'two-ton' Luisa Tetrazzini, just as the 1906 earthquake hit, sang a high C, instantly promoted to high F by the impact. Pure legend (the earthquake hit at

7:15 AM) but what are legends for? Merola brought opera magic to San Francisco for half a century, including Claudio Muzio and Lily Pons. He inaugurated the new SF Opera House in 1933, introducing Kirsten Flagstad and Lauritz Melchior in *Tristan und Isolde* in 1935 and conductor Fritz Reiner in 1936, bass-baritone Ezio Pinza in 1937, and conductor Erich Leinsdorf in 1938. He brought Kurt Adler, former assistant to Toscanini, as assistant manager and conductor in 1943. Adler was ably assisted and socially mentored by James Schwabacher, scion of a wealthy SF family devoted to SFO, a promising but light and not wide-ranging tenor who sang two seasons early in the 1950's. He later abandoned any attempt at a singing career, devoting his entire life to SFO as supporter. The Merola training program became his hobby, where he could impose his Francophile bias.

In December 1980, I attended a public relations workshop in Washington, complete with keynote speaker Tom Peters of *In Search of Excellence fame,* guru of the executive management transformation then emerging, a largely bogus reframing of *How to Win Friends and Influence People* for corporate consumption, an uplift pitch curiously appealing to personnel managers. Buying a new suit and tie would be more economical but would lack the travel and hotel time so dear to itinerant executives. My attending the workshop was indicative of the progressive management style of the Forest Service so surprisingly reviewed by Peters in his book as an outstanding example of government agency excellence.

A bit should be said about this agency because few people inside and none outside government have any idea of the differences between parts of the federal government. The Forest Service, Marine Corps, and FBI are unique organizations. Each has high morale, strong traditions, internal solidarity, much independence due to strong lobby and citizen support, tight line of command, and encourages initiative, up to a point. The Forest Service was founded in 1905 by Teddy Roosevelt and Gifford Pinchot, Eastern patricians, for a noble cause, environmentalism, and never considered itself a 'bureaucratic' agency dedicated to routine functions. Pinchot pursued 'forestry' as a profession and promoted the Yale Forestry School in emulation of European examples. He was part of the timber famine outcry in the late 1890's when fires and irresponsible harvest seemed to threaten the very existence of forests in the United States. Professional forestry backed by the Forest Service would introduce scientific management to demonstrate and carry out responsible use and management of forest resources on a renewable basis. Pinchot was a close friend of John Muir who founded the Sierra Club, and he served as first Vice President of the club with Muir as President. The Chief of the Forest Service by tradition served as Sierra Club VP until the late 1920's when a final split became inevitable.

The split began in 1910 over Hetch-Hechy Reservoir in the Sierra, supported by Pinchot to provide water to San Francisco and opposed by Muir as a desecration of pristine wilderness conditions for the benefit of urban convenience. By 1916, the split led to the formation of the National Park Service and system, designed to remove from Forest Service control those parts of the National Forests that were of high natural beauty and worthy of preservation. Gradually parts of the National Forest System were designated National Parks, a form of pillage of its turf the Forest Service bitterly opposed. The Forest Service began as a high class agency with ready, capable and trusted employees. The chain of command was short and simple: Chief, Regional Foresters, Forest Supervisors and District Rangers. Everyone else was support for the link it was hired to support. This led to tight, integrated, consistent management and considerable insularity, since the agency was within the Department of Agriculture which had little interest in or knowledge about forest management. (The very reason Roosevelt and Pinchot kept it out of the Department of Interior). Committees in Congress that dealt with Agriculture Department appropriations and programs were headed by Congressmen and Senators from farm states, equally indifferent to forest issues. So the agency and its clients had almost total independence of outside supervision, except the irritating comments of environmentalists and their organizations. The agency was however driven by a stewardship ethic and professional standards which limited abuse of resources until the late 1940's. Then the postwar housing construction boom and demand for federal timber got so tempting as a means of expanding agency grades, salaries, and personnel that rather irresponsible clear-cutting harvest practices were adopted and their consequences overlooked, but not by the Sierra Club and other groups. The battle continued through the 1970's and 1980's and I got to be part of it.

The Forest Service in California was progressive, experimental in its approach to management. They would 'try things'. They sent employees to Esalen Institute near Carmel for personal and spiritual 'growth', an enlightened approach that led to several divorces as women employees liberated themselves. As the agency hired more hydrologists, wildlife biologists, plant scientists, landscape architects and other professions to mitigate the effects of timber harvest they introduced an entirely new kind of employee and attitude that eventually turned the agency away from traditional uses. Ranchers and timber mill operators were very uneasy. Tom Peters mentioned this enlightened management in his books, so we were 'hot' and known, open to new ideas, approaches, initiatives highly unwelcome to the timber-range cadre. I was a factor in this mix, as will be explained later.

The Bennington Alumni Association of Northern California (BAANC) was an early contact for us in the Bay Area. Dorothy and Ivan Cousins were the most notable members, since her sister Julia Childs had gained international fame as a TV cook and Ivan had been a roommate of 'Beat poet' Laurence Ferlinghetti in postwar Paris. 'Dort' was lean, lanky and about 6-feet tall, Ivan agreeably fat, personable and short, about 5'6". Dort was abrupt in her gestures, a reflection of her peremptory style, friendly when not crossed, and clearly 'in charge' wherever she happened to be. Dorothy MacMillan, Julia, and a brother were children of a successful Southern California businessman who kept his money during the Depression. Dort and Julia attended good schools, got European vacations, and were spoiled rotten during a period of national privation and social collapse. Being homely made them all the more insufferable when crossed. Dort had the proprietary air of someone who, however dissembled the arrangement might be, bought and owned the people and organizations she associated with and made sure they knew it. She graduated in 1940, one of the Bennington Incunabula. The school went co-ed in the late 1960's, so alumni from the purist period were ever after distinguished from the later raunchy (as reported) period.

The Cousins built a home in Sausaulito in the 1940's, one of those wood and glass, in-the-woods things with indoor-outdoor patio. It was rather dark and damp because of the trees and fog but I suppose it was worth a fortune. I observed the Ivan/Dort dynamic at close range. Apparently someone was expected at the airport and Ivan was to pick her up but forgot. I never saw a woman trash a man as Dort did Ivan, all the accumulated arrogance of wealth and probably marital contempt delivered point blank, my presence not cause for restraint, rather a goad to greater dramatic effect. She probably liked an audience for whatever she did, her early bias was toward theater and acting, in fact the reason they met in Paris in the first place. Ivan had opened an oriental knick-knack shop in Sausalito in an earlier period, apparently a toy shop to keep him busy, and lots of tasteless Sino pottery was littered around the downstairs rooms. He kept telling me dirty jokes of a rather queer bent, and I later concluded that he probably went over the side just to escape or annoy Dort. He 'worked' as an actor, mainly TV commercials. With his portly body, pink and vanilla complexion, thin white moustache and hair, he was usually cast as the elderly grand-daddy fishing in a boat with lures dangling from his sun hat. He was a personable guy but I had the feeling he was trying to find the right occasion to make a pass. He had been a Navy officer in WWII, went to Paris on the GI Bill, got into theater, which was Dort's thing, and probably concluded that marrying money was better than trying to earn it. Big mistake usually. They had a son and daughter, the latter unfortunately looked very much like Dort.

The Bennington Presidency was in flux. The 'President' from 1966 through 1971 was a diarchy, wife and husband soon distracted by marital discord, she drifting into a relationship with Rush Welter, history faculty, her husband into whoever would tolerate him. The college went downhill financially and the only mark they left was coeducation in order to expand the applicant pool. Following an interregnum came Joe Murphy, 1976-1982, whose wife soon departed Bennington leaving him to his favorite pastime--drinking in student dorms. The standard of executive conduct, never rigorous but at least not flagrant, soon unraveled. He took up with student Susan Crile, although we missed the connection in 1981 when we attended her opening at a gallery in San Francisco. In 1982, BAANC Chair Doris Muscatine gave a welcoming dinner for newly appointed Bennington President Michael Hooker. Her husband had headed the UC Berkeley academic revolt against loyalty oaths for professors in the early 1950's which gained him liberal fame, although as a specialist in Chaucer his academic purview was narrow if deep. Renee attended as co-chair, sat at the left hand of the anointed one, Doris at his right. Renee wore a 'folk' dress, fitted cotton print, high armholes, very new age Bennington or French Provincial, absolutely gorgeous, Certainly even more so as she was the only flower in the weed patch of homely, middle-aged, plump alums. Hooker looked quite enchanted at the whole occasion but this didn't deter him from accepting the position of President at Rutgers four years later. Heading Rutgers, a huge New Jersey State University, a much more impressive career move than shaky quirky Bennington. When he left Bennington, the Muscatines entered into the search for a new President, advancing their candidate Elizabeth Coleman, New York shrink who wanted to 'get into' education. She got the job in 1987 and remained until 2013.

Meanwhile, back at the ranch. *Futuring* was a management fad partly spawned by I*n Search of Excellence,* but driven mostly by the managerial revolution caused by globalization of the economy. Detroit was first, then steel, clothing, fabrics… Inability to compete with cheap Asian labor and high end Japanese design, US and European corporations were moving offshore, overhauling managerial systems, you know the drill. The Forest Service, a federal agency included by Peters in his lectures and books as a government innovator, had to keep up appearances. We did in California, the seminal State. *Futuring* became the buzz word of the mid-80's. I believe in nothing but behavior, action, performance, results. But I love words and am an actor, I will take my part and run with it, upstage if I can, get the best review as well. Forest Service was desperate for words with which to describe, understand, and shape the new era. I joined Futuring as a co-star and ended up center stage. So what is it? Basically, putting a new label on old bottles. The idea, which applies to anything you want to do, is to look at the current situation and imagine a future *desired* condition or outcome. *Desired* is the key word. We all imagine the worst. Futuring just asks you to imagine the best, then believe it, practice it, and think of nothing else. Good therapy whatever its intrinsic merit. Like *'Every day in every way I am getting better and better'. Plus ca change, plus c'est la meme chose.*

The lead in this undertaking went to Personnel Management Staff (later called Human Resources), no other staff wanted anything to do with it. Fools! I teamed up with the personnel guy given the assignment to make it work. They needed me because no one else had a clue what to say and how to interpret and translate into FS-ese the aspiring exhortations of which the whole Futuring gambit consisted. I wrote *Future--1995,* projecting a 10-year agenda for imperative change to meet the 'challenge of the future'. Trouble is the 'future' hardly figured in bureaucratic thinking past or present. Everything was based on doing the same thing in the same way with the same budget (or more if possible) and focusing all energy on maintaining the status quo.

No more. Congress was shaking things up. Budgets were insecure, sunset clauses were being drafted, closer scrutiny of cost-benefits, with Reagan's amiable but alarming attack on government spending ringing in their ears. Once we got their attention, which means once you scare them, you can indoctrinate. I went on the road to regional meetings to explain Futuring. The jargon caught on, once I demonstrated the parlous, certainly risky situation we were in. I became the guru of Futuring. After all, I had heard Peters in person in 1980! Great fun and I was pumping out statements, speeches, doctrine for the Regional Forester, Zane Gray Smith, who bought the program right down to the waste baskets.

Sexual harassment and women's rights were part of Futuring discussions of desired outcomes. I was aware of the fairly common assault on clerical staff by agency leaders, especially in the Southern Region and Mountain Region. Our own Deputy Regional Forester had provoked harassment rumors, handing one of his staff his motel room key at a meeting in Sacramento for example, or the very low couch in his office which allowed him to peek as ladies uncomfortably tried to keep their skirts below the knee. The Regional Forester of the Southern Region was notorious for moves on clerical help, the ones most likely to need a job and least likely to complain. I was personally outraged and decided to do something about it. As part of Futuring, which allowed me wide scope in generating new directions, I published a long feature publication on sexual harassment. The publication, intended to clarify beyond doubt what was not to be tolerated, was distributed throughout the Forest Service and the Department of Agriculture to uniform acclamation. It was recognized outside government by women's groups as a major contribution to the cause of women's rights, and led to numerous grievances against supervisors within the agency by women who until they read the publication had no idea they had been victims of legally accountable harassment. Many secretaries and clerks had no idea what was done to them was illegal and actionable! The Southern Regional Forester retired discreetly. Our wayward Deputy was transferred after nineteen women in the Region filed grievances against him. So, I had quite an impact and no one was about to get in my way. The

Regional Forester loved the favorable publicity and agreed with the policies advocated in the publication. How could anyone not, publicly?

The capers and misadventures of dysfunctional families are common themes in literature, opera, theater, movies, song. *Anna Karenina, The Godfather, Lucia di Lamermoor, Hamlet,* the variety of plots and characters strike a chord in all of us, because we are born and raised in a family, and all families share a spectrum of situations conflicts and cares no matter how extreme individual variations. 1985 was the year of Dysfunction. Renee and I attended our first Ring cycle and had our first Engel family reunion in California, very similar in conduct, however different in characters, costumes, props, and degree. Overwhelming, beautiful, puerile, funny, bombastic, witty, ludicrous, inspiring, profound--we could have seen all four performances of the complete Ring cycle if enervation had not set in. James Morris the greatest Wotan of all, Gwyneth Jones and Eva Marton as overpowering Brunnhilde, Rene Kollo Siegfried, Edo de Waart conducting, marvelous traditional sets, Nikolaus Lehnhoff's superb direction, Walter Berry's Alberich, 16-hours of bliss, awe and exultation. As a *coup de grace,* we attended the special uncut showing of Richard Burton winking and sulking his way through the film *Richard Wagner,* eight hours of Rhinemaiden T&A, greasy hammering dwarfs, pyres, salons, 'toesies' under the dining table, orchestra rehearsals, and guileful close-ups of THE MAN fiendishly cogitating an aria, seduction, or pinch accompanied by the Nibelheim equivalent of Musak, or THE MAN walking at 14,000-feet elevation through trackless Alpine snow to the magnificent redemption-through-love motif.

As if the squabbles of the Walsung family *et alia* were not enough turmoil for one summer, The Donald, Winifred, Paul, his wife Debbie, Karen and her daughter Cindy came to California in July for the proverbial crossfire of expectation, resentment, dissimulation, and ritual--a family reunion. In most respects they reenacted (*mutatis mutandis*) plausibly similar scenes made fresh in our minds by the domestic entanglements of that better known if more contentious Walsung family in June. Cindy (15-years) looked like a punk rocker with wild too-blonde hair and pool sized blue eyes. She read Danielle Steel novels most of the time. Both Karen and Cindy spent all

day shopping in San Francisco so I abandoned plans for a musical and theatrical survey of our Bay Area haunts. Paul, now a millionaire wire and cable manufacturer (Quabbin Wire & Cable) in Ware Massachusetts (I had worked with an eponymous Henry Ware at LOC), and his wife Debbie, and Donald and Winifred stayed in San Jose with Mark and Sandy. Paul successfully defended his wallet against predatory pauses that followed presentation of the check during restaurant excursions. Paul organized a trip to Yosemite National Park from Massachusetts, insisting that everyone stay at Yosemite Inn. Since he insisted, I assumed that he was paying the fare, although I had misgivings about making a raid on his wallet. When I found out that he expected everyone to pay his own way I pulled out, concerned about the raid on my wallet. A free ride, even if uncomfortable is better than one you pay for. Levels of competition and aggravation slowly increased toward the end of the Engel family reunion. Just as they were about to leave Yosemite, Donald decided to abandon the reunion and go to San Luis Obispo to see someone he hardly knew in Athol who had retired to the West Coast, stranding Cindy and Karen at Mark's house. They ate in their room and had nothing to do with their hosts, while frantically calling us to see if they could return to Oakland. Sandy Engel finally told them they couldn't just take food to their room. Karen and Cindy couldn't avoid going on a trip to Monterey with Mark and Sandy and the children, on which they nearly had a nervous breakdown. As I had predicted to Renee, things got chaotic and conflicted. After the first day when we went to San Jose for a swim and visit, Renee and I remained in Oakland apart from the warm family reunion.

Meanwhile... Futuring didn't expressly affirm transparency as a key element of reform, but I decided to assume that objective, which gave me unusual access especially to awards given employees throughout the Region. The Forest Service like the military has different grades: clerical/administrative/professional/supervisory rated GS 1-15. In the military there are company grade officers (2nd Lieutenant/1st Lieutenant/Captain), field grade officers (Major/Lieutenant Colonel/ Colonel), and general grade officers (Brigadier General--1-star/Major General--2-Star/Lieutenant General--3-star/General--4-star; 5-star is reserved for theater commanders like Eisenhower/MacArthur.) Awards to employees in the Forest Service at Grades 1-12 are usually given for exceptional performance that is described and made know to all. But annual bonuses, for which a special fund was established, are given to GS-13 and above just as a supplement to presumably modest salaries paid for higher skilled managers who keep the show on the road. I did not know about this special slush fund until, as Futuring guru, I asked personnel for all awards for all grades. They assumed I had authorization and proper use for such data. I didn't.

I saw how much more the canopy received for no explicable reason, just that they worked so hard and were so essential that an annual bonus needed no explanation or special justification. I was especially annoyed that the delinquent sexual harasser Deputy Regional Forester received $5000, nearly a third the annual salary of a GS-3. I decided to print everything: name title and bonus amount, all the way to the top. Consternation understates the effect. All employees were astounded and delighted that such a racket was exposed. I received dozens of emails praising this disclosure and commending me for the courage and audacity to publish it. The average firefighting grunt could see just how much the overhead got compared to him or her. Management was embarrassed that I had rolled the log, or pulled up the rug, to show what was under it. The Regional Forester was clearly irritated but the transparency pitch constrained any adverse action he might take against me. I had made him a hero in the fight against sexual harassment and in the knightly endeavor of managerial reform, plus the majority of employees were commending him for such bald disclosures of the doings of top level managers. Employees knew who deserved and who didn't such benefice. He suggested we not disclose the sums next time. OK.

Casualties were kept to a minimum in 1987, despite a severe fire season and Stock Market crash. Renee headed the local Bennington College alumni fundraiser, an exercise largely guided by the principle '*Let the candied tongue lick absurd pomp and crook the pregnant hinges of the knee…*' in which thrift did not follow fawning, but rather an exhausting series of calls, pledges, equivocations, and dropouts for at least three months that spring. The benefit event was a performance at a theater in Ghirardelli Square of Pippin Pocket Opera's English version of Mozart's *Entführung aus dem Serail* (Abduction from the Serail) renamed *Yanked from the Harem,* in which 1970's US college students are detained in Turkey for traces of controlled substance and the second act drinking song is not to Bacchus but to Classic Coke (pun intended). Houston Opera did the same translation in 1987 with great success. The Bennington benefit included lunch at Paprika's Fono, a Hungarian touch. Evidently the whole gig offended Mozart purists (maybe one person), libbers, and people who don't like paprika, clearly a solid majority of any graduating class. Hardly half the tickets sold, but the show was more than (T)okay. As Renee said afterward: '*Never again!*'

I bought a 1980 Alfa-Romeo Spyder Veloce roadster in August about a month before the market meltdown. The Alfa, or Alfalfa as we called it, cornered better than I do and got better mileage. It certainly brought California's secondary road system into perspective and improved hand-eye-foot coordination combined with the mildly aerobic effect of open air at high coefficient of drag. We completed a 10-opera season nearly as arduous as two weeks at a fat farm. Prisoner choruses for two weeks in a row depressed a fairly well-dressed audience (rather like being sung to by panhandlers on the way to Maxime's), but a good looking Traviata (with commendable top as we say in vocal training class) and an elegant 61-year old Romeo in the form of Alfredo Kraus (who clearly is the answer to Auden's question: Is there anyone nowadays who could descend a Baroque staircase?) made up for that. We went to literary readings where the harried author arrives late from the airport, breathlessly reads from his/her latest book, and then looks around defensively for questions with occasional peeks at his/her Casio. Ivan Doig was a treat as are his books. One shy authoress in Charles Aadams black produced a novel with enough technical orality to qualify as a medical school text.

I congratulated Doug Bellis on getting his wife Alice a leather miniskirt (congratulation is the 'civility of envy' as Ambrose Bierce claims), aware of course that sarto-psychoanalytically leather above the waist is *macho*, and below is what above is for. The leather miniskirt was worn by maidens in Germanic tribes because it was 'convenient', easy to care for or replace according to Mommsen. Bierce didn't offer a definition of 'convenient'. Maybe I read too much.

Wildfires were the worst since 1977 when we first arrived in California. I wrote a speech about their disastrous effect on the National Forests and the State for the Regional Forester to give at the Commonwealth Club, a major venue for movers and shakers in business. It was published entire in the Commonwealth Monthly magazine and circulated to thousands of members. It got statewide coverage and made the Regional Forester a public figure and pundit, plus it put the Agency in the public eye and generated bucks in public contributions for reforestation which we promoted through a PR program. Not bad for a 10-page speech.

At the center of the web

He of course was thereafter entirely dependent on me for anything he said publicly. Convenient for me in some ways, in others not. But it increased my immunity from outside interference since I dealt directly with him and nobody wanted to get in the way of what he needed and I was providing. My kind of deal. Much of the burn occurred in forested areas of the Sierra Nevada and Northern California, not as usual in the volatile brush land of Southern California. The fires hit timberland and wildlife habitat, notably for the Spotted Owl. As an indicator species you could not pick a cuter bird. Mating pairs need about 2,200 acres of habitat to survive and raise their young. Multiply that by every horny pair of owls in California and you have a bunch of acres. By 1988 the issue of Spotted Owl habitat protection hit the chainsaw when 'scientific' analysis by wildlife biologists in Oregon revealed the threat timber programs presented to Spotted owl survival. The Forest Service in Washington D.C. and Oregon suppressed the report but it was leaked to environmental groups who filed a lawsuit in Seattle seeking to enjoin timber harvest until the issue was resolved. I had by that time been assigned to the California Spotted Owl team and sat in on phone calls between strategists in Washington Office (WO) and the Region.

The WO was pro-timber and trying to figure a way to get the court to withdraw the wildlife biologists' report as 'confidential and nonpublic material' improperly obtained. Such stupidities provoked by timber industry touts in Oregon, Washington and the WO were undermining California Region effort to do what the Threatened and Endangered Species law required: Protect the damn birds!

Hi there!

In the period 1988-1990, I got very close to environmental group leaders and became a guru and unofficial ambassador between them and the Regional Office (RO). This started casually when I attended an RO staff meeting. A number of topics were covered and then they turned to me to see if I had anything to report. Renee and I had gone to a poetry reading in Berkeley the past weekend by Gary Snyder, Zen poet and environmentalist who taught literature at UC Davis. Gary lived near Virginia City in an enclave of independent former Hippies and individualists who formed the core of an environmental 'Mafia' in the Sierras, several of whom attended the poetry reading. Their leader was Steve Beckwith, a bright dedicated hawk to all us Forest Service chickens. Gary read poems, there was a discussion, inevitably the Forest Service was mentioned, unfavorably, and much lamentation over timber rape in the Sierras ensued.

I reported on the reading as an indication of the kind of adverse comment we get from people like Snyder who have considerable clout in California shaping public opinion on forest issues. A poetry reading was the last thing anyone in the room had or would attend and certainly would not consider significant. With this rather esoteric angle and its major significance, I got them to reconsider their bias and take steps to deal with it. It sounded to them that I had an insider track on the source of their headache and so I was assigned the aspirin job of setting up informal get-acquainted meetings between the Regional Forester and staff and regional and local environmental group leaders. Sensational success! Everyone got along famously, issues were discussed reasonably, reasonable proposals to settle them were worked out, and the groups agreed to work with FS managers in implementing them.

The Washington Office *never willingly* invited these groups to meetings, only if they had to. They had no regular meetings to exchange views and work out agreements. We did all the time after the initial meeting. When I insisted that any meeting the WO held in California involving issues of concern to environmental groups must include them, they were initially stunned but complied, at least for part of the agenda. I told WO and the Regional Forester that we had to provide equal access to enviros as we did to timber and other interest groups. That was the only way to find out what concerned them without their having to bring a lawsuit to do so. As it turned out, environmental groups helped us get data or look into problems and as an added bonus reduce their paranoia. A good example was herbicide use, an issue for which I identified the problem and got it resolved. FS stipulations with contractors hired to spray herbicides set minimum effective rates of application to prevent inadequate coverage. Application of more than was necessary was not considered. Environmentalists objected that field applicators often exceeded adequate rates, just to be sure, thereby increasing adverse impacts on surrounding water resources and habitat.

Greater field supervision was put in place to make sure the adequate amount needed was not capriciously exceeded .

Herbicide use on forest lands was adamantly opposed and made a major public issue against the Forest Service. In 1989, we held a meeting at UC Berkeley to figure out how to deal with the issue. Most were members of the timber staff. Discussion went on and on about environmental groups and their effort to get a court injunction. They asked what I thought. I said we are looking only in the most obvious direction. By way of preface I should mention that the Forest Service used herbicides authorized by the State for use on agricultural crops, namely Roundup (similar to Agent Orange used for defoliation during the Viet Nam was) commonly used by homeowners to clear their lawns of weeds. The State presented data as innocuously as possible. Only application by crop was listed, not totals. The totals were astonishing: hundred thousands of gallons of undiluted active ingredient applied to farmland throughout the State. Monsanto, the manufacturer had added forestry use to augment the market and sales. But the company came under concerted attack by environmental groups. So concerted that the company was concerned about adverse affect on its public image. I told our group that the company would likely **delete** forestry use in order to end further controversy. The group groaned and said that was ridiculous. Two months later Monsanto did just that. In 1991, the Regional Forester suspended all use of herbicides on National Forests in California. I mention this controversy, which is otherwise of limited interest, to show how assumption is the common flaw in collective management of any large organization with an agenda to defend.

Many Regional Office staffers were in favor of environmental protection. One example was the Clavey River on the Stanislaus National Forest in the Sierra Nevada, a candidate for Wild and Scenic River (W&S) designation. The Stanislaus delayed because the river cut right through the center of the forest and recommending W&S designation would limit or preclude some multiple uses. Enviros lobbied furiously to force the issue. The Forest tried to sector the river, protecting the upper part but allowing 'appropriate' uses including timber harvest along the lower, a ludicrous proposal. How do you divide a river!! The Deputy Regional Forester, a woman, wore a **Save the Clavey** button in the Regional Office, hardly disguising her preference. This was a sign of the change under way. From 1989 on, the Region got more and more 'environmental', much to the chagrin of less progressive minds in the WO. But the trend was irreversible in California. Smaller battles raged in Ranger Districts, where volunteers of the Sierra Club and other groups spent their evenings and weekends working on protecting resources. An amazing group of people, true grassroots representatives of the rather posh national organizations. Grassroots were more aggressive and 'radical' than the overhead organization but I always admired their intelligence, dedication, and competence.

You've read about it, seen pictures of it, expected it, and in 1989 the SF Bay Area finally got it. A 7.8 Richter scale earthquake. I had passed under the upper span of the Bay Bridge just twelve minutes before it collapsed, but can't claim any transforming sense of Providence at work. I was standing at the back door, just home, Renee at the sink in a suitably Home and Garden vignette involving potatoes, when the tremor struck. The house rocked noticeably in a slow, random rotation but no pictures fell, no glasses shattered, the vases stayed within the dust rings they occupied. We planned to take a potluck to an artist friend Patti Heimberger in the lowlands and started out. We weren't listening to radio and we didn't have television so we had no idea of the scope of the damage. Traffic lights were out on the way but we didn't sense anything major had happened. We got to her studio and saw people milling around but still didn't get it. Finally someone told us the bridge had collapsed and houses in the SF Marina had collapsed as well. The great benefit of the earthquake was that ferry service was the only access to SF from Oakland, free of traffic, stop/start and acceleration, which removed any tension associated with the commute. Nothing so conduces to taking work lightly as a morning cruise.

Lack of the bridge made attending the SF Opera's annual contest with composers' intentions more difficult, but we did see Boito's *Mephistofele* with a nude chorus (the best definition of 'mixed blessing' I have encountered) in which Samuel Ramey kept performance standards higher than the music deserves. We also saw an *Aida* of aptly hippopotamic proportions and eight seminude male dancers doing a log roll for an inattentive Amneris. A few cracks were evident and a bra was hanging from the chandelier, but (to redirect your thoughts) the Opera House was otherwise structurally undamaged by the earthquake. In September, we went to Ashland Oregon for their much touted Shakespeare Festival. Horrible mistake. Nasty redneck town in the desert flatlands of Eastern Oregon with temperatures in the 90's, instead of the Sherwood Forest setting we had been misled to expect.

In 1990, the Region was cornered, without a clear path out of the Spotted Owl, Clavey River, herbicide and other environmental muddles. The new Regional Forester, Paul Barker, was particularly concerned that the Region had no response to the mounting environmental storm created by Earth Day held every March 15, to mobilize national attention against the environmental slaughter going on in the water, air, soil, forests, farms, grasslands of America! You name it, we had an issue. Stumped, dumbfounded, no ideas, staff sessions to deal with the crisis yield zero results, where to turn? To me of course. As a solution with heavy public pizzazz to get ahead of the criticism, I proposed we announce a new page in National Forest management in California, an **Environmental Agenda**. Relieved, ecstatic, he loved it and we did. I wrote the entire thing, setting policy goals and intentions clearly in the direction of environmental responsibility, ecosystem management, and protection of most valuable wild and scenic resources. It just accepted the environmental facts in California and told the Forest Service to get on with dealing with them. The Agenda went over extremely well in the press and with the public. The Los Angeles Times called it '*a major reversal of FS policy and a commendable step in the right direction*'. The SF

218

Chronicle and most TV stations said the same thing. We were popular, big news, and the Regional Forester could walk the streets again!

In June 1990, the Region held a week-long region-wide management session at Northstar Ski Resort, North Lake Tahoe, to discuss implementing the Agenda, yours truly participating and even captured on video, now long lost. The session proved the folly of summering at a winter ski resort that has no need of air-conditioning. However, we did have a few nice dinners in Truckee and attended a picnic of FS employees from Regional Staffs, Forests and Ranger Districts who met me and Renee for the first time and were of course stunned by her beauty and charmed by her friendly down-to-earth style. A guy never comes into complete focus without seeing his wife.

In January 1990, we joined a life drawing group, the first time since 1972 I had a legitimate excuse to be in the presence of a naked stranger. Sessions were held in the studio of our artist friend Patti Heimberger. This was an 'artist studio complex' (both architectural and personal) that was slowly being taken over by a marginal category of 'musicians'. At first the drawing sessions went pretty well until our host Sally began to show signs of malice, first expressed as intensive kneading of a lump of clay, and latterly by acquiring a boa constrictor left in her care by a traveling friend. We never saw 'Bruce'. Sally kept him in a glass cage in the upstairs loft near her bed. Before each drawing session she would release a boxed rat into the cage, club it into live submission, and let Bruce do the rest. We found this depressing. So we welcomed her announcement of the last session in June. We next attended life drawing sessions at the Oakland City managed Artist Studio near Broadway Avenue.

Sunday, October 12, 1991, we left around 9 AM to visit Renee's brother Mark in San Jose. I noticed how incredibly hot and windy it was. Returning about 3 PM we saw what appeared to be heavy fog or clouds. It turned out to be the big (5,000 homes gutted) wildfire in the East Bay hills. Back home, we packed essentials and waited. Fortunately for us the wind was blowing strongly due west toward San Francisco where much of the ash and soot ended up. The fire remained about 1 ½ miles north of our house. Hearing about disaster averted is pretty boring, but it was mildly interesting how one goes about choosing what to save. We packed two boxes of high value books, a $500 watercolor brush and three of my best watercolors, three oriental rugs, enough clothes to get to Paris if the fire handed me an insurance bonanza, silverware and photo albums. When the danger passed we went to bed. Monday, I stayed home just in case the winds shifted. Tuesday, it was mostly over. Friday, a Berkeley radio station had a call-in show so the community could offer sympathy and support for the victims (the fire was at high elevation and gutted some of the most expensive and distinguished homes from the early years of the 20th Century in Berkeley and Oakland). During the show, callers from the lowlands (mostly Blacks) said the victims deserved what they got, they never did anything for the poor, they were all insured and taken care of whereas the homeless and unemployed.....Entrenched social antagonisms never die.

At the Opera we saw two rogues, *Attila and Don Giovanni* balanced by two roguettes, *Electra* and *Carmen*. We also saw *Tristan und Isolde* waddle around in each other's vicinity for several hours, reminding us physically and at times vocally of the Sea Lions at Pier 39 (living proof of the need for sharks). The season had one anomaly. In July we were at Tower Records in Berkeley trying to find a Callas pirate recording. I filled out a form for KKHI, a commercial classic radio station, to win a dinner and opera tickets. I forgot all about it. Then on November 1, we received a phone call. The Hispanic lady had a thick accent and I nearly hung up when she somehow conveyed the fact that we had won. For the rest of the week, unbeknownst to us, our names were broadcast all over the Bay Area by KKHI. We rarely listen to that station because commercials constantly interrupt the music.

The prize, as with most prizes, was a mixed blessing. Dinner was at the Carnelian Room in the Bank of America tower beginning at 6 PM. The opera, *Electra,* began at 7:30 sharp. So the race was on and there was a torrential down pout I mean pour to add local color to the occasion. We got through dinner by 7:10, the KKHI-hired limousine picked us up out front and then plowed through driving rain to the Opera House, where we dashed in and to our seats just two minutes before the opera began. We sat through 75 minutes of Greek torment, after went to the local garage where I had parked our car that morning, and then drove home, wipers at high speed. We were barely damp dry, lucky not to catch pneumonia. Even more aggravating was to hear later from opera friends who listened to KKHI how envious they were that we had won such a wonderful prize. On the other hand offering the ambiguous pleasure of faking overwhelming satisfaction at this good fortune to augment their envy and our coincident esteem.

The most dramatic event of 1991 was our trip to Athol in August for the Donald/Winifred 50th Anniversary. After fifty years there isn't much you haven't done or had done to you. The 1985 reunion was a disaster, this one hardly better. Winifred vented her long sublimated hostility toward Donald by acting like an idiot nurse to Paul and Debi's newly adopted baby boy. Constant baby talk made her ridiculous and me nervous. News of Karen's separation from husband Gordon, probable divorce, and mysterious new love entanglement bothered Renee and interested me. The Donald was retired and restless, scheming to sell the house at 188 Highland Avenue, move to a cheap trailer park in Athol, and live six months of the year in Florida near his brother David. Even Winifred wasn't so supine as to accept that arrangement. I was irritated having to smile so resolutely and so long at this extended family banquet paid for by affluent and peculiar Paul. He and Debi had been seeing a shrink for years and always seemed never quite plausible as a couple. The kid didn't look like simplifying or consolidating the situation. The more money Paul made the more fishy he seemed toward family members, perhaps rightly fearing a raid on his treasury. Karen was complacent, like the cat that ate the canary, partly because she was enjoying some success as an artist but mainly because of the 'love interest', a figure of some speculation, said by Mark to be a 'prominent Pennsylvania politician', by his wife Sandy 'a rich industrialist', and so on. Later we learned that her love interest was the chairman of the art department and her first counselor when she began art school in 1975 at Millersville College, PA. He was separated at that time from his wife who did not want a divorce, just wanted to see as little of him as possible. Not a bad situation for a guy working the fauna at the local academic deer park. Question was, just what was going on between Karen and Ron for the past fifteen years, since they remained in touch as it were as student and counselor/teacher. We got out of Athol alive, but just.

San Francisco Chronicle was the cultural forum in which the vital art, music, theater, dining, and social transactions of the vibrant city were announced, reviewed, critiqued. There was an art critic, theater critic, music critique, food critique, social reporter, topped by Herb Caen, inventor of *Baghdad By the Bay*, a three times weekly cursus of social doings, sex scandals, culinary discovery, what Wilkes Bashford and Willie Brown were up to, that a certain prominent person was seen with a certain other prominent person's wife at the Kon Tiki bar. Art was in bloom, at least two dozen commercial galleries of slight to major scale. The big kahuna being John Berggruen, his gallery the venue for Hockney, Diebenkorn, Park, Manuel Neri and most established artists (his art dealer father had an affair with Frida Kahlo!). Emerging gallery challengers, some hanging by their toenails, pocket intruders in closet size venues, all selling art to buyers from LA, Tokyo, Seattle, Taiwan, SF being the emporium for the best of everything for people from everywhere.

Members of the Museum of the Legion of Honor and the Museum of Modern Art had opportunities to visit artist studios, meet the artists, buy at bargain rates. We met Oakland-based Squeak Carnworth at her studio and had a long conversation, leaving thirteen members of the visiting group to listen and learn. San Francisco art galleries once had an open house one Thursday a month to attract buyers. Every year, San Francisco and Oakland had open studios for two weeks so people could check out hundreds of artists based on sample paintings displayed at a central location. I participated in SF once and Oakland twice. Optimism in some cases delusion sustained many artists, some having a knack or theme that attracted enough sales to keep them going, others hanging from a cliff of just not quite good enough, sustained only by marginal employment for marginal means.

Aphrodite Washington Square

I had by late 1991 completed a sufficient backlog of paintings that it seemed feasible to enter the East Bay Open Studios and show them to the public. What made the Bay Area particularly inviting to artists was the enormous amount of studio space available if you weren't too fussy. The disuse of former industrial properties throughout the flatlands of East Bay and the commercial industrial areas south of Mission in San Francisco made available large factory and industrial buildings for subdivision into studio spaces. They did not attract hi-tech startups until the dot-com boom of the late 1990's drove most artists out of their studios. The Paperbox Factory at 43rd Street in Berkeley was a typical example. A large, oddly divided building with an enormous central water vat, the factory had been acquired by a group of architects to be redesigned into artist studios, but at a pace that suggested completion was not an urgent matter for the owners or more likely a sufficiently promising prospect for their bank. The project manager had an office and living quarters on the premises. The intent was to sell studio space, completing each section of the building with funds generated from sales of studios completed earlier. The project was in a state of pause in 1992, so the project manager, whose artist wife had a studio in the building offered free space to show during Open Studios. We took one and hauled twenty framed paintings weighing at least 15-pounds each in our Mercurial Cougar across town and mounted the show on the unpainted drywall of a fairly large room. I designed a small map in postcard form which we sent to friends and also made available at the central open studio exhibit. The artists showing at the Paperbox were friendly if occasionally perplexing. Anna Stavropoulos, who was quite pleasant and seemingly uncomplicated, proved to be deeply Greek in her work, apparently capable of imagining Sophoclean levels of hematic tragedy. She painted scenes of rape and disfigurement in black and white on gauze fabric, mostly images of women being violated in unspeakable ways, liberally spattered with red paint and stenciled feminist texts. An architect drew hypothetical buildings in such detail as to suggest a serious dearth of paid commissions. A very self-important German woman painted abstracts. She was evidently married to an abundant source of money, wandered around quickly categorizing and dismissing most of us as rank amateurs. The wife of the manager used gold foil extensively in her vaguely Chinoise prints. Another woman showed piles of rope twisted in original shapes and died in earth tones. The fellow across the hall from us produced small *objects d'art,* for example a meerschaum pipe with an eyeball in it, of sufficient distinction apparently to earn praise from the art Nazi as *'ganz original'* or something to that effect.

Many friends showed up to view my masterpieces. My subjects were entirely people in daily situations in San Francisco venues, such as Washington Square, Embarcadero Plaza, and the SF Waterfront. They had a certain familiarity and charm so I got compliments such as: W*hat relief not to get reflections in puddles type watercolors!* One woman liked my 'Aphrodite' painting charging back and forth looking at it from all angles and then asking the price. I of course had no desire to sell so it was a bit of a problem when confronted with an offer. Which raises the question of amateur vs. professional artist. Most artists showing at the Paperbox and elsewhere were attempting to make some money if not a living out of it.

GREECE

After the Oakland Open Studios we prepared for our 3-week fly-drive trip to Greece. I studied modern Greek enough to get the numbers down and emit a few phrases in case of need. Most Greeks speak English. But I never travel anywhere without learning the language to some degree, either to make them less confident in attempts to take advantage, or to impress them in my favor with my effort to meet them culturally half or at least 10-percent of the way. Greeks are scrupulously honest with tourists, their main meal ticket, so the latter was the main benefit, on the few occasions it worked. Western Civilization began with Homer and the Greeks. Queer dons at Oxford and Cambridge extolled Ancient Greek culture, Plato, Pericles, ideals, dialogs, stark white Ionic monuments and nude male statues, the icons of our cultural origins. They would take a select number of students for rubble roams, reading Aristophanes, immersed in an aesthetic stupor of idealism ouzo and homo-Eros. Modern Greece would have none of it. A third world armpit of poverty and conceit. Years of Plato, Praxiteles, Homer, bouzouki, the entire amalgam of myth, marble and expectation crumbles into bureaucracy, cinder block, indifference. The first impression of Greece is dismal. We walked through passport control into the waiting area. Airport staff have the charm of rubber stamps, noting but not remarking your arrival. A commando in camos, Groucho moustache and sling ouzi scowls vigilant for terrorists. We move outside to taxi/bus stops. The bus is cheap, 300 drachmas vs.1800 for a cab. The bus moves slowly between two- and three-story cement and cinder block buildings that wall in the route to central Athens, a narrow congested gauntlet through which Vespas, yellow Mercedes cabs, and diesel trucks whine, honk, and grunt in a haze of exhaust and dust. No color no trees no space. Just the grey monotony of cement. Billboards tout a Michael Jackson 'concert', ASSO cigarettes. Finally the Parthenon, like an ultimate billboard hovers above the buildings as the driver shouts *Syntagma*, stops, and dumps us into traffic and a four-block trudge to our Hellastours arranged accommodations. We give the unsmiling clerk at the hotel our certified reservation. *Is this all they gave you?*, raising the prospect of homeless and abandoned. He takes our passports and says Room 421. Efharisto. Parakalo. No smile, no welcome, no well-wishing, no interest, no nothing.

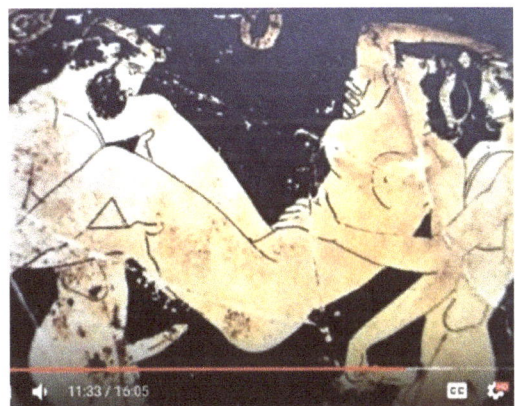

5ᵗʰ Century BC vase

In Pandora's Box, Hope was counted as one of the evils of mankind, one of the fundamental differences between the Classic and Christian temperament. There is a clue here to contemporary Greece and Greek character as well, which in this respect appear to remain entirely Classical. The room isn't just spare or sparely furnished, not simply understated or charmingly uncluttered, the *'diklino'* (twin beds) aren't simply 'Scandinavian' in design, the bare walls not simply 'monastic' in spirit. The room and furnishings are a carefully calculated subtraction of any trace of human appeal, a subtle shading of the functional into the penal, a deliberate withholding of the indefinable touch that shows you intend to house rather than store the unwitting tourist. The effect is dispiriting because the entire effect is based on 'absence'. No definite accent reveals this as intention, so you are deprived of a motive for anger that would save you from despair. Perhaps a more charitable explanation is that Greeks live in public places and are so indifferent to home furnishings they don't share the upholstered and cozy preferences we have acquired. One further horror mentioned in only one guidebook but hardly to be believed was the matter of toilet paper. A sign near the roll showed an X over a hand poised to drop paper into the toilet. The general inattention to domestic comfort apparently included a willful miscalculation of the carrying capacity of sewer pipes such that the entire city endures the curious practice of putting TP in the wastebasket rather than down the drains! If the drains can handle the other stuff, why not the paper?

After a short tour of the Plaka and dinner we return to the hotel for showers and sleep. The Greek shower consists of a hand-held nozzle from which cold to luke warm water flows under low to medium pressure in a hypodermic needle of water. The entire floor is soon covered with water which empties into a drain hole in the middle of the bathroom. The theoretical basis for this arrangement is that the entire bathroom is designed as a shower stall with a central drain hole so water can be sprayed in any direction. In practice, this is extremely inconvenient, requiring us to wade around in shoes that muddy the floor and track into the room. Constant street noise combined with the lack of double beds, bathtubs, shower curtains, hot water, and full capacity plumbing over a period of weeks provide discomforts only the most Micawberish could overlook. The night is hot so I turn on the air conditioner. Nothing happens, so I call the front desk. I mention it is not working. He says he will check. He says it is not connected. I ask if it can be connected. He says he will check. A few minutes later it goes on. All this is practice for the taffy pull for services we confronted throughout the tour. *Efharisto. Parakalo.*

A great breakfast of boiled eggs, rolls, marmalade, cereal, excellent coffee restored spirits if not faith. The Plaka was commercial, seedy, lots of Priapus King-of-Cock figurines, junk leather wallets, all to the sound of blaring acid rock, the edgy vain Greek shopkeepers looking desperate and hopeful in a contorted attempt to attract while ill concealing their indifference to the wandering horde of tourists. I didn't hear a note of Bouzouki the entire trip. We had dinner at Eden vegetarian restaurant.

On the way back to our hotel we encountered a common but seldom witnessed scene. By way of preface, for English Germans and Scandinavians, Greece is the ID country to go to for sun fun sex and liberation from cold, gloomy, 9-to-5 monotony at home. Girls bring their contraceptive pills so they can enjoy the sultry dusky love making for which the Greek male is so well praised. These lovers are called 'Torpedos' locally and take pride in keeping score. We saw an English girl and a Greek arguing near a Honda motorcycle. He paced around nervously. *'What did you expect?' 'You raped my heart...' 'You wanted sex and you got it.' 'Why do you walk like that?'* He was walking long exaggerated steps, obviously agitated, to and from his Honda beside which the girl was standing. *'I walk normally.'* She was attractive in a subdued English manner, intelligent. He was a Raf Vallone stevadore type, hairy chest, thick curls, muscular, good looking in the Greek gaucho way but also older and intelligent. They were not addled teenagers. The situation was absurd and embarrassing for both. I had read about this sort of thing but was incredulous that any intelligent female would fall

229

into it to the extent of taking it seriously. To see her in this situation and taking it seriously seemed absurd, especially since the guy was basically right. She had no right to impose the requirement of love on her sexual excursion. No European female could have the slightest doubt about what is going on. The more interesting side was his. It was flattering that she had fallen in love with him, an unaccustomed outcome for a Torpedo, setting a higher standard of evaluation and expectation than sexual satisfaction. He wasn't a bad guy. I felt sorry for him because there is a kind of dishonor in failing higher expectations in these matters, even if they are not shared. The issue wasn't sexual performance. She challenged his self-esteem by taking him seriously, which is a greater compliment and higher expectation of himself than he anticipated. Even if he later bragged about or mocked the situation, disappointing in any way hurts the ego of a professional. On the other hand, what did she honestly expect to happen?

Next morning Renee wakes up craving to fuck. We strip, throw off the covers so we can tangle over both beds. Maybe it's something in the air or the statues of Priapus with his magnificent prick and smiling bearded face (I had a beard, so maybe confused by a dream of sexual passion she assumed that he and I shared his other major attribute). We christened our trip **Priapus Tours** in his honor.

Crete was marvelous. Knossus the center of Minoan Civilization beautiful fascinating, especially the small theater where Odyssus saw an enactment of his and his cohort deeds at Troy, the origin of Greek theater. So moving to be seated exactly where he sat 3000 years ago. I swam in the Aegean at the far eastern end of Crete. I could lie on my back and not sink, the only time in Greece I could truly relax.

Auto travel in Greece is made difficult by bad maps, poor signing, and deficient guidebooks. You have to credit the Greeks for providing an English transliteration or translation for every sign, if you can see it in time. Street signs are posted on the corner buildings, white on blue, in type just small enough to make reading from a car in motion difficult and located just far enough from the street to make seeing it in time nearly impossible. Highway signs usually are placed exactly at the intersection, demanding extraordinary reflexes for timely response. Where these two handicaps don't suffice, a tree or shrub is normally planted three feet in front of the sign, limiting the viewing interval of a passing car to less than a second. But the most ingenious device for foiling a tourist is incomplete maps. No map showed every street, road, town, site or landmark. In Iraklio Crete we had to rely on the guidebook or Hertz map that gave main arteries but left out the veins and capillaries. The commonly low-rise urban landscape provides no landmarks to beacon the driver in a general direction. The main streets marry at intersections and abruptly change their names, and sometimes direction.

Tourist contacts are mainly with waiters, hotel and airport staff, shopkeepers and gas station attendants. The Greek waiter can't be making a killing but he seems contented and very professional. We like the unceremonious dispatch with which the order is taken and the meal is served. They talk a lot together and smile ingratiatingly where thrift may follow fawning but are not 'servile' in any way. In spite of the practice of accosting you, they are overall a sympathetic group, doing a necessary service with dignity and speed.

There are two Greece. The Greece of classical culture and the contemptuary every-day Greece of streets, towns, people and aggravation. Classical Greece had been a subject of study for decades. During the Priapus tour, we saw the original 'scratch' stone start line for races at Olympus and site of the original Olympic games dating from 750 BC, center for annual gatherings of people from throughout the Classical world, like a Disney World of entertainment and monuments. The Oracle at Delphi, the Crusader castle ruins in central Greece from the 12th Century, the temple at Soulian, the Spartan plain, and yhe fascinating virtually unaltered Venetian town of Monemvasia with its lanterns and multicolored doors and stone walkways. Mykonos, Delos, and Santorini where we had a delightful dinner in the white stucco jewel of a town at night, stars above and not bad imported Bordeaux red to reconcile any conflicted impressions of the day. A trip that reordered my understanding of Classical Greece. Good value for the money.

Greek men are egotists, feisty, quick to take offense, in a state of constant one-upmanship vis a vis each other, never willing to let the other guy gain or overtop. This makes social order difficult, even at the simplest level. (Better however than Ancient Greece where city states frequently were at wars of mutual annihilation.) Concerts, plays, any public event that sells tickets and has seating order never starts on time because as a matter of ego and self-esteem, appearing on time is *infra dignatum*. To arrive late has status cachet, forcing an entire row to stand and defer to late seaters a triumph personal and social. An example of this egotism during the Priapus Tour occurred in Monemvasia.

Monemvasia (one gate) on the Southeastern coast is on a rocky island promontory connected by one road over a narrow isthmus. No cars or trucks can enter and even Vespas and motorbikes don't go in because the streets are jagged uneven cobblestones that would tear tires to pieces. Transport is by donkey and cart. The entry is a 'chicane' gate-- enter straight then turn 45 degrees right to get through the gate. The crenelated walls have outposts and guard turrets. A wooden main gate held together with iron bars and protruding iron spikes clearly discouraged attack. The town looks Medieval Italian, obviously, having been built by Venetians, with winding cobbled 'streets', wrought iron lamps overhanging the narrow pathway between pastel stucco and wood buildings. Absolute charm and unspoiled by motors, but not exempt from radios.

We walked to the Monemvasia Hotel, which had been restored to provide beautiful rooms overlooking the Aegean. Wall hangings, opulent blankets, bolsters, cushions, wooden bed and furnishings, latticed windows with heavy wood shutters with iron fasteners, thatched ceiling held by large beams. A picture book for 6200 Drachmas, including *proino*. We have to lug our baggage all the way to the end of town to get there but there is no question of staying anywhere else. We settle in, enjoy the incredible view and cozy room. We eventually go back to the car parked outside the gate and go to town for dinner. We find a taverna near the waterfront and have moussaka and pastitsio. Returning in darkness under a nearly full moon, the town is beautiful. The yellow light from iron lamps and the play of color on the cobbles, on salmon, ochre and white walls, on the green and red doors and window frames. It's like being on a set for Othello or Taming of the Shrew. Unfortunately, when we return to our room we hear loud American jazz from speakers set out on the patio.

I go downstairs to try and get it turned off. The reception area's only occupants appear to be a family group, an old guy with sourdough moustache and bright red sweat shirt with Harvard seal, a teenage girl, two middle aged and one elderly woman, likely the family of one of the two clerks I am about to deal with. I go through the door to the patio bar. No customers. One speaker placed at the building wall below our second floor window. I check the bar--a separate room with bar, stools, tables where the stereo system is set up. The speaker is on a long cord wired to the indoor system. Nobody in the bar. I notice the dark guy on the patio. *'Could you turn down the music?'* He asks: *'Why?'* I say it is loud. I can hear it in my room. He says he isn't in charge and has to ask the blonde guy who is. The blonde guy comes out. He looks German but is Greek. I ask if he can turn it off or at least down. He says the bar is open and they play music for the customers. I say nobody is here so you don't need the music and it is too loud. He says it isn't loud. I say I can hear it in my room and it is. He talks at length in Greek to the dark guy, obviously stonewalling. He walks back into the reception area. The dark guy says they have a legal right to play music until 11 PM. I say I am not a lawyer or a neighbor. *'I am a client at the hotel and am asking you to turn it down. There are no customers at the bar and no one is out here listening'.* He says customers are coming later and they won't turn it down, much less off. I say: *'What you are telling me is that, although I am a client, you don't give a damn what I think.'* He says that isn't what he said. I said you two guys are real clever. He senses insult and asks in a hostile manner: *'What did you say?'* I go back into the reception continuing the argument. *'I'm a client and ask him to turn down the music. No one is on the patio and music is unnecessary. It is disturbing us in our room.'* The blonde says it is early, only 9:30. Some of the family group chuckle agreement. I turn to the old man in the Harvard sweat shirt (VERITAS) and say: *'Here is an educated man. He's been to Harvard (unlikely but what the Hell). It's perfectly reasonable to want quiet in your room. This is a beautiful place, and you don't need a lot of noise, etc.'* The old guy, probably the patriarch of the motley crew, doesn't look at me. I say it is a question of attitude toward clients. They say the bar closes at 11 PM. I say, *'Then you turn the music off at 11?'* The dark guy says: 'Maybe.' Then he says: *'Maybe you should change rooms.'* I say there are no rooms and besides you are telling me I should move to another room at considerable inconvenience in the middle of the night instead of turning down the noise? He asks: *'How long are you staying?'* I had already checked out but the records are locked up and he wouldn't know one way or the other. *'I had planned to stay for several days.'* The dark one says: *'Maybe you can change rooms tomorrow.'* I repeated that there was no reason why a paying client should have to change rooms when they can simply turn down the noise. Renee, who was with me through all this, outraged, stomped out of the room shouting *'We'll never come here again.'* I turn to everyone in the room and say that Ancient Greece was distinguished by its hospitality to strangers. I muttered a few phrases in Greek including the opening lines of the Iliad to gild the lily. *'You are not living up to the great standards of Plato, Aristotle, and the noble heritage of Greek culture.'*

Throughout this long and nasty incident I remained completely calm, never betraying any anger or raising my voice, appearing reasonable and firm in argument, and addressing everyone in the room, not just the two punks. I used Greek to the extent feasible: *'Mono thelo isixhia*

234

sto domatio. Then ine distixos na katalavo? Monemvasia ine poly kala,
then xhrisasome musika. Katalavenete?' Blond said little. Old guy said
nothing. Dark guy did all the talking. I left with complete aplomb on
the bit about attitude toward guests and classic hospitality, and returned
to our room, assuming we would have to put up with the damn noise.
From our room we could hear a heated discussion going on in the
reception area, women joining in! The older guy talked quite a bit. After
about five minutes the discussion and the music stopped. Dead silence
for the rest of the night! What happened? The guidebooks talk about
Greeks' love of argument and refusal back down. On the other hand
there is the so-called '*filoxenia*', liking of foreigners. I don't think they
like us, but they want to appear favorably to us, maybe! More to the
point, '*filotimo*', which is a kind of 'face', makes them vain, wanting
approval and to appear justified. It also makes them touchy about
personal challenge and inclined to fight rather than switch. On the
other hand they are pragmatic and if bluff doesn't produce results, they
tend to drop the subject. It is likely that the older generation persuaded
the younger to defer to foreign guests. The younger Greeks are entirely
self-centered and wouldn't accommodate anybody without advantage.
Another possibility is that the combination of my complete aplomb in
arguing in the presence of a group of them and even using some Greek
phrases raised admiration for astute argument, esteemed by the Greeks.
Whatever the reasons, we were relieved and vindicated that standing
up is always better than standing down. Greece is not a place we would
return to any time soon. Too many Greeks are basically unwelcoming,
argumentative, egocentric and unlikeable. So there!

Soulian

Back at SF Airport we encountered an elderly couple who told us how much they enjoyed Greece, especially because she was clever enough to learn a little Greek. When she spoke it everyone fell to the ground in wonder and admiration. Amazing. We got to our car and notice the Greek speaking lady and her husband driving out of the parking lot. The license plate read *PROINO. Parakalo. Efharisto.*

In 1993, I again participated in East Bay Open Studios. A central exhibit in downtown Oakland displayed an 18-inch square sample of each artist's work, which allowed visitors to select studios to visit. I displayed a watercolor of a girl changing the sparkplugs and oil filter of a beat up 1972 Pinto. This was the only painting I had that fit the 18-inch rule but it turned out to be a savvy choice. The politically correct theme drew a fair crowd to 4125 Fruitvale. The experience of hosting random individuals working through a list is mixed at best but there were enough favorable comments to make up for the indifferent and in-a-hurry and a surprising number of people chose 4125 out of the more than 200 artists participating!

GAY PARIS

In November 1993, we rented an apartment in Paris for two weeks at 117 Rue Notre Dame des Champs, about a block from *Cloiserie des Lilas,* one of Hemmingway's café/bar hangouts, two doors down from James McNeill Whistler's studio, and Ezra Pound's apartment. We ducked through the bakery across the Rue from our apartment (Hemmingway used to so we wanted to do the same) to get to Boulevard Montparnasse and roam the literary topography, including Luxembourg gardens, Gertrude Stein's place at 27 Rue des Fleuris, and so on. We went to Comédie Française and saw Moliere's *Dom Juan,* probably his least significant play but done extremely well, and we understood most of it despite the thick patois of peasant characters. Plus we enjoyed seeing the theater Sarah Bernhardt played in, all bordello-red plush chairs with lots of gilt and chandeliers. The chair into which Moliere fell when he died of a heart attack onstage during a performance of *Malade Imaginaire* is displayed in the lounge. We saw Madama Butterfly at Opera Bastille in a stilted production where every sliver of emotion was meticulously eradicated in favor of metronomic motions in slow motion and slower impact. At the Theatre des Champs Elysée, where Stravinsky premiered *Rite of Spring* in 1913, we saw Lully's baroque opera Roland (complete with a Goddess of Love on a concealed wire ascending to the rafters through pastel cardboard clouds) starring Anna Papagoulas of Merola Opera training program fame in the elevated leading role. An organ recital at night in Notre Dame cathedral with moonlight streaming through the stained glass would have converted Mohammad. We also visited the new Louvre with the Japanese glass-paned pyramid and the Leonardo *Mona Lisa* as chronological contrast. Throughout the visit we had cool sunny days, no rain, just one morning of gently falling snow like the 3rd Act of *La Bohême,* and wandered Paris by bus and on foot. Our top floor apartment was well lit by skylight windows and the heater and plumbing actually worked. A kitchen and dining area proved economical and convenient given the timing (late) and cost (high) of restaurant dining, and made us feel more resident than tourist.

Nudity has become a standard feature in opera productions. Over the years we noticed that gay stage directors (probably the majority) undress the boys and cover the girls, a counter intuitive move with respect to sales, whereas the straight directors are inclined to undress everybody. Most years the gays call the shots, but in 1994 it was our turn. In Tannhauser, nude couples rolled around on stage surrounded with mirrors to indulge their narcissism and suggest a comically Playboy version of Hell under Satanic management. Far more realistic and overpowering was the ultimate experience in the last act of *Fiery Angel* by Prokofiev in which fifty erotically possessed nuns stripped and gyrated on stage and climbed the scaffolding while a perplexed Grand Inquisitor tried to repair the spiritual damage during 10-minutes of musical bedlam that defies description. The chorus of Russian ladies with bodies that would make Hugh Heffner cry with envy provided every possible posture, gesture and exposure of their magnificent assets, while my binoculars were screwed to my face trying but failing to see every gorgeous body in full writhing glory. Every male in the house was doing the same. A live YouTube in spades!

Buying the Steinway. I resumed piano in earnest after nearly twenty years of not being able to play a scale. During our trip to France in 1974 I pulled or fused the tendons in my right hand and subsequent attempts to free them up failed. In 1993 I found that weight lifting seemed to help, probably by stretching the tendons, although it hadn't done much before. Articulation in the ring and middle fingers was still impaired, but I got to the point that I could play tolerably if I warmed up and shut the door. Hoping for further improvement to justify the move, I started looking for a grand piano in the fall to supplement or replace my Yamaha upright. Steinways run $15,000 used to more than $75,000 new so I began looking for a vintage (1910-1940) Knabe, Chickering, Sohmer or Baldwin. This took us on a search to all parts of the Bay Area, until we found my magic carpet, with original bill of sale in NYC 1920!

Robert Pierce lives in Los Angeles where he owned a piano store. He was also a pop-music 'Liberace' playing solo or with small bands at various gigs private and ceremonial, getting photographed with celebrities, selling pianos along the way and himself in the process. In 1994, he had thick wavy hair even at 75-years and was still full of himself. The type seems to settle in large numbers in LA. In the course of all this hype and mini-glamour he compiled a list of serial numbers of all makes of pianos. His book, *Pierce Piano Atlas,* is the only guide available that records the makes, serial numbers and date of manufacture of every brand of piano current and extinct since the mid-1800's. Typically the $28 book, which he sells from home, is made up half of biography and photos of himself in obscure locations with now dimly recalled or entirely forgotten semi-celebrities, usually with a white grand piano in the foreground or background. Page 286 lists the Steinway serial numbers that include #196584, Model O that I purchased. It was built in 1919 and sold November 16, 1920 at the Steinway showroom, 107-109 East 14th Street, to J. A. Easton of 599 West 190th Street for $1475.

Steinway Model 'O' 1919

It took me two years to find the right piano, looking as far north as Sacramento, east to Danville and of course all over San Francisco, Berkeley and Oakland. The Berkeley-Oakland fire of October 1989 had a major impact on the piano market nationally. Hundreds of pianos were burned in the fires that swept the high value homes of the East Bay hills. A friend lost a Steinway Model M when his house was destroyed. The owners were educated successful, wealthy, including many amateur players. The loss had to be made up and hundreds of Steinways and lesser brands were imported from the East to meet the demand.

Steinways cost more than other pianos. So I began looking for other brands considered pretty good in the 5-to-6 foot grand range. A piano store in San Raphael had a beautiful Knabe for $16,000. They also had a beat up Steinway Model O circa 1910 for $13,000. It looked battered, the hammer felts were worn down to the nub, but it sounded like heaven. I listened hard and memorized the sound. In addition to cost, the mahogany was a major negative. A grand piano should be black. It is the only color worthy of its dignity. So I looked for several more months, usually seeing 'restored' Steinways in which everything original was replaced, something that changed the entire character of the sound. Then one day I saw an advertisement in the SF Chronicle. A piano store in El Cerrito had a Steinway O for sale. Renee and I drove there. This could be it! What then? I brought a money market check unbeknownst to Renee. I saw the 5'11" Steinway O 1919 and fell in love at first sight. The owner left it on consignment for $16,000. I offered $15,000. He called the owner. Done deal. Including concert bench in naugahyde. Renee didn't pass out. There wasn't room to. So many junk pianos one could hardly walk much less collapse. Investment or folly? Since 1995 it hasn't lost value, there are simply fewer of them now. Of course there are fewer piano students, except for Chinese who are the last best hope of classical music in the US. I wouldn't part with my O for anything but a Steinway B, an offer no sane Steinway owner would make.

We waited for as long as possible for something to happen in 1996, but nothing did so I will improvise. I refer mainly to the US Government buyout which, if approved, would have given me an incentive bonus, released me January 3rd, 1997, from further employment at your expense, and allowed me to pursue my piano, which improved remarkably thanks to the beloved Steinway acquired in 1995 and the old reliable Yamaha upright acquired in 1968. My main victims were Chopin Mozart and Beethoven, especially the Raindrop (Op 25/1) and Revolutionary (Op 10/12) Etudes of the former and the Pathetique (Op 13), Waldstein (Op 52), Moonlight (Op 27), and Appassionato (Op 57) sonatas of the latter. I use the von Bulow tags since one rarely keeps the numbers straight. Apparently, the Steinway power was audible by neighbors four doors away, they commenting that I must be a concert pianist whereas my playing was more like driving the coast Highway 1, slow down on the uphill and curves and make up time on the straightaways.

We did consider a trip to England, but like Des Esseintes in *A Rebours* never got beyond trying on our plaids and drinking Earl Grey tea. I was on detail to the Washington Office for about three weeks in summer, which brought home the utter boredom and futility of airports, hotels, restaurants, and travel in general, a contrarian view among bureaucrats. We visited New England, Donald, Winifred, Paul, Debbie and their son Greg. Had a surprisingly enjoyable visit which cheered up Renee a great deal. We rented a one-bedroom suite near Dupont Circle, with full kitchen, separate dining and living areas private bedroom, where we entertained Flora Moroni, Renee's High School friend then working for IRS, and her husband Shorty for dinner after work. The logistics were that I would pick up the entrée on the way from work and Renee would have the salad and other requirements ready when I arrived. We had a fun time, drank too much wine, and planned to visit them Saturday at their home on the Maryland western shore of Chesapeake Bay. They seemed unwilling to part with us, since they don't get much company in the boondocks. Lots of blue fin crab cakes, white Zinfandel and laughs.

The 1996 opera season given at Civic Center as the opera house was being earthquake proofed was outstanding, including the best Lohengrin we have seen. Normally Ortrud takes the show, in this case Leonie Rysenek in a stunning performance, but this production was absorbing and balanced throughout. Former Merolini Patricia Racette was in the Tales of Hoffmann, gorgeous, passionate, intense, and under 130 pounds.

China figured prominently in 1997. I arranged tours for several delegations from obscure Provinces and tried to learn a bit of Mandarin along the way. Entire departments came over, focused mainly on seeing Disneyland, San Francisco, New York and if possible Washington D.C., the incidental business along the way just an excuse to justify the boondoggle (bureaucrats everywhere catch on fast). I spoke my imperfect Mandarin to a group of sixteen from Hebei Province bunched at the end of the conference table in the Regional Office emitting Chinese tobacco smells as sour as their looks. They were all homely middle-aged bureaucrat men except for a charming woman interpreter with whom I sympathized traveling in such company, tailor tags still on the sleeves of the cheap suits they bought in Los Angeles. I made special eye contact with her and we timed my talk and her translation so she could easily keep up. I made a few remarks but started with *Xuan ying ni zai Jiu jin shan!* (welcome to San Francisco) when they exploded into applause and laughter. Apparently, an attempt at Mandarin on my part was an icebreaker! Mandarin has four tones that entirely change the meaning of any given word (each is one syllable) so I attribute my unforeseen gift for Sinic comedy to the range of verbal antics and puns the tones make possible, a talent one can inflict with or without intention. For all I knew my pronunciation of Xuan ying ni zai Jiu jin shan may have sounded like 'Beat your Johnson' in my mispronounced Mandarin. No matter.

Things went famously. Soon they were in stitches and taking photos, always pulling my sleeve to get in the picture. A large group photo had me at center, arm around the translator (very pleasant duty), and all the delegation fawning over me. I looked good in blue blazer, white shirt, tie and Kennedy smile so they probably thought I was the top banana. I imagine my face is still featured prominently on the walls of the Hebei Forestry Division but I have no interest in making sure. Emboldened by this success, I hosted a second session with a delegation from Shandong Province at our experiment station in Berkeley to be followed by meetings with UC Forestry faculty. I gave a bit of Mandarin followed by discussion with our Chinese speaking specialists. At the end I gave a valedictory shout: *Zhong guo ren he Mei guo ren…PENGYOU!* (Americans and Chinese are friends!) to which a standing ovation and applause. How little it takes!

SF Opera returned to the earthquake- proofed but unaltered House with a great season. Even the Flying Dutchman achieved liftoff. A dramatically moving Evgeni Onegin was a pleasant surprise, since I always thought of Tchaikovsky operas as grade-B musically. I arranged to retire January 3, 1998, having demonstrated little aptitude for steady work for many years. We planned to look for friends with extra rooms to facilitate our prospective travels. Pushkin says habit is a substitute for happiness, so replacing work with *La Vie de Boheme* may suit me. If not, I would be in a real *'pungente* salsa' (Inferno, 3).

My exclusive theme and interest in painting is the beauty of women, which can be pursued more leisurely and perhaps safely in paint than in person, or in writing for that matter. Which introduces an odd year-long interval provoked by the film Persuasion released in the US in 1996. Based on the novel by Jane Austen, it tells the story of Anne Eliot who fell in love with a naval officer without fortune and therefore deemed unsuitable for marriage who late in the Napoleonic War retuned from the West Indies with a fortune in captured booty. It was authentic as to detail, costume, manners, and locations, a brilliant recreation of the period 1816, with anachronistic musical background of a Chopin *Prelude* I play myself, by the way. I was frustrated and wanting to get out of government and Renee was having trouble with her heart condition, two sticky mitro-valves that depressed her.

I suppose I was looking for an escape and was smitten by Amanda Root who played Anne Eliot in the film. I was also pent up with creative energy, just needing a prod to get going. I wrote Amanda via BBC that produced the film and where Amanda frequently worked in television. She replied and we launched a pen pal relationship in which I contributed poems and screenplays with plots I thought appropriate to her talent, in addition to letters. Unlike Hollywood actors, British actors are quite willing to write to fans. I wrote to Amanda in March 1996.

Dear Amanda.

Thank you for your lovely presence in Persuasion, so beautifully interpreted by brilliant artists, fond direction, adoring camera, and sustained devotion to immortal Jane. Among the many delights of the film was the astute choice (entirely apt if anachronistic) of Chopin Preludes, which I play as amateur pianist and will forever adoringly associate with you and your incomparable Anne Elliot. Should there be a romantic revival in the US, I and your countless admirers here will hold you entirely responsible. I send this to RSC in hope that it may be forwarded to you to join the outpouring of love and

affection you have unwittingly inspired, richly deserve, and hopefully do not find too importunate to accept.
Christopher

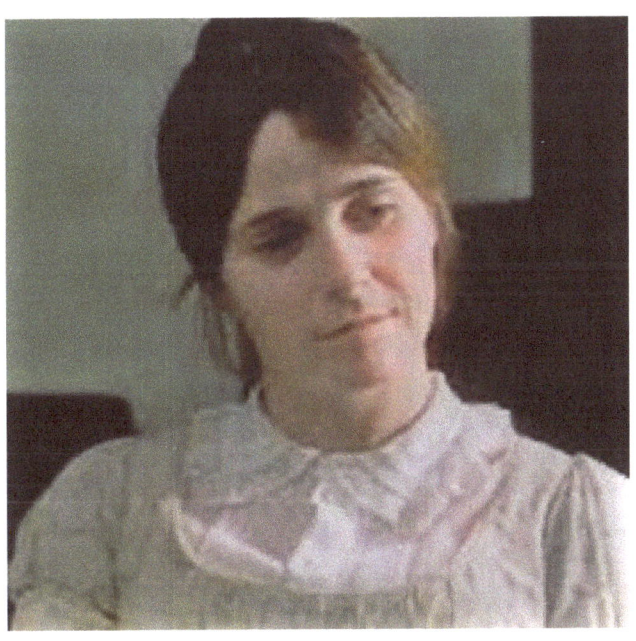

We corresponded until June 1997, when she went on a shoot to Wales. She inspired me to write poems (a few follow) and screenplays and long adoring letters which she seemed to welcome as encouraging and supportive. I tried to imagine a role for Amanda in a character as outwardly unlike Anne Elliott. I wrote a film script *Alumni Fund* to liberate her from pious and restrained roles like Anne Elliot to play another lady, rogue at heart, an antidote to Persuasion. My film script Alumni Fund involved Jessica Hyde (alluding to the dual personality of R. L. Stevenson's Dr. Jekyll and Mr. Hyde), an English girl, daughter of a bus conductor, and currently head of the alumni fund at Abington College in Vermont. She wears tweed suits, cameo collar pin, sensible shoes, and is adored by the alumni and board of directors. The college recently went coed and in dire financial condition hired tough-talking Sarah Goldrock, a butch Jewish PhD from the Bronx, as President to regain accreditation, complete antipode to the genteel ivy League ethos of Abington. Unknown to the alumni and board, Jessica came to America broke, got work as a stripper in a mafia club in Manhattan, was hired as au pair by a Mafia Godfather, and through his help (forged qualifying documentation) got her position at Abington. He has in fact established similar plants in a dozen colleges, including Bryn Mahr, Vasser, Holyoake, Radcliffe, using the alumni directory for each to identify the hits. Amanda attracts large pledges to Abington and arranges through a mafia hit man to cull a select few donors each year to boost college funds, from which she earns a percentage. She has a clandestine affair with the wealthy husband of an alumna, and conveniently terminates his wife so they can marry. Much else goes on but that is the general idea. It is a funny noir comedy with ample characters and scenes for Amanda to show her stuff, including a celebratory striptease in front of her bedroom mirror when all her plans finally come to fruition. I sent her a copy. She replied.

Dear Chris

My goodness where do I start? I have just finished reading your consummate, witty, and 'deadly' script. What a good ending, the whole thing is delightfully dark and intriguing. Do your talents never cease? It's a terrific script and very funny. I really enjoyed the character of Jessica and I loved Goldrock too, in her unceasing butchiness and coarse rationalism. Your last poem was waiting for me as I arrived home after a particularly distressing incident, and yes fuck it, it did move me to tears, it was just the tonic I needed, because someone was thinking of me, and thinking enough to write such things. My agent in LA sent me a script of a remake of an old American movie 'The Parent Trap'. I think Hayley Mills was in it. Anyway, Disney has got this new draft and my agent thought I'd be good for the Mum in it. I'm being confirmed on Sunday at St. Martin in the Fields, Trafalgar Square. It's a very big day for me as it's something I have wanted to do for simply ages, and my family and friends are coming too. I am content and happy and very grateful to these terrific scripts my door.

Sincerely with love,

Amanda XXX

Amanda wrote in June that she was going to Wales for several months to shoot a new film. I retired on January 3, 1998, my last day in office. A very elegant tea party was served as a farewell, and about 3:30 I left for the last time. About 4 o'clock Amanda showed up with her boyfriend. A colleague at the agency called me to say she was staying at a hotel downtown and could receive my call there. Amanda had other business in San Francisco but it was flattering that she would bother to actually go to 630 Sansome rather than call ahead. The circumstances required more than casual evaluation. After a beautiful enchantment that led to a spurt of creativity I had not experienced before, I figured the intensity and purpose of our correspondence would now lag, probably to pro forma Xmas cards once a year. My romance was over, the marvelous fugue she inspired mostly at its end. I was entering a new phase of retirement and the circumstances that led to the Amanda interval were now behind me. I never heard from her or she from me again.

SE14 5PP

18v April '96.

Dear Christopher,

Thank you so much for the lovely letter you wrote to me about 'Persuasion', and my performance in it — I was deeply touched by the things you said.

I hope you are aware of the encouragement and support you give by taking the trouble to write how you feel, it's so appreciated and I am very grateful. I loved working on 'Persuasion' and had a fabulous time with all the actors and the crew — everyone got on famously so I have very fond memories of that time. Doubly nice therefore to receive such a response as yours.

I am steering clear of the R.S.C. for a bit, and theatre in general to try and avoid the stereotyping that inevitably occurs. I'm determined to make a break into the film world, so although it's tough at the moment, waiting for a good film part, I'm trying to stick with that decision. So unfortunately I will not be praying in harder if you come to England this year!

However I hope it won't be too long before I'm back on the screen — with such encouragement as yours it gives me that bit more strength to stick out the fallow periods.
Thank you again.

With very Best wishes

Amanda Root.

Gift

What can I give, what thing of use
that you might see or wear
would long remind so lovely you
of so loving me--
since fondness tied to use
soon fades by daily handling.
And what of words that have no use
whose meaning all depends?
Might they find passage to your heart.
place there a sight or sound
so gentle loving fair
it now and then must rise
like music to your ear
or sunlight to you eyes
til I am part of what you see
or part of what you hear?,

My Love

Thought tells me you are no more fair
than sunlight seen through dappled leaves
your walk bears no more startling grace
than fawns at play in morning air.
The colors of your cheek no more surprise
than flowers on a wild green hill
and stars amaze the velvet night
as much as I am by your eyes.
Your touch falls no more gently down
than butterfly upon the rose
the Celtic harp at twilight sounds
as lovely as your voice at dawn.
A lingering Summer's day in June
spreads as much warmth as does your smile
your strands of hair combine with no more grace
than branches dancing beneath the Moon.
But thought compares what it can see
heart hears songs that thought can never see.

Autumn Song

Winter's wind begins to cull
our lovely pregnant aching Autumn
swollen with Summer fruit
and wild wind-sown berries of Spring.
Sun drunk pears,
startling all the wild amazed birds,
leap through frosted air
like rainbows, yellow, red and gold,
to spread their final sunburst
over chill-threatened Earth.
Autumn is almost more than we can bear,
all memory of beauty, grace and light,
of promise kept or not, and ripeness in decline.
Smells of slow decay hint at April's green
and rusting leaves recall
branching glories of the Spring.
The pears were not taught, do not expect.
harbor from ice-bladed wind.
So gathered by your hands they glow
wondering, silent, through slanting afternoons
amazed to the end by the warmth
of your voice, your touch, your love,
their second, un-hoped for Summer in the Sun.

RETIREMENT

The word itself is pejorative, passive, and inapt for what I had in mind. Retire may apply to those whose job had been their life interest. Jobs never were for me. I had wanted to retire at least since I was 21, and let everyone know it, especially Renee. The prospect became official in 1993 when I reached the age of 55, eligible for full retirement benefits, no deductions or reductions, all of it. It may seem puzzling that someone so dedicated to the idea would wait five years to do it. The reasons are interesting, well mildly. So long as you can't, you yearn for the day you can. Once eligible, a new perspective reveals itself. When you reach the point that you can walk anytime, urgency vaporizes. I had a great job, lots of interesting contacts and activities and could pretty much write my own work schedule and projects. Renee and I were enjoying travel (Greece 1992. France 1993) and showing art (Open Studios 1992-1993). We were attending life drawing sessions and our usual theater and opera events. The work routine was familiar, lucrative and enjoyable. Why leave? They made me an offer I couldn't refuse.

In July 1997, the agency offered a buy out and I decided to go for it. The departure date was January 3, 1998, the buyout amount $25,000, no golden parachute but be grateful for what you can get, and subject to income tax in 1998 when income and the tax obligation would be less. In 1998, after overcoming initial doubts that they would actually shove the money under the door, retirement seemed quite agreeable. We resumed life drawing in January, during the day this time. Renee set up a studio in the downstairs bedroom and enjoyed tai chi with her friends, but retirement took some getting used to, mainly because my retirement entailed no great changes for her daily routine. I kept at Mandarin, which given the odds was madness. Most scholars agree it takes five times as long to learn as French or German and the *pons asinorum* on which I was stranded midstream seemed correspondingly long. If nothing else, listening to Mandarin improved my French! Don't ask, I don't know why. Piano and guitar also figure in this retreat from occupational engagement. I was working on the *Waldstein* sonata, particularly the last movement. Playing this more or less as written gives me an aerobic workout and spiritual lift nothing else can, well almost. I also relearned long-neglected classical guitar Bach suites, Albeniz, Sor, Tarrega and began looking for a concert guitar to replace my old student model.

Our opera gig started in June, attending operas and Merola training program events. Although Tennessee Williams is not our favorite playwright the opera version of Streetcar Named Desire by Andre Previn wasn't bad. His score evokes the corrosive loneliness of Blanche Dubois, although the spermy meatballs surrounding her resist musical interpretation or aesthetic redemption. The British soprano we heard as Blanche in the second team performance conducted by Patrick Summers sang her to perfection, a deeply wounded lost soul in a marvelous final soliloquy. Previn conducted the first team with Renee Fleming, too hyped to be authentic. Previn has written a cash cow, definitely good for small houses, small-scale productions, and even small-scale voices. Main problem is to find a baritone in good enough shape to play Stanley. Vocally he poses no challenges whatever. Speaking of opera, the Clinton impeachment soap opera was ongoing. Caroline Casey, a Berkeley astrologue and astute radio commentator on public events, wrote: *It makes working in the Oval Office sound like hitchhiking through Italy.* Clinton followed Emily Dickinson's advice: *Always tell the truth, but tell it slant.*

In June 1999, we did our second RING, cast with two of the fattest sopranos (Deborah Voight and Jane Eaglen) in two of the most romantic roles in opera, requiring suspension of disbelief nearly unsustainable. RING tickets combined with purchase of a mid-level concert guitar amounted to the price of a Toyota Corolla. The RING seems to be invincibly moving no matter what visual accommodations one has to make to get voices able to go the whole eighteen hours. My new guitar provides opportunity to work on *Recuerdos del'Alhambra* at about 1/3 concert speed which is the pace I seem to do everything. The Steinway turned 80-years this year, a magnificent thing to look at and play which I do to no one's satisfaction but my own. The *Moonlight Sonata* showed most improvement. I can get through the third movement at various speeds, rather like driving coast Highway 1, with intervals of slow hairpin turns and uphill climbs, pick up speed on the straight-aways.

The 20th Century ended with a hi-tech panic about how to correct computer-based programs for finance, research, economic and other fields that depend on data processing designed for 1900 to 1999, unable to accommodate the new century of 2000+. Scores of programmers, many brought in from China burned midnight oil, to borrow a 19th Century metaphor, to solve this 21st Century problem. I had no programmer to reprogram my life for the new Century. As Woody Allen once said: *In movies the story can cut to the next scene. In life you have to live every fucking minute of it.*

21st CENTURY

Florida hanging chads, 9/11, Afghanistan, Iraq, 2006 recession, just a few early indicators of what has become the century of disintegration now in its 22nd year at this writing. Shrub, a mix of the moronic (he nearly choked to death eating popcorn while watching a Dallas Cowboy game) and the sophomoric (his favorite song is *Wake Up Little Susie),* was elected President in 2000 by Justice Scalia on appeal. He started by failing to prevent two unending wars (Afghanistan 2001, Iraq 2003), was re-elected in 2004 (proving the failure of sub-cephalic American public education), botched hurricane relief, and bankrupted the Nation (2006 recession). Truly *Mission Accomplished,* depending on how you define 'miss'.

Public inanition provided background to private tragedy. My wife Renee died June 5, 2004, due to two mitro-valve failures. Long story, too maddening to relate. She was informed of this condition in 1979, which tightened like a vice over time, a gradually approaching threat choking her optimism. For me, the end of our world. Her death left me completely disoriented, depressed, irrational. If I attended an opera or play, I left after the first act to hurry home to her urn (she was cremated), a crazy way to be with her. I had witnessed her death at Kaiser Permanente Hospital in Oakland. I wished I could follow her. I couldn't be away from the house for more than two hours, I had to be with her. I half believed she might walk into the room. I was crazy and alone. Her family were egoists, entirely self-absorbed in their anxieties, phobias, obsessions and even sibling rivalries. They all turned up for a ceremony at the Funeral Home where her casket was on display before cremation. No one was crying, except me. I was glad to see them go.

I got 'creative' to the extent of getting back to painting including Renee (below), writing a book (Freedom vs. Equality), beginning a 1000-page memoir of our life together, and playing piano frenetically. After nine months I recovered enough to consider looking for women to share interests with. After 39-years of marriage, I was culture-challenged with respect to dating. Like an explorer in his first encounter with Hottentots, I didn't know the idiom, the frames of reference, and for the most part didn't much care. I just needed to kill time since time is something I had plenty of.

Renee died June 5, 2004, a day after her 61st birthday and two weeks short of our 39th Anniversary. I always wanted to marry, I was happily married. It was love at first sight and I did not once in 39 years make it with another woman. I did come close a couple of times. The first a co-worker married to an older stiff. She would stand at the copier (an erotic venue if ever there was) and let me push my knee into her pussy and rub it around. At an afternoon office Christmas party we were sneaking out the back entrance to be alone in a car, hallway, loading dock, behind a bush, in a dumpster when a fellow worker came in unexpectedly and feeling 'caught', we soon returned to the party unfulfilled. Upon reflection I realized that would have been the dumbest thing I could do and was relieved that it ended before any damage was done.

Ten years later in 1982, I was on a field trip and a woman I met at the local office took to me. She had a huge beehive hairdo, very blonde, hourglass figure and wore a tight dress with a Mason-Dixon line just above the knee. When she sat down I had a view of her legs close together. We had drinks at my hotel but she had to go home. *'Let me know when you are coming next time. I can keep the evening free.'* I doubt that I could have gone through with it. I loved Renee and would have been too guilty.

In April 2005, I tried internet dating sites. First domestic, later foreign. The domestic talent was appalling, freakish, quietly mad. I had no idea such losers existed. Obesity, lethal homeliness, emotional hairballs disqualified most. Two obsessions, religion and vegan dieting were most peculiar. A vegan devotee near Palo Alto had a guru who kept her on an all-leak diet. Her refrigerator crammed with jars of leaks in various stages of modification: raw, chopped, shredded, soup, puree. Her online photo showed a typical muddle-class divorcee in business suit, not bad looking, slender, early 40's. Face to face she looked like a Dachau survivor, all bone like three sticks tied together. Another lady I 'met' on a Christian website loved Jesus and mentioned him in a creamy voice every four minutes, casting occasional suspicious glances at me: *'Does he really love Jesus or is he just faking it to get in my pants?'*

Not once did I find a normal attractive sexy American online so I decided to reappraise my strategy and focus on foreign markets. I redid my photo album and strengthened my personal/income/academic write-ups. I used three main photos presumably attractive to ladies seeking a 'professional' companion but with enough macho to appeal to what happens after work. In general, I did not appeal to American women. I either knew too much or made it obvious that I thought they knew too little. They are so formed in the American High School-College matrix that I have little access to the assumptions and expectations they have formed. Another problem is that so few American women appealed to me. During my later travels in China I would see at least a dozen women every day who turned me on. Here, maybe one a semester. So foreign travel was in order.

RUSSIA

I first tried Russian Love Match where for a nominal $14 a month I could write and receive responses from ladies throughout Russia Ukraine and the Baltics. My written Russian was pretty good so no language barrier or misunderstanding was likely to impede or mislead my explorations. I contacted at least two dozen Russian women, an education in amorous philandering and prevarication on an International scale. This was absurd. I had no affinity for Slavic women or they for me. They are completely without charm, any attempt to affect charm being so entirely and obviously fake as to gull only the willing. But it was amusing to play the game. Anna was a Russian working in Yalta, Ukraine, once married ten years to a doctor who became increasingly alcoholic and 'uninhabitable'. I painted her picture based on a photo she sent me.

June 15, 2005
Greetings! About! You are the artist still. You will be the first man which has written my portrait. I always envied creative people. I cannot at all play, nor sing, nor draw. But I can create in the kitchen. I was married 10 years. A fine kind person, but it drank every year increasing more and more. Here 6 years I live alone. I finish university as programmer. Now I work develop network of mini-café, 'French Bakery', in Crimea. I wish to change work in

tourist business. Travel, new countries, cultures, the nature, customs, to new people is my passion. I study independently Italian, French, English. I have in head a porridge--all words of all languages mixed.
Anna

Anna1   ***Anna 2***

She wanted most to meet an Italian and 'enjoy life', make up for time wasted. Not sure where she got the Italian obsession, but I wasn't dusky enough apparently, and during my phone call to Odessa she made not even a shred of effort to establish a connection. No great loss, although her bikini photo, interesting hips, and emphatic stance was provoking, as though saying 'I'm not Bardot, but my equipment will give you the ride of your life.' Another Anna in Moscow led to a brief correspondence and a photo for a portrait à la Matisse in pure cadmium red yellow green, an experiment in nonrepresentational portraiture. I gave her the wrong Hotel I had reserved in Moscow so no possibility of meeting when I got there later in 2006.

She wanted most to meet an Italian and 'enjoy life', make up for time wasted. Not sure where she got the Italian obsession, but I wasn't dusky enough apparently, and during my phone call to Odessa she made not even a shred of effort to establish a connection. No great loss, although her bikini photo, interesting hips, and emphatic stance was provoking, as though saying 'I'm not Bardot, but my equipment will give you the ride of your life.' Another Anna in Moscow led to a brief correspondence and a photo for a portrait à la Matisse in pure cadmium red yellow green, an experiment in nonrepresentational portraiture. I gave her the wrong Hotel I had reserved in Moscow so no possibility of meeting when I got there later in 2006. More interesting was Alina in Tallin, Estonia. Her photos have an irresistible 'so-what?' look I couldn't help find challenging. Alina wrote poetry, a further incitement and complication that seemed to deepen possibilities. She sent me several of her poems and I reciprocated. She wrote and understood English well, had visited the US and France. After a long logistical discussion via email, including the prospect of a visit to St. Petersburg (unrealized), I bought a Lufthansa ticket for a flight departing August 29, 2005 for Tallin via Stuttgart. Thus began my Quixotic adventure with Russian women, in the sense that I, like the Don, was a romantic who imagined marvels, riding a stallion only to wake up on a donkey or wearing a crown only to wake up wearing a chamber pot. Not that I wasn't warned in an email from Alina.

  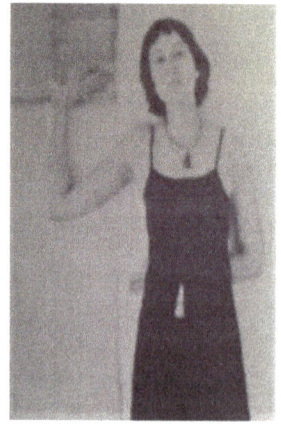

Most likely I am not the best to walk with for hours as it's as Freda Khalo used to say: 'I'm damaged all the way, but the leg is the worst.' Actually I

know my body can be a turnoff—for guys less smart than you are. And in the opposite way, for others who are smart, it can be something they get the highest pleasure from. But I know that you're smart enough to deal with that as it should be and after all I am pretty sure that you need me just like I need you. Just remember, looking in my eyes it's me and don't judge the book by its cover no matter how pretty or ugly the print is. I'm sure you will like the content much more if you start reading.

Tallinn is a tiny Baltic port city, now half Estonian and half Russian, with predominantly crude cement soulless Soviet-era apartment buildings and military installations and historically attractive gothic German and Scandinavian town square, cathedral, public buildings suggesting its Hanseatic League connection that relieve the oppressive Soviet gloom. Alina met me at the airport and we drove by cab through the unprepossessing landscape to the dismal Kruschchev-era apartment she had rented from its traveling occupant visiting her British lover in London. A major revision was immediately apparent. Poor Alina was deformed, her upper body bone structure twisted out of shape. Full length photos showed nothing of the kind. She was saving up co-pay for surgery (radical) to straighten the spinal dislocation, one shoulder above the other torqued asymmetrically and one leg shorter than the other causing a major limp, all which made it difficult to establish how, if indeed one wished, to seduce her given that she had to wear a hard plastic thorax prosthetic to maintain upright balance. She had traveled to the US and needed a sponsor for a return visa. I suppose I served that function, any physical encounter being the price she might have to pay for such endorsement but probably unenthusiastically. I was willing to try once I got her undressed but that seemed to be something strategically possible but tactically uncertain. An even greater complication for this misadventure was her demented 'spiritual' affiliation.

In the US I encountered different degrees and kinds of 'madness'. Alina had a new one for me, astonishing because I had read about it but only once encountered the phenomenon (tambourines/chants/bare feet/jingle-bell ankle bracelets/shaved heads/beads) during a stopover at O'Hare airport in Chicago. A Hare Krishna compound/temple/whatever existed in Tallinn not far from my apartment. It turned out that Alina is an avid novitiate and regularly dines, chants, and attends whatever equivalent 'religious' ceremonies are therein performed. I was still ignorant of this when she proposed the next day that we have dinner at a 'restaurant' she often goes to. Alina entered the building first while I waited outside, unclear why that was necessary, but apparently she needed 'permission' to invite a stranger into the holy sepulture.

While waiting I heard what can only be described as a herd of people chanting, dancing, and shaking tambourines with a few flutes, at first distant, then closer and closer. I thought: *'Who is making this insane racket?'*, until they showed up at my feet. A random sort of mostly men and some women in colorful gauzy robes and obligatory sandals. Apparently, they did this lap dance every day to drum up interest (more likely annoyance) among the Estonians.

Inside, the temple was agreeable enough. The leader was young, personable, outwardly sane, good looking, rather short, slim, no long beard or 'penetrating' guru eyes, with a bright and welcoming smile and manner. We hit it off. He spoke only Russian so my speaking their language impressed the babushkas in the kitchen who prepared dinner at the complex as 'charity work'. I offered to teach him English, без платно, which inspired admiring twitter from the shy babushkas, 'free of charge' always a winner. I invited the leader to San Francisco where I jokingly said he would go unnoticed among the other crazies, perhaps not accurately translated into Russian so no offence taken. He privately told Alina I was a 'good guy', which heightened her regard for me.

Which prompts an aside. We all have a range of variation in mind as criteria for what is acceptable. What is within the brackets of that range is 'normal', viable, 'one of us'. What is outside the brackets is not. Over time, the range for most of us expands. Once religious fanaticism was so entrenched that Catholic and Protestant would under no circumstances tolerate intermarriage. I considered Hare Krishna as a mild form of lunacy but not entirely disqualifying, a sort of temporary aberration of otherwise sensible people eventually to be abandoned for more sensible forms of the 'search for meaning'. The leader was a very personable and rational seeming guy and whatever oddities of costume or locution he may prefer were harmless conceits, much like being a Shriner who wears a red fez and Turkish balloon pants to march in parades down Broadway and mumble secret oaths in occult meetings. But seeing Alina jump from foot to foot and chant whatever mumbo jumbo they preferred was at once so comic and so undermining of confidence in the intellectual reserves of the participants as to end further interest in long or short term involvement.

Of course, no matter what the impediment, a man conjures images of how to and how often. I had already run that screen test through my mind, so when she planned an overnight in my apartment it provoked a re-screening. I was actually eager to fuck her, having no chance for six days, but mainly out of curiosity as to her configuration. Perhaps she was right. It would be a turn on, like a refined form of sadism, to see her twisted body with smooth skin, erect nipples, and moist pubic triangle writhing helplessly under the throbbing instrument of my insatiable passion. I managed to sit beside her on the living room sofa and attempt a kiss and fondle. A major impediment was the metalo-plastic exoskeleton back brace she wore. How to sustain passion while removing the prosthetic device imposed greater demands for mind/body separate activity and motivation than I could meet. One afternoon we visited the US consulate where she submitted my invitation as sponsor and US contact to obtain a visa. This shiftless and inconclusive excursion finally came to an end. She accompanied me by cab at 5:30 AM to the airport where we held hands and talked about her prospective visit to the States. I felt elated that I would soon board the plane and get the Hell out of Estonia. I didn't contact her again, happy to return to Paradise in California.

For the balance of 2005 and most of 2006 I pursued desultory connections in the US and email probes in Russia. A mutual exchange of an extraordinary amount of amorous bunk. They seeking a kind reliable spouse, looks don't matter, money doesn't matter, practically nothing matters but sincerity and honesty, of which there was little enough on both sides. I contacted Bernice online. She had a video cam and lay in bed showing her phenomenal breastwork. She lived in Canada but was planning a visit to her daughter in San Leandro, a few miles south of Oakland. Her father was Chinese, her mother Canadian Indian, member of an officially registered Native Canadian Tribe. The brevity of their encounter, of which Bernice was the collateral damage, meant she was raised in reservation poverty but through remarkable determination she moved from beautician to psychologist to include marriage counseling and doing psychological evaluations of indicted individuals required by courts. Her daughter was living with a Hispanic guy and had a son via a Black student she met in High School. Bernice had worked as a 16-wheel intercontinental truck driver for three years, traveling extensively in the US and Canada. She had been in the Caribbean, a liaison with a Black politician there. She was never married but in frequent varied contacts, a very game girl.

She was borderline plump, but still had a definable waist, pleasantly full and compliant figure with a bold pair of 38C's, for which we went to Victoria's Secret on our first encounter to select a suitable bra, my opinion of course helping her decide which ones to buy. We settled on pale rose see-through with enough tensile strength to support her substantial well-formed superstructure. The prospect of fondling and fucking her overrode any qualified judgment I might have formed as to our compatibility. In the dark and in a hurry thinking is not an option. It was Christmas 2005, so we spent the weekend at my house lying in front of the fireplace, toasted, erect, moist and frequent. She liked doing it but had the most alarming habit of going total inert, no reaction, no response, as if passed out, something like making love to a warm corpse. At every subsequent meeting she seemed to have gained five pounds, so at the last the earlier physical charm was largely overwhelmed. It ended amiably and I wished her well.

I attended a few operas and plays, in particular David Mamet's *American Buffalo,* a tiresome complicated altercation about an American coin! of interest only to see capable actors attempt to breathe life into a thespian flat tire. California Shakespeare had moved to a new outdoor stage in Orinda, now directed by Dan Moscone (son of the assassinated SF mayor) whose first production in 2002 was Chekhov's *Seagull* in the most brilliant and idiomatic staging of that playwright I have seen. Costumes, sets, characters, direction were spot on. Unfortunately, as years went by he became more eccentric, a final blow in 2006 was an all-Black cast Hamlet, following a theory of counter casting that logically would require a White Othello. Hamlet was more like Uncle Tom's Cabin than Elsinore. Other tiresome politically correct stage tricks and the appalling punk casts incapable of delivering a line of Shakespeare led to fewer plays of the Bard and increasing reliance on Wilde, Wilder and Whoever? The Merola opera training program collapsed entirely by 2006, no special events, no remarkable training session, no mainline talent hired to instruct. Battle fatigue? Hard to tell. Just the final descent into irrelevance that afflicted San Francisco after Herb Caen retired in 1997.

I have read a great deal of literature, especially Russian literature (in Russian). Online I chanced to meet **Elena Titova,** resident of Berdsk a town 25-miles south of Novosibirsk in central Siberia. Elena had certainly read Tolstoy, Pushkin and all other great Russian novelists and poets. Half the girls in Russia are named Natasha (*War and Peace)* or Tatiana *(Eugene Onegin).* The Soviet regime was scrupulous in publishing all major Russian authors regardless of their political persuasion at the time of writing. I bought a 1953 two-volume illustrated edition of *War and Peace,* as high-end as they could manage, published by direct order of Stalin to commemorate Tolstoy's anniversary. If you have not come under the spell of Russian romantic/fatalistic love and sacrifice by age 15 years you are not likely to. It's not much compatible with contemporary Western attitudes. The French have a bit of the Russian love/loss in them, although the French have more irony whereas the Russians have more fatalism. I read the Constance Barnett translation of War and Peace when I was 12-years old, so I was early inoculated, only much later to read it in the original Russian.

Elena Titova

Elena and I shared recent tragedy and loss. I had lost the love of my life two years before and she had suffered a disappointed 'love' with the bum who fucked and abused her. She wrote often that I was the last love she would have. If I didn't prove real, she would abandon all hope of love in her life and so on… Misery does love company and can provide a strong bond absent other motive. Which placed a rather one-sided burden on me in that she would determine what standard to apply when deciding whether I lived up to expectations. The feeling that she was every minute 'testing' me to that undisclosed standard pervaded our relationship in person and threw me off my game. More of that later.

Elena did not have a computer at home, she used one at work to write to me. No weekend messages possible. Our correspondence was long and bountiful, sometimes twice a day. She was brilliant, sensitive, educated, soulful, articulate. She disclaimed any resemblance to a *'photo model' or* 'empty headed doll'. Rather she said she was somewhere between *a clam and Aphrodite*, nice Classical touch. She had to confess she was not a contemporary lady, much preferring the old days. *'I wish I had been born a century ago, and regret the misfortune of being born in our dangerous and corrupt era.'* We got our parameters straight and I tended to agree with her in principle although I did not detest cities or dining in fine restaurants to the degree she did. Here is her beautiful and confiding second email to me. It gives some idea of the depth and interest of our correspondence. (I did not have Cyrillic alphabet on my computer so we both wrote in transliterated (Latin alphabet) Russian, which I translate into English.)

Thursday, September 28, 2006. 1:15 AM
I think of you. Don't cry my dear Chris. We are not lost in our vile and corrupt world. We have found one another, and that is marvelous! We are friends and understand each other perfectly. Notwithstanding we are thousands of kilometers apart, that does not separate my thoughts about you. Of course, I regret that my daughter has no father, but that is better than having a drunkard for a father. My husband was 5 years younger than I. We lived together 4 years. I was everything to him: mother, nanny, lover. But he did not value that and betrayed and destroyed my love. When Irina was born he drank even more, was jealous of my love for Irina, and cheated on me. He played cards and lost everything: money, car, my new fur coat. He brought me only bitterness. When Irina was 7 months old, I left him and returned to live with my parents. He drank for 2 more years and then pulled himself together. He asked to be taken back, but I felt no love for him any longer, only contempt. I thought I was through with love forever, but now I feel differently. I now see that life just begins at 40. In general I am very strict with myself and with those I love. I try to live with a clear conscience so I have no shame or regrets about whatever happens. Sex is not important in my life, although far from being a matter of indifference. For 12 years before I married, I was never with a man because I did not want a casual relationship without love. All my life I waited to find an intelligent man, much older than I--a friend, helpmate, sympathetic, with whom I would be

interested to go through life. But by some irony of fate I was a prime idiot--my husband for reasons I do not fully understand, was able to seduce me. That was probably God's way of punishing me for my pride. Dear Chris, I am so happy that I can converse with you and entrust my deepest thoughts to you. Our friendship is only by email, but I believe it can grow stronger. Perhaps, at this moment, a true love is born between us, that like a tree will put out roots and grow ever stronger and stronger. My thoughts are with you…
Elena

She said she was amazed at how well I could write and understand Russian and how I resembled her father:

To master Russian so well you would have to live in Russia at least a year. Have you lived in Russia? I love your face. You strikingly resemble my father. He too has a moustache, is slim, and as you, is almost totally 'foxy'. Chris, I am now so happy that I have another marvelous friend. That's YOU! I don't feel alone now and forgotten by everyone. I now have a distant, soulful, understanding friend, for whom I am indispensable, it is magical that we, coming from different worlds, found each other, and our lives have shared meaning and happiness and that happiness will never be forgotten.

By now I am completely in love and mesmerized by this beautiful, articulate, interesting, passionate person. Our letters are long, involved, confessional, confiding, intimate and loving. It's like a Russian novel and as I reread them I am amazed at their beauty and meaning and ultimate tragedy, I love her still. Time neither diminishes nor erases the marvel of Elena. But back to business. Our correspondence was deeply confessional. She told about her feelings, thoughts, anxieties, dreams, delusions. We gradually wove a complex web of interchanged thoughts and feelings making us more intimate than is possible face to face because one rarely talks so reflectively and at such length in person about the subjects we discussed. Long correspondence is the most intricate explicit and inclusive form of love making. It is the best prelude to a lasting relationship and the most devastating reminder of an unhappy ending. Elena came out of the shell she had surrounded herself with in defense disillusion and despair. She opened more and more as our correspondence continued.

October 4, 2006:
Now is the best time in the World. I no longer want to be alone night and day. Live without tenderness, without love, without hugs and kisses, without a protector and a man's shoulder to lean on. I see that a woman's happiness is to be with a loving caring husband. If I will be your wife I would every evening listen attentively for your footsteps and greet you, tired and hungry from work, prepare a delicious meal for you as you tell me about your day at work, and later look fondly at you as you help the children with their homework and lightly scold them for any mistakes.....hahaha! How marvelous to go to bed and wake up with you, my lover, and joke and laugh together, go out for all to see our happiness. All my life I waited for my 'prince'. I think everyone deserves happiness, but not everyone can find or perceive it. People are prevented by fear, distrust, and past mistakes. Unfortunately, 'princes' exist only in story books. But I realized recently that dreams and happiness are something one has to accomplish oneself. I long ago became disillusioned about Russian men--who don't deserve to be called 'men'. They always turn out to be boorish, drunkards, irresponsible, not compassionate, inclined to betrayal and perfidy. I am not superstitious but lately I have become interested in astrology. Your sign is Aquarius which I love. I am Leo, and Leo and Aquarius rarely break off their relationship. Irina is also Aquarius so I can show up as a twinkle between both of you stars…hahaha! With warm and tender feelings for you.
Lena

This was the ninth day of our correspondence, which continued to 22 November when I departed for Russia. Forty-seven more days! Sometimes two messages a day, and with increasing intensity because from now on it was love Russian style! A headlong romantic gallop in words. Confronting the greatest threat of all to love: Boredom!

Beaumarchais in his play *Barber of Seville* has Rosina say: *L'amant n'est pas dûre sur les productions de l'amour,* but there are limits. Face to face, a stud with big hair, big teeth, OK looks and a fat cock has the advantage. There is little a smaller, quieter, more thoughtful guy can do to compete. But at a distance, through correspondence, he can shine. IQ matters. Even the most benighted girl can get weary of repeated phrases, initially thrilling because they convey conviction, devotion. Suppose over two months a message every day says: *I love you.* Suppose also for variety the moron adds one more *I love you*, such that the last message contains sixty of them. A girl has to interpolate different meanings and nuances for each. Beyond ten it gets tiresome. Quantity never makes up for lack of quality. For an intelligent lady well-educated and leading an examined life such trivial expression early becomes disqualifying. Elena is intelligent, well-read certainly in Russian, sensitive, hyper alert to fakery and inattention. She is very beautiful, has very exalted views of love and marriage and has wounds to remind her of the perfidy most likely to ruin any commitment she makes. She is skeptical, wary, disillusioned, which makes her the perfect target for the perfidy she almost reflexively anticipates. She is so consciously armed to prevent it that she is incapable of recognizing it before it is too late (viz. her failed marriage).

I have always loved complication, ambiguity (I like the endless convolutions of Henry James' paragraphs) and found it quadratically with Elena. Fortunately, I am a word guy, not a numbers guy. I love algebra and the quantitative precision of number but I was early mesmerized by vocabulary, the descriptive/expressive power of words, probably because there was so much dreadful in my family life that I needed words to shape my understanding of the emotional havoc that surrounded me. One cannot discuss at length subjects that do not interest one. Even if obsessed with a subject one requires introspection and vocabulary to distinguish and weigh the merits and complications. In other words, without a great deal of internal cogitation one is not prepared to correspond in depth about love, marriage, betrayal, all favorite subjects of meditation and judgment of Elena.

First, I need to 'do the math' as it were of who Elena and I were at the time. Elena was 44 years old, had a daughter Irina 4-years old, was permanently separated from her dissolute paramour, lived with her parents, relatively poor but surviving pensioners, with a married sister nearby and a brother somewhere in Siberia. She hadn't *'been with a man'* in any capacity for twelve years before she 'married', in that she officially 'registered' the guy as Irina's father. That leaves a lot of ground for speculation. If she moved in with him around 38-years old, she was twenty-six when the last experience of 'being with a man' occurred. She said she had an *amour fou* with Irina's father and delivered Irina when she was 40-years old. Maybe the reproductive clock set off an alarm and she desperately wanted to be a mother, hence the abandon. We are not talking about a deceived teenager. I turn up on Russian Love Match website that she must have joined, perhaps a considerable time before. Given her mistrust of man in hand there must have been some impulse that drove her to seek one in the bush. She had visited a friend in Germany, met a guy who wanted to marry but it didn't work out. Germany was the only country she admired and wanted to move to because as T. E. Lawrence said of Arabia: *It's clean.* She was conflicted, maybe even horny, and I walked into her inner theater to play a leading role.

Which comes to me. I was 68 years old in 2006. For decades I thought I was 5'10" until my father in law measured me in 2001 at 5'8". I weighed 140 pounds. In other words, small, slender and as Elena said 'foxy'. I looked very Anglo-Saxon, a losing proposition in the USA but a winner abroad. So many English and Hollywood anglos (Errol Flynn, William Powell, Cary Grant) had paved the way into the hearts of Russian and other foreign women that much seductive groundwork had already been done. I am half Swede so signs of age come slowly. I appeared to be 10- to 15-years younger on a good day, even in my 40's.

I am an autodidact, asocial but extremely easy in company, speak well and try to engage other people, have charm and presence as needed, am tenacious and a fighter but look peaceable and non-confrontational. I am spiritual, emotional, sensitive, intellectual and romantic, often amoral where sex is concerned. (A view from the inside, likely not what others' see from the outside.) I truly sought love and marriage in all relationships, but would cut and print the 'take' when that outcome was unlikely. I am not a sexual athlete or a stud but I have been told I am a 'great lover' by a practiced lady who has many occasions on which to base qualifications for that title. I am not that confident of my overall appeal but have enjoyed some very beautiful and intelligent company so I am grateful about the gifts I have received. In most cases I was prepared to marry, wanted to marry, and would have married if they agreed. I can't include our entire correspondence here, but a number of excerpts from Elena's emails will convey the intensity and passion aroused, expressed and experienced on both sides.

October 2006:

Chris, you love me truly? I love you even more. With each of your letters I sink deeper into that abyss of love. I don't sleep at night always thinking about you, about me, about us together. I love you so much. I yearn for you, think of you constantly even when working and sleeping. When I read your letters, I hear your voice, see your smile, feel your breath. You are master of my feelings. You bewitch me. I love you, I love you forever. You have bought tickets? What decisiveness! That means no longer hesitate. Only forward! I do not have my own small corner where I can invite you to stay with me, I am obliged to look for another's dirty smelly uncomfortable and furnished by alien tastes 'apartment'. I am ashamed of my humiliating position. All my life I have been dependent on someone, and so it turns out I am not master of myself or my own life!! All the meaning of my life is to write you and read letters from you and in that way be closer to you my dear Chris. I, like you, feel this is my last chance at happiness. I hate my weak character, my dependence on others who cultivated in me over many years dependence and submission. I always comply with others' wishes and beliefs. So I am willing to lock myself up in the 'monastery' and act against my will just to keep the favor and respect of people close to me. I am without will power and without rights. Living is very hard for me, dear Chris. I have seen little good in life and so I do not value my life. I never expect anything and never believe in my 'Lucky Star'. The stars have not yet smiled on me. You are the only one, who with your words tries to bring happiness back into my life. Every day I love you more and more strongly and never imagine how I could live without you. Our meeting is either God's gift to me or his punishment. And I am ready for this! Dear Chris, I can with one glance tell what someone thinks of me, and whether I can have some relationship with him in future. My intuition has never deceived me. But I have at times betrayed my intuition and not always listened to what it had to tell me. And I fear that this time I may make the same mistake again and betray her.... because I do not want to lose you. Because I love you! And because I believe that a new life begins for me now. And that will be a real life. Because it will be OUR life.

Your Elena

I had tickets for Aeroflot flight 327, 23 November 2006, Los Angeles to Moscow, with a follow through flight Moscow to Novosibirsk November 25. I planned a stopover in Moscow to see the city and compose myself for the big debut. Any perspicacious reader of her messages will have observed certain shadows in the otherwise idyllic romance unfolding. I will not address them or even identify them in case they escaped your attention and would deprive you of the surprises ahead. Her last message on November 22 was encouraging, everything verbal and emotional choreographed and scripted. If only I can remember my lines!

We meet soon--I repeat that like a prayer. I know you are on your way to me, my dear Chris. My thoughts are only of you. I will wait for you, friend of my life, and will have everything, the charm of first meeting, smiles, gentle hands and tears in the eyes. I will see you and forget about fatigue and misery. My soul will enjoy a new spring...and you will be beside me.

You are my love, my light, my star! Come quickly to me, to everything that calls itself LIFE!!
Your waiting Elena.

The Los Angeles to Moscow flight took off at 4:15 PM. I was seated mid-ship. Rather comfortable interior, belying all the putdowns of Aeroflot travel. The flight was smooth, November weather calm all the way to the east coast. Storms over the Atlantic did not appear to be a risk. Mid-Atlantic, heavy rain/thunder/lightning created drama outside but the pilot assured us in Russian and English that there was no problem. We bounced around a bit. Lightning seemed to be targeting my window. Then one hit the left wing engine. It began to flame out. The controls became irregular. The pilot ordered everyone to drop oxygen masks. The plane lurched down, then sideways, then up, then seemed to plummet while we were thrown side to side in hopeless panic. A last vision of loveliness appeared before me, Elena, smiling, saying 'I love you', as the plane plunged into the black Atlantic and eternal night.

Report of the crash mid-Atlantic reached the US almost immediately. Within hours, Moscow news also reported the crash. Elena was at home in Berdsk watching TV with her parents when a news broadcast announced that Aeroflot flight 327 from Los Angeles had crashed. She immediately burst into tears, trembling. Her parents had no idea about me, that I was expected in Berdsk on the 25th. Elena had told them nothing. She went to her room, lay on the bed, and sobbed uncontrollably. Next day were reports--no survivors. Eventually debris from the plane was recovered by helicopters from ships sent to the crash area. Among the debris was a water tight satchel, mine, with a letter to Elena just in case.

Elena my beloved!! I will soon be with you. If for any reason I cannot reach you, I write this letter to tell you my love is now and forever. I will always be with you. I will always love you. I will always remember.
Chris

By a circuitous series of officials and agents this letter was delivered to Elena two weeks later. Her parents wondered why she wore black since the crash. Reading the letter confirmed our timeless love, and she wore black ever after as a sign of our implacable love known to no one, and devotion to my memory. So fitting and tragic an end to the 19th Century romantic story of our love and letters.

That is how things should have turned out. This is how they did.

Getting a visa to enter Russia is a major project, consistent with the paranoid, hermetic, defensive tradition of Russian Slavs. If you know their history you understand why. They were conquered circa 800 AD by Swedish Vikings who set up the Kievan Empire in the eponymous city. They were conquered again circa 1300 AD by Genghis Khan and his Mongol Hordes who took goods and slaves as tribute for 300 years. Then by Poles, Lithuanians, Teutonic Knights, Napoleon and finally by Hitler. Worse, they have always been ruled by bureaucrats: Tsarist, Stalinist, Federal. Everyone is watched and controlled on the principle that everything is forbidden that is not expressly permitted. Russians have always had internal passports, citizens are not allowed to travel within Russia without a government visa that requires a written statement of justification for such travel, destination, exact dates of departure and return, accommodations, means of travel to and from, and proof of adequate funds for the trip. Almost as bad as getting a visa into the country. A Russia travel agency in San Francisco arranged tickets and visa, which required sending my passport to Moscow!! The Foreign Ministry would issue the visa only for the precise dates of arrival and departure, introducing further uncertainty in an already uncertain and inflexible enterprise of travel half way around the World. Maybe my Aeroflot reservations expedited the process. I doubted I would ever see my passport again, but within a week all was returned, tickets, passport, visa, and I got geared up for Siberia.

The first leg of my trip was to Los Angeles where I stayed one night and hooked up with my sister's son Patrick, aspiring actor, an occupation self-attributed by half the population. LA was 101 degrees F, Siberia was 5 degrees F. I had to carry an LL Bean goose-down parka to LA airport where stacks of Russians were preparing to board the same flight. I met two Romanov's from Moscow who traded precious gems. One said Russia would lose Siberia within 25 years. No people and 1.4 billion Chinese who claimed it was stolen from them, to say nothing that they were eager for land/oil/minerals/water. He thought I was 'sly'. Asked: *'Why go to Russia in Winter?'* I said I wanted to see the Russian Winter I read about in Tolstoy/Pushkin/Turgenev. We boarded the plane and after a very smooth flight and exactly on time we arrived at Sheremetevo International Airport Terminal No. 1 in Moscow.

I planned to stay in Moscow two days. I had reserved a room at the Mandarin Hotel, taxi from and to the airport for the flight to Novosibirsk, and a guided tour of Moscow for the following day. I was groggy after the 14-hour flight. I got through customs and went to the reception area. An ***Intourist*** agent was supposed to welcome me, carrying a sign with my name. No agent, no sign. I was milling around concerned, tired, and uncertain when a frowning stocky guy who looked like a KGB hit man approached me. (Everyone in Russia frowns, a habit of centuries to discourage contact or notice.) He was a taxi manager. He asked if I needed a ride downtown. I told him Intourist was supposed to meet me with tickets and a taxi downtown. Unexpectedly he cordially offered to take me to the Intourist desk. They told me the agent was now waiting for me at the reception area. The taxi manager said to contact him if things didn't work out. Very friendly and reassuring. Can't tell the book by its cover sort of thing. I did find the Intourist agent who took me to my reserved taxi.

Adding to my gradual reassurance that Russia wasn't a total criminal conspiracy assigned to fleece me, the taxi driver said he liked to watch the Chicago Bears football games on Russian TV. His daughter was learning English and studying for a career in business. Very friendly. Loved America! No English, so I spoke Russian. We got to the Mandarin Hotel, quite elegant, and after the usual desk clerk *pro forma* delay in finding my reservation, I received my key and a porter took me to the elevator. On each floor is a 'concierge' who checks arrival and departure of tenants. I joked a lot with her, even saying I was an American spy, but not to worry. She laughed uncertainly and reached for the phone as got on the elevator to go to the BIZNEZ room where computers were available. I emailed Elena, expressed urgent love, and went to dinner in the hotel restaurant. Quite decent menu, well cooked meal, and personable service from what appeared to be recent High School graduates, mostly girls. I took a quick walk around the block after dinner and then went to bed. My movements were observed and reported (to whom?) at every location. About 10-minutes back in my room a call came. Pleasant voice in English with thick Russian accent: *Would you like a sexual massage?* No thanks, but thanks for the offer. Upscale hotels in Russia and many in China have resident or itinerant sex workers available for clients. I saw the lady next morning having breakfast.

I had booked an Intourist tour of Moscow. Two guys, very agreeable, English speaking, took me to the Peter/Paul Cathedral, Kremlin, other sites. Moscow is very attractive, pointy Cathedral onion domes painted bright colors like Easter eggs, wide avenues, Red Square (from the bricks, not the politics), the equally bricky Kremlin not very sinister looking despite the high walls, and of course the Lenin Mausoleum, with a frowning bronze bust of Stalin (demoted and removed from his bedmate) and busts of other Soviet era heroes including the American John Reed aligned in a row behind. Where building construction or restoration was under way they mounted in front very attractive photo billboards of the finished version to conceal work in progress. I liked Moscow but it was a bit soiled by snow, slush and impacted traffic.

Afternoon of 25 November I went to Sheremetova II, the domestic flight airport, and the epic meeting with Elena. Moscow-Novosibirsk flight is about five hours, comparable to Washington DC-San Francisco. I got into Novosibirsk about 7:30 PM. It was cold, 3 degrees F. It was dark. Daylight in the middle of Siberia runs 8:30 AM to 4:30 PM. I was alone. I had no cell phone (the I-phone had not been invented yet). I had no reservations, only whatever Elena had arranged. I entered the reception area expecting to find the love of my life, not entirely sure what that might amount to however. No one. I looked left, right. After fifteen minutes I was getting a bit panicky. I checked before leaving San Francisco on hotel reservations in Novosibirsk and every hotel was booked, no vacancies. I looked at the taxi drivers soliciting fares (they looked like they would kill for a ruble) and I began to calculate whether at this late hour I could just return to Moscow and later California and forget the whole thing. I was not in the best mood, after twenty minutes truly concerned whether I would have to sleep on a bench in the airport, assuming I could get away with that. I walked around the entire reception area again, and returned to my entry point.

Standing there as if dropped by helicopter was an erect not to say stiff lady staring blankly in the direction of arrivals. She was tall and slender, wore 3-inch high heel boots, a form-fitting parka, no hat, her hair tied up in a bun. I approached, the resemblance to photos sufficient to justify such a move. 'Elena?' She turned and we had our first eye contact. I was smiling, she wasn't. Given the importance of 'eyes' in romance, love at first sight and that sort of thing, our first contact kindled little expression or emotion. Almost a flat tire metaphorically speaking. No love at first sight, no lust, no amorous impulse, no nothing. No electricity, not even a spark. I attributed this to the late hour, my fatigue, her lateness, the cold dreary airport reception area. She was expressionless, attractive enough but without any trace of enthusiasm, anticipation, or welcome.

She asked: *'Is anything wrong?'* I replied much too emphatically, 'NO!', which just reinforced the suspicion that something was. I recited such excuses as long flight, long travel, tired. I exuded as much feeling and enthusiasm as I could and kept smiling, like pumping air into a punctured tire. It took several minutes before we got into a rhythm of minor questions: *How was the flight? Is it far to Berdsk? Great to meet you!* The sort of polite chat you might have with a total stranger while waiting in line for a taxi. We left the airport and walked about half a mile through slush and snow in miserable cold semi-silence, she advancing energetically on her 3-inch stilts and I straggling behind trudging exhausted through the unyielding snow dragging my 300-pound suitcase behind. We got to the bus stop and by some miracle a bus arrived, something I doubted would happen before 5 AM. On the bus we got a bit more conversational, I relaxed, and began an easy bantering with her. I asked about the apartment, Berdsk, how she survives in this weather. Anything to evoke response assuming the practice of question and reply would generate energy for a more spontaneous exchange. After about twenty-five minutes we arrived at the stop in Berdsk and walked 100-yards across a park through even more snow to the Krushchev-era dreary cement dungeon/apartment building. She opened the door and we walked up concrete stairs one flight to the furnished apartment. It was warm, the bathroom and kitchen were modernized and given the alternatives this late at night it looked like the Mark Hopkins. We got a bit more friendly. She remarked that I wasn't as tall as she expected and that my hair was rather white. I refrained from corresponding anatomical comparisons. She looked good, but cold, not just thermally speaking. She said there was food in the refrigerator. She had to go home now, her daughter needs her, but she would return in the morning around 9 AM to fix breakfast. I said that would be great. Clearly a decline in eloquence as between writing letters and carrying on conversation (if you could call it that) was inevitable. Two months of love, tears, doubt, confession, passion, for this?

So there I was in the middle of Siberia without a cell phone, in questionable straits, with a bland not to say discouraging encounter and no Idea what to do next. Elena showed up the next morning much changed. We laughed and chatted and she fixed some eggs and toast. I got my juices flowing and my affection restored to nearly epistolary level. I got up while she was putting out the cutlery, went up to her and hugged her. No major sexual assault, just an affectionate reinforcement of our weeks of devotion and pledges of love. This brought on a storm of surprising, unexpected, even shocking passion, quite contrary to the nearly spiritual tone of our online correspondence. She grabbed my arm, dragged me to the sitting room bed/sofa, began ripping off her clothes with breaks to help me divest my own, in a wild uncontrollable urge to fuck. We were both naked, she lay down on the bed/sofa. I got on top, when suddenly she said 'Давай', rolled over on top of me and inserted my cock in her insatiable pussy. She pumped away on top of me, eyes shut, mouth open, groaning and sighing loudly, pumping her pelvis wildly, trying to get me inside her as far as possible.

She was completely uninhibited and by deduction from such purposeful dispatch, presumably well and often experienced in the *modus operandi* she preferred for our encounter. It crossed my mind that she might be nymphomanic, given the rigid features and defensive posture, the guarded persona I saw at the airport, typical of such women who cannot resist, in fact desperately want to fuck, but don't want that to appear publicly. This Elena was not drifting in the clouds, admiring the stars, seeking the elevated sphere of pure and devoted love. She wanted and loved having a cock inside her, she stroked and stirred energetically, hysterically, groaning and saying *Да Да Да!* while I provided the tools needed for her self-absorbed project, in which I observed rather than participated. It was too much, too impersonal, ultimately what anyone else could provide no longer has any intimate and loving or even lustful sustaining appeal. Even at the technical level a man needs some foreplay, warm up, pump prime, even if short prequel to the main course. I enjoyed watching her, eyes closed, mouth open, groaning, leaning back to thrust her pussy forward, getting me in as deep as possible, pushing and rotating, a kind of frenzy, something I once imagined I wished, but somehow felt had nothing to do with me. She was on her own trip and where she started and where she ended, I was nowhere in sight.

.

After, I took a shower and then she followed. We crossed in the hallway and she smiled and said in English: '*I could eat you up!*' I said: '*Me too!*' Another surprising glimpse into her store of experience and even English sexual lingo. Things were looking up. She was on leave, but for propriety stayed at home, daily arriving around 9:30 AM and leaving around 9:30 PM to be safe from the 'hooligans' who tended to emerge at that time of night. I supposed she had informed her parents of my arrival and our intentions. I also supposed every night she gave them some account of our day together. Days were easy. Breakfast. Lots of talk about her predicament, misery, physical decline. '*My breasts are shrunken/I am worn out from work and poverty/I feel trapped living at home, never independent*' and so on. I got to really like her. I told her she was beautiful, she was the most important thing--a mother. I told her I wanted to marry her. I told her almost anything positive to offset the self-defeating remarks about herself.

We would walk in the park, shop in the local supermarket, where about three entire rows of shelves on both sides were dedicated to vodka in ½ pint, pint, fifth and gallon jugs. In the park, men would carry flasks and take a swig from time to time. We went to a currency exchange and I got $1200 to pay rent for our apartment. We shopped at a department store, looked at furniture, she eyeing my reaction to the rather tacky high-priced beds, chairs, tables, checking for condescension, which I concealed as best I could. I looked at toys for Irina. She discouraged any purchases, although I told her I would like to meet her daughter, a loveable cute and allegedly introverted beauty. I wanted to meet Irina but she kept putting it off. I figured if I met.

281

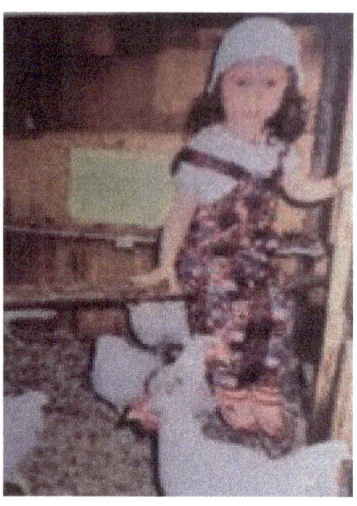

Irina we would become great pals and that would win Elena over to a more positive outcome to our improbable encounter in the middle of frozen Siberia. I knew I would love Irina, so cute, engaging, and introverted, just my type. But her parents warned Elena about Westerners abducting, kidnapping, raping unsuspecting women and abduction and sale of young children to European hospitals for organ harvesting. (In a Russian comedy film titled *Poor Liz,* villagers mentioned a TV documentary on abduction of Russian children for organ harvest when speculating on the intentions of a Canadian visitor courting the heroine.) They frightened Elena into keeping Irina safe at home. She said she always followed her parents' advice. No exceptions here. Her mother, father and grandmother constantly warned her that my eagerness to meet Irina proved my diabolical intentions. Eventually she believed I was after Irina for sale to organ harvesters. They obviously were mounting a campaign to undermine this latest and most threatening challenge to her continued submission.

Evenings we watched Russian movies and news on a black and white TV. She liked Soviet era films about young people enjoying holidays at Soviet summer camps: fishing, bonfires, songs, chaste amorous touching and glances. We sat on the bed/sofa. I chatted about how nice the Soviet era was. I held her close but she was averse to much physical contact. She didn't like hugging, caressing, or kissing. Almost autistic in this respect. Apparently all the fucking she could manage was expended on our first encounter. I arrived on a Thursday. By the following Wednesday I had proposed marriage and been refused. She said it was not working. I said I regretted that. As a parting gift I wrote her a check for $1000 just as a gift for the visit. I packed, she told me where the bus stop was, accompanied me there. I took the bus to the nearest hotel where an Aeroflot ticket office was presumably. They booked flights but did not do changes, so I had to move on to Novosibirsk.

I got a taxi. He was a jolly born-again Christian, liked America, and we chatted the whole way. He went out of his way to be helpful, finally dropping me off at the Aeroflot office. He said he would wait and take me to the airport. The clerk was most cooperative, changed my Moscow-LA flight to two days ahead, and suggested I could stay at a local hotel and take the Novosibirsk-Moscow fight day after tomorrow. I thanked her profusely (all this in Russian) and said I should leave for Moscow today. So off to the airport where the customs lady detected something metal in my suitcase. Smiling and joking I said she could look the whole mess over. We found the culprit, my moustache electric razor, and both laughed. I was getting the amiable side of Russia on my way out.

I finally got on the plane to Moscow, arriving 6 PM. This was the domestic flight airport an entirely different animal from the international flight airport. No courtesy, no attempt to make your experience agreeable, and every attempt to rip off the stranded refugee. I see why Elena was so concerned about local travel. These guys would as soon shoot me as fart. I did take a taxi (at larcenous rate) to the Mandarin Hotel on the chance of getting a room, but they held no favor for my earlier visit. After nearly an hour they said they had no rooms. I went out into the Moscow night and tried a few adjacent hotels, all booked up,

Finally, I took a taxi to Sheremetova International. They had a room for two nights, $350 per. Lovely. The room was well appointed and I was grateful for being nearer the flight rather than in Moscow. The hotel restaurant was very good and breakfast was included in the punitive room fee. I could lounge around comfortably for the remaining hours in Russia. On the second day I left Moscow for Los Angeles. Never to return! But the story didn't end there. I wrote Elena to tell of my regrets that it didn't go as planned (understatement) and that I did love her and hoped possibly we could start again in a more realistic and sensible fashion. Apparently the organ gatherer interpretation of my motives had been reinvigorated in her family post mortem discussions.

29 November 11:17 pm
Epilogue Hello Chris,
If you read this email, I feel content that we separated. You tried very hard to be lovable, but you were poorly suited to playing that role. You brought eagerness and needless self-confidence. I would like to give you some advice for the future. If you want to again play the role of suitor, play the role much better and conscientiously, so your potential spouse will believe you and not think you are some dangerous maniac or organ tracker occupied with selling children for organ transplant. Nevertheless, I am genuinely sorry for your next victim. Now I know there is a God on this earth. He is my God! He saved me from you. And your God, the Devil, betrayed you this time so you couldn't carry out your evil plan. And you lost your despicable game. I told you it was sufficient for me to simply look at a person in order to know him. I knew you three days, but I knew you well. And now I know what love American style is worth. I am personally persuaded how awful and base Americans are. But you said goodbye to me. Not everything is open to sell or buy. There are things much more valuable than money. Honor, integrity, uprightness, all of which you lack entirely. I am sorry for you. Your blighted inheritance from your parents has corrupted your soul, made it black and evil and savage. You are incapable of understanding the true Russian soul, with its love and worthiness. You Americans will never break the will of the

Russian people. Even if we have to live alone, real Russians, Russia will live!!
Only with the death of the last Russian will Russia perish!!!
Elena

Persuaded by her parents that I was trolling for children's body parts (among which her daughter's) and ascribing the corresponding moral decadence of such a cad to yours truly, plus a nationalist anti-American riff, Elena confirmed my supposition regarding the influence of her mother and father. Such outrage on supposed but false assumptions fit well with the paranoid cast of Russians and claims of superiority based on the 'Great Russian Soul', a subject of legend and self-congratulation throughout the population. It is exemplified by Maria Bolkonsky in War and Peace, who gives food to wandering 'true believers' exiled from society by the government and church administration for retaining the traditional method of crossing themselves with two fingers instead of three imposed by a Synod in 1695 or thereabouts. A form of giving the middle finger to authority unfortunately with sometimes fatal consequences (e.g., the burning of their church with parishioners inside at the end of the opera *Khovashchina)*. More to the point, it shows the minute and seemingly insignificant concern with formal details of genuflection unrelated to more substantial doctrinal and spiritual concerns. Russians, unable to organize their society for worldly success, lay claim to a moral ascendance based on their temporal suffering and misery that confirms their superior spiritual quality compared to for example, me and others in the West. I replied with my own interpretation of the catastrophe, and her reply to my reply extended the reversal in epistolatory tone that preceded our first meeting.

December 3, 2006 9:17 pm The last
Hello Chris
My surprise knows no bounds!! You still have the gall to write me and swear your love for me! I can't find words to express my indignation!!! You will say anything to justify yourself but I draw my conclusions based on my observations and facts. I noticed that you were more interested in Irina

than in me. That made me suspicious even during our correspondence. You also displayed gross ingratitude when you abruptly left Berdsk. You made no effort to defend yourself, or dispel my doubts about you. It was as if you agreed with everything I accused you of. You spent a fortune on the trip and left with nothing in return. And that also seemed strange to me. It looked like a failed business deal that meant nothing to you and that you could do again with anyone else. When you so easily left me I was in shock. But not because you gave me a phony $1000 check (you knew that perfectly well), but because you abruptly dropped your love and me. It seems you not only gave me a phony check, you brought me false feelings. In a word, everything looks completely contemptible. And I am happy that everything ended for the best. I see no sense in our further correspondence. Anyone who loses my trust is forever out of my favor. You are for me a 'dark horse' and I will never again take risks or trust you. And after all, it is very sad that it turned out this way. I truly believed you and thought of you as the uniquely wonderful man of my life. God, how I am punished for my naivety and stupidity! It is a real lesson for me. I learned that LOVE is a land of deception and everyone living there is pretender and deceiver. And I never again want to submit to such an experience. With that our lives take different paths. Seek another lover. I will devote myself to the one person who loves me, my daughter. I need no one else. Enough disillusionment!!! And finally! You killed my love. And to love again is impossible. Goodbye forever. I have said too much already.
Elena

Love it! I always enjoy turmoil. And the reasons for her rejection seem to have been: 1) I had designs on Irina, even evident in our antecedent correspondence. 2) I was a corrupt organ hunter of the worst kind. 3) I did not truly love her and dropped her without care or concern. 4) I gave her what I knew to be a worthless check for $1000. None of which was true, but the constant negative reinforcement and undermining by her parents allowed for the most dire and unflattering interpretation of her 'observations and facts'. Her father told her the check was phony because it did not have watermarks. She believed him. So why didn't they just tear it up? It was clear evidence of my perfidy. The local bank could not cash it or process it internationally. She would have to go to Novosibirsk to a national bank capable of such a transaction. The father was obviously a loser from a long line of welfare-state losers who never attempted anything and curled up in a defensive pit of self-pity and fear in which he managed to keep Elena. But she kept the check and eventually traveled to Novosibirsk. The bank said it was entirely valid and they would process it through the international banking system SWIFT. Within weeks she had the money!

Which presented a moral dilemma. If they were wrong about something so tangible and beneficial as $1000, where they equally wrong about the other nonsense so carefully contrived and cultivated to divert Elena from a real prospect? If she wanted one, which was by now doubtful. I interpreted her behavior as possibly related to nymphomania, a bit crude, but her rigidity combine with her violent uncontrollable sexual performance opened the possibility. In any case the following messages expand this line of inquiry and resolved the matter of the check.

December 7 11:39 pm
The very last
Dear Chris [Back to Dear!]
You convert everything to sex. I didn't want to touch on that subject because it is very delicate, but you yourself brought it up. You do me the honor of describing me as a nymphomaniac. I have an entirely different opinion. I am a rather frigid woman, not the hypersexual type you consider me to be. I do not want to dispraise your male self-esteem so I will not offer my opinion of you. I will disillusion you if I talk about myself. I can live entirely without sex. I know that sex is more important to men than to women. And women must sometimes submit to male desires against their own preferences in order not to lose his 'love'. Surely you know that. As many times before, I sought something different in my relationship with you and thought I had found a loving heart; spiritual love would be more desirable to me than sexual lust. You failed to understand me. What happened between us was normal and

I was happy to give you pleasure. No offense intended. I found it strange that you expressed your dissatisfaction. I did not satisfy you. And that is very important for you. Again, you are wrong about the men I have been with. I don't intend to make any confessions. You are not a priest. I will say one thing, every person thinks in proportion to his depravity. If you lead a disorderly sex life, you should not assume others do the same. If you do not meet respectable ladies, you shouldn't assume such women do not exist. Let's not slander each other. Let's part like intelligent people. We know each other well enough to know we are not suited to each other. Why waste words? I wish you success and hope you find your special person who will be worthy of your love. Be happy and please don't judge me harshly, if I offended you. Elena

December 8 11:53 pm
Forgive, goodbye
Dear Chris
I also want to part as friends. Some evil force interfered with our relationship and divided us. It was a delusion, absurd! Above all, I want to beg your pardon for accusing you of deceit. Your check turned out to be valid. The

bank in Novosibirsk told me so. Every bank in Berdsk told me the check was phony because it didn't have a watermark. They had never seen such a check. I even decided to throw it away, but reconsidered and decided to keep it as a memento of you. I went to Novosibirsk and was told the check is valid. But I must wait about two months to receive the money until they 'check it out'....ha ha ha, like the movie How to Steal a Million. Forgive me!! I will keep the money and later I will tell Irina who gave it to us. I am hurt that our relationship ended so stupidly. I concede, I was mistaken and my nerves were overwrought. But you also were to blame. You didn't even try to change the situation, show me that I was wrong. You simply packed and left...as if to another city. Up to the last minute I waited for you to stay. An hour after you left I ran after you. But the hotel Golden Valley Hotel told me that you did not check in. I then concluded that you had gone directly to the airport, so I returned home. Now we are again on different continents. We parted and life goes on as before. That means 'God is satisfied' as my granny always used to say. You did not fight for me and Irina. We are not 'done for'. We are like everyone. We are not the only ones with problems. And we will somehow survive. I have a brother and a sister. And I will never go to America, not for a million dollars. I am afraid of America, and of you in America. I was born here and I will stay here. As a remote possibility, if I meet a good man, I might move to Germany. But that is a future prospect. Goodbye dear Chris. After all, there was much that was good between us. Let the good remain in our memories. And let's forget the bad parts. I truly wish you happiness. Understanding. God protect you!
Elena

In 2016, ten years after our adventure, I wrote Elena just to see how things went. Her daughter was 14-years old and doing well in school. Elena had grubby jobs and was eaking out a living. Her parents were still huddled in their Soviet era 'house' where Elena still lives. It was an agreeable exchange of messages, but her perhaps typically Russian fatalistic view of life remained under the comfort of habit and low expectations. Her final words were: *I trust nobody. I hope only for myself.*
Elena

CHINA

This period, 2007 to 2012 deserves a special heading, because China is such a significant part of my life. I have already reviewed the nine months in 1948 I lived in Qingdao. Sixty years later in 2008, Go-Ahead Tours in Boston offered 14-day tours to Beijing-Xian-Shanghai all flights and accommodations included. China Love Match (CLM) an online dating service offered access to ladies throughout China for $14 a month. I had studied Mandarin since 1996, and could speak enough to order food, check in to a hotel and exchange money. The Chinese were invariably welcoming and friendly unlike the Russians invariably opposite. My contacts with visiting Chinese delegations the last two years of my employment gave me somewhat current experience. I decided that for the first visit I should join a tour to reduce logistical demands to a minimum. Reserving rooms and air travel on my own was just too onerous and opaque to risk. I reserved a tour for February 2008, but Go-Ahead had to cancel for lack of takers. As I discovered later, winter in China is bitterly cold. Go-Ahead got me on a tour beginning in September 2008, well booked and definitely a better seasonal choice. My main job in 2007 and much of 2008 was arranging to meet ladies via CLM.

Chinese girls may be as calculating as others but they preserve a feminine charm that makes whatever they think they can get away with tolerable, even amusing, certainly not a matter for disillusion or phony resentment. I didn't much care if *'I love you'* or its equivalent was for real or not, given the extraordinary gifts on offer. A remarkable number of Chinese girls and women are petite, svelte, beautifully proportioned, foxy and irresistible, with warm smiles and gentle Asian grace. Every day I would see at least twenty ladies I would like to meet. And given an Anglo preference in China, they were forthcoming. Some would approach me! I know what you're thinking. Who cares? Most I corresponded with were independent and employed in good jobs, many divorced, an epidemic in China since women can now make careers and do not have to put up with the scrawny egoistic males they once had to marry. Many want to move to America or are at least willing to. Many, if they like what they see, want to try us out. Willing victim to their wiles and intentions, I began my extraordinary venture into the deer park of Chinese women.

Which poses a literary and aesthetic problem. One prefers to remain at a reasonably civilized and urbane level of discourse, especially with respect to women. The fact that China is a marvelous deer park of easy and delightful fulfillment makes relating the course of one's amorous encounters difficult unless salient features are left out of the account or rigorously curtailed. My much admired favorite author, Jane Austen, simply confined her narrative to the upper region of human faculties and endeavor, a Victorian imperative as well. The reintroduction of sex in English literature ran a gamut from Wilde to Joyce, whose Ulysses was banned and subject to final litigation as to whether literature that dealt candidly with sex was exempt from criminal charges of pornography. Nowadays there is only the issue of taste, not morality, in writing about such antics in what aspires to at least a modicum of literary merit for a sophisticated audience. To summarize, I found a delightful compliance and absence of Puritan resistance in all regions of China. CLM offered online contacts with women all over China. I have a stack of paper showing messages from more than three dozen women. I figured I should arrange contacts with ladies in the cities my tour would be visiting.

The tour rendezvoused at Beijing Airport and traveled to the hotel by bus. I don't like tours. Too much time with Americans dilutes local engagement. But for my first venture to China I figured arranging for prepaid accommodations, internal flights, and meals was better than trying to reserve by myself in unknown territory, Go-Ahead Tours did a remarkable job of coordinating arrivals from the East and West Coasts to Beijing within an hour of each other. Our guide, a very attractive personable girl of 25-years, distributed green Go-Ahead bags and neck tags with the company logo. Easy to identify and keep together the flock. We boarded a bus and headed for the Beijing hotel that would be our home for the next three days.

I prepared for the trip by corresponding with ladies in the three cities or nearby, arranging to meet upon arrival. For Beijing I arranged to meet Zhao Wenwen, who worked for a construction company in Tianjin, some 50-miles south of Beijing. She was divorced, had a daughter 19-years old preparing to attend the university. We didn't write much, or very eloquently or erotically but she agreed to meet and I figured any port in a storm. She was 42-years old, had married her much older professor from college and after the child they divorced amicably. She probably hadn't had male company since. I got to my room and about twenty minutes later there was a knock at my door. Wenwen arrived with an overnight case, no coyness about where she would stay and no awkwardness as to our being total strangers. Although more mature than expected, she was extremely happy to meet and combined with the implications of her overnight case, any shortcomings looks-wise that might work against a long-term relationship were vastly overcome by the short-term consent her overnight case implied and turned her into a Mitzi Gaynor so far as my intentions were concerned. Her charming protest, *'Don't push'* a delightful variation on the classic sequence, *'Don't! Stop! Don't stop!'*, made our encounter passionate and delicious, surprisingly so. During the intervals we visited the Great Wall, attended Beijing Opera and parted amicably when the tour left for Xi-an.

In Xi-an I arranged to meet Xiaozhi, with whom I had had a long and romantic correspondence since June, made charming by the very unidiomatic and tortured linguistic curlicues of her computer's translation of Chinese into English:

Dear Chris

I affirmed that we will fall deeply in love, you are natural, outstanding, sincere. I think you am the life companion who frequently I must seek. Your letter, I feel excited, thinks you with the fervor, I is submerged by you. I saw your healthy good looks. I think of you frequently, whenever I think of you, I have one kind of fervor, is unable happiness which described with the language, loves you, wants to kiss you.

Xiaozhi

Encouraged by Wenwen's reception in Beijing, I was overwhelmed by Xiaozhi's, again the overnight case accompanied by an enthusiastic embrace and eager mounting of the elevator to my room. Our next tour stop was Shanghai. Confusion over names and phone numbers and addresses thwarted my plans for meeting a lady I had corresponded with. I love Shanghai, a beautiful city astride a large river, marvelous architecture, the Bund, a shore line series of 19th Century English designed buildings used during the British management of China's foreign trade. Where FDR's father in fact worked for a decade along with other traders from the States.

FDR loved China and hated Japan, with dire consequences for Japanese in the homeland and California many years later. Walking the city was marvelous, wide broad avenues, not the tight alley-like streets of Hong

Kong. The French quarter was distinctively Gallic in architecture and mood, although long time since it was a French colonial outpost. It had a very expensive two-star restaurant, Michelin gets everywhere. A river cruise, something like the bateau mouche gig in Paris, was enjoyable to the extent we could keep away from the acrid diesel exhaust which shifted direction depending on the wind and forced urgent passenger realignments below deck. A further difficulty was there were so many passengers and the boat was for some reason so nautically unstable that we had to take turns going up to the sightseeing deck to avoid possible tip over.

My first trip back to China was a homecoming of sorts. I had lived in China so nothing was entirely alien. What was a pleasant shock: the incredible buildup and modernization, plus even more the fact that no one was starving, as was the case in 1948. The traffic was still impossible, but now instead of donkeys, mules and honey carts there were Hondas, Toyotas, Mercedes. That thousands of bodies wandered the streets was unchanged but they were well dressed and no beggars in sight. And at least 20-percent of the women were good looking, in obese America maybe .02-percent. Upon return to California I immediately started planning my return.

Intelligence is the greatest aphrodisiac, at least for the intelligent. I saw this photo of Vijuan on China Love Match and fell in love. That she wore glasses made her even more attractive. Vijuan Is a petroleum engineer with CNOOC (Chinese Exxon) headquartered in Dajing, forty miles NW of Harbin. That is the 'oil region', sort of the Texas of China close to the Russian border. Harbin, the regional Capitol, was once a Russian city known for its ice sculpture displays indicating the arctic prevailing temperatures in the region, as when I arrived at Harbin airport in a snowstorm and 5-degrees F. She operated a Hewlitt-Packard computer program used to document and analyze all the technical/seismic/other data related to her work, including remarkable displays in color of graphs, tabulations, geologic strata (she had everything on her home computer so I was able to see a good deal of it). She described, suitably impressed, the group of HP engineers who came to Dajing to help her and her coworkers set up and operate the hardware/software, a contract for maintaining the system part of the sales package. She had married another engineer and had a daughter 15-years old. She divorced her husband because he had caused her to 'lose face' by lunching and traveling on business with one of the secretaries in his office. *Infra dignatum* for a professional to be compromised by a mere clerk although he protested that 'nothing happened'.

I arrived in Beijing and transferred to a domestic flight to Harbin. It was snowing. It was a bit disconcerting to land at Harbin airport 11:00 PM in a blizzard (How the hell did they manage to land!) and get a cab to Harbin train station where we planned to meet. I arrived at the train station at midnight with no accommodations and relying entirely on arrangements made by Vijuan. I left the bus and entered the station reception area. All concern vanished when I saw Vijuan waiting as hoped. Encounters entail doubt and even anxiety, suppressed but always latent. It's like showing up for a new job, a little too smiley, chatty, friendly in the insistent way that can be so annoying. We had as it were gone all the way on line with photos and chat, much of the ground that lay ahead had been explored, mapped and described so the encounter was not entirely virgin as it were. One dreads a complete turn off. A few shortcomings are tolerable if sufficient compensating assets are evident. But Vijuan exceeded all expectation, finding everything anticipated and more that could not have been imagined. I liked what I saw and apparently she did too. It was gangbusters!

She told me the last train to Daqing had left at 11:45 and we would have to wait to 5:00 AM for the next one. Five hours in a train station, a venue well suited in literature and film for romantic arrivals and departures (check Anna Karenina) but not for extended delays. It worked out quite well. We talked constantly and hugged as much as decorum in a crowded station would allow, and when decorum got in the way, we walked to a secluded area where we necked, fondled, and talked dirty. She spoke fluent English and even more fluent porn so we had a grand time egging each other on. I already decided I wanted to marry her, which settled the big question in my mind. Only trick was how, in what sequence,.

At 5 AM we boarded the train for Daqing. Trains reflect the character of a country's people. This was no different (only the advent of hyper-speed bullet trains in China has ended this convention). Squalor would not begin to describe the feeding, shouting, spastic movement and clamor of a Chinese local train. The smell was particularly acute, exotic food, defecation stench from nearby johns, beer, sweat, onions. The people looked appalling, babies screaming, sweaty fat drooling kids, distorted faces, bad haircuts, staring (at me). Vijuan and I clung to each other on a bench and endured the trip of about 1 ½ hours with a few laughs at the preposterous situation. I had been under way for about 24 hours so although not tired I was a bit groggy from all the bustle.

In Daqing we took a cab to her apartment building arriving about 7:30 AM. Her apartment was in a modern high rise beside a small lake a few miles from central Daqing. It had a nice kitchen, adjoining dining area, fair sized living room, two bedrooms and one bath. She told me an Indian oil executive in his 60's bought it for her. He was in love with her, but ill and unable to perform. He wanted to marry her but his family strongly opposed. She liked him. He died a year or so after they met. She kept the apartment but inherited the mortgage.

The daily routine was not ideal. She went to work at 9 AM, returned 6 PM. I was left in the apartment all day. Nowhere to go in the vicinity and even if I had a key I probably couldn't find my way back. The area had many apartment buildings and a very exclusive 'Royal Estates' housing development. We ate out a number of times or she would cook dinner, very domestic. She had a married sister in town who owned a hotel Vijuan helped her buy. Her parents were pressing her to marry the fat spoiled son of the local CCP leader, which would give the family cachet and social advantages. The leader lived in a massive elegant home within the Royal Estates, given him by the property developers in return for prompt permit approvals. Vijuan did not want to marry the son. She told me about her divorce, her job, and the Sheik from Dubai she had met in 2004. Her plan was to work in Dubai for five years at much higher salary, save enough money to retire, and return to Daqing. The Sheik had three wives so he stayed within the Islamic standard of four. Each wife had her own villa, an inducement for Vijuan. She also liked Arab eyes, dark and deep, as it were. I was beginning to feel tangential but willing to wait and see where I might fit in.

Evenings we took a cab to restaurants and weekends we went downtown. There was a Walmart and a large computer technical center for computers, cell phones, cameras, and the rest. I bought her a new keyboard and mouse, not much but a gift carries weight and guanxi advantage. I met a number of curious Chinese unaccustomed to meet Americans and Europeans in Daqing, hardly a tourist attraction. All were friendly and welcoming.

She liked our being together, liked being held and caressed. She would say *I love you. Don't leave me. I want to marry you.* I replied the same. She said I didn't have an heir, so she wanted to have a baby for me. She repeated this often enough as though it should be our immediate priority. On the other hand she said we shouldn't make love so much or she might get pregnant. Unlike most Chinese ladies she wasn't much interested in going to the USA. She suggested that I could live in China. I said that was definitely possible. Before I left we talked about meeting again soon. She accompanied me to the bus stop. I had the uncomfortable feeling that she had finally decided to do the Dubai gig. Very difficult to sort out this relationship. I loved her, wanted to marry her, and ended leaving for good. When I returned to Oakland, I planned to return to see her in March. She temporized for a while, saying she did not want to marry and I should find someone else. Yet her last email was dated Friday, February13, 2009, 1:14AM.

Dear Chris
I love you deeply. I cannot sleep nicely just for thinking of you. I get up early just want to chat with you before I go to office. You are so attractive to me. I love you with all my heart, and I hope you will love me with all your heart also and I will do my best to make you happy in my life. Nothing is difficult if you put your heart. I want to hold your hands all my life. I am really sorry for misunderstanding you. I love you. Kiss you.
Juan

She did go to Dubai. She told me her daughter had graduated high school and was going to join her that summer. She said she didn't marry the sheik but was engaged to an Arab businessman who bought her a home on Hainan Island. She sent a photo. I look at her in her lovely black dress, imagine her wandering the dunes of the Arabian peninsula, swimming the blue gulf, sipping cocktails in the palatial hotels, basking in the absurd affluence of the Arab Shangri-La and wish we had made it. I still hear her soft loving voice in bed our last night together. All

298

meaning, beauty comes like music through the ear. *'I love you.'* I will hear her music always.

I had the ticket to Shanghai-Harbin but no Vijuan. Rather than cancel the flight I sought another contact, Lucy. She lived in Tianjin, about a 2-hour drive from Beijing. We contacted online and her photo clinched the deal. Those lovely apples and the artful way they are sort of exposed and sort of concealed made her irresistible. Tasteful but fetching.

Lucy was divorced, had a son and daughter, worked for a dating agency in Tianjin and was willing to arrange accommodations for me in Beijing. She agreed to meet at the airport. I had purchased a cell phone of sorts that worked more in the breach than the observance. I arrived, got my bags, and tried to call her but the damn thing didn't work. I was in half panic thinking it was 10:30 PM and I had no reservation. I went to the reception area and tried to identify her in the mass of faces awaiting other passengers. Finally someone said in a tentative weak voice '*Chris?*', and there she was.

Vijuan had explained how Chinese women often use photos from their fetching 20's on websites when searching for mates while in their 40's. Lucy was recognizable once I calculated required revisions of an earlier version familiar from her website. She had put on some weight, the main difference. She must have intuited from my facial expression the recalculations and re-estimations going on in my head. I was more transparent than I would otherwise have been, because I had been 14-hours on the road as it were. Recalculation confirmed on balance that there was no disqualifying change, the face the same, the more mature figure acceptable and the clincher, the apples were as fetching and augmented by added weight to delightful proportion. I quickly smiled, said *Lucy?* and we were on our way.

The hotel was in an outlying newly developing high rise district southeast of central Beijing. We checked in and took the elevator to the 20th floor. The paint had barely dried, the room new in both good and bad respects, some finishing touches remaining to be made. The room was ample, attractive, with a view of the Beijing region twenty stories up. I took a shower, explained that I was a bit tired after prolonged flight, and went to bed. She eventually joined me in her pajamas. Fatigue willingly yields to compelling alternative interests, and I made the usual hand tour of her body. I will pass on the details only to relate an amusing rather archaic defense mechanism I hadn't seen in years, definitely not used by contemporary ladies no matter how perilous the circumstances.

Lucy was very feminine, wanted to please for fear of offending, and too shy to rely on verbal commands or manual interdictions in the face of male insistence. Conflict was absolutely something she could not stand and determined resistance was not something she could possibly undertake. Hence she relied on material support in the form of a tight rubberized girdle, something like a chastity belt, to put off probes I so obviously intended. Her miscalculation was to assume that such an obstacle would, as it were, speak for her: *'Please, I do not want to fuck on the first night.'* In fact three days later she did say *'I don't usually do it on the first date.'* Her second miscalculation was to assume that such an impediment would reliably put off attempts at paradise, not realizing that obstacles incite as often as discourage initiative. I did what males have done with girdles since their invention, I simply started a roll and then summarily rolled it down over her hips, pulled it over her thighs and ankles and flung it in humiliating shriveled defeat to a corner of the room. Resistance and effort tend to heighten the reward.

Next day we moved to an inexpensive hotel (this one was remote, areas of interest far distant and not easily reached) near the main shopping district in Beijing, small but comfortable. We of course went shopping, walked endlessly. She arranged to meet her daughter and son. The daughter was married, sulky and asking for money. The son lived with the father and was spoiled, lazy and ungrateful. I sympathized with her. We planned my next trip to include visit to Dalian a port city and main naval base and other adjacent areas for possible apartments to buy. I reconsidered and while she met her daughter I went to China Airlines and changed my ticket to leave two days early. Lucy was nice and cooperative but I realized it wouldn't work out for the long run. I told her I had to get back to California right away. She accompanied me to the airport where she could get a bus to Tianjin. We parted, but unanticipated by me we were destined to meet again not long after!

Beauty is truth, truth beauty, that is all ye know on earth and all ye need to know, John Keats. Dead wrong. No equivalence. Add *Goodness*, and you have the triad of human ideals: ***Truth Goodness Beauty***. *Goodness* the most compatible, extensive, subjective, endearing. We all praise goodness, we all are capable of it to some degree, and people who offer it are usually well liked, even loved. Truth is austere, objective, absolute, blind (conveys no favors), unchallengeable, and coercive. Fortunately, what we call 'true' in everyday life is a mixed bag of evidence, argument, preference, opinion and point of view that falls short of that pure undiluted concept. We are fortunate that truth in general human association is not susceptible of mathematical/scientific levels of precision. It is always an approximation, never definitive, although in narrowly circumscribed context it may be acceptable as sufficient proof, as in courts of law.

Which is a long winded introduction to Beauty, a word, if I had to define it, I would simply say: 'Sherry'. I am especially susceptible to the *beauty* of women, which I define as a recognition by the soul, not a cognition of the eye or brain. It is an involuntary, breathtaking, overwhelming surprise when first encountered, entirely detached from the common assessments of salient features and expression. It has nothing to do with

302

measurement, appearance or sex. It is like confronting divinity: stun amaze, awe. Obviously this is not an everyday experience, maybe a few times in a lifetime.

It has happened to me four times. First, with Harriet Mether, next with Renee Engel, next with John F. Kennedy and last with Sherry. JFK was an outlier. I had seen the 1960 debates, the press photos and conferences, the Berlin media coverage, the photos. So it was astonishing when I saw him in person that I was stunned by his beauty, not 'handsome', not some queer thing, just the sheer Greek God-like impression his glorious appearance and vitality inspired. With the three women, I realized the distinction between adoration and love. I loved Renee while being astonished by her beauty, whereas I adored Harriet and Sherry with a sense of an unattainable beauty never, if only for a time, to be mine.

Sherry, beautiful, graceful, to die for, lives in a high rise 2-bdrm/1-bath apartment in the Western (hi-end) of Shenzhen. She has a daughter, then about to take college entrance exams. Sherry is svelte charming lovely slender. Improbably her daughter weighs 140 pounds tall large fat and unattractive. Sherry works for a construction company in sales and client services, nearly an executive position in that she charms and wheedles clients who sign contracts for windows, the main product of her company. Her married sister lives in Shenzhen, her parents in Nanjing, her father a retired admiral in whatever form the PRC Navy takes. She married a tech entrepreneur whose main recommendation was that he came to her recovery bed in the hospital after she had a serious auto accident. Such loyalty bred obligation and she agreed to marry. He then started a company making hand held translation devices, cashed in her car, fur coat and savings to keep the startup viable, and in the end went bankrupt. For this she divorced. A question arose later: Was she so injured or disfigured by the accident that she was reluctant to expose her body? Just asking. Her smile was devastating! It was as if the sun came out from behind the clouds and all creation depended on it for life and survival. She was magic! No one comes close, except Renee. She and

Sherry were similar in this power to enchant. I found her on CLM and wrote I would like to meet her during my trip to Hong Kong in May.

2/05/09
Dear Bowen
I am happy to get your letter. I would like to meet you in Shenzhen. My phone is 137243570058. Look for you to call me sometimes.
Sherry

This was my first trip to Hong Kong/Shenzhen. The procedure is you land in Hong Kong International Airport northwest of the city, then board a van/bus to Shenzhen. Passports are checked at the mainland border then you go to Shenzhen customs for visa checks and baggage. Once through you take a cab to your local destination. Sounds simple enough, but late at night with a cell phone that didn't work I ended up a bit stranded. Sherry had booked a hotel for me but I still needed to talk to her first. I explained my predicament to a cab driver, he called her number for the address, I got to the hotel and waited for Sherry in the lobby.

Glamour is an ambiguous compliment, suggestive of superficial even flamboyant attractiveness. An alternative meaning might be total and irresistible attraction without effort or special effects or intention to impress. I had used the word loosely a number of times without having a settled definition in mind. Were Harlow/Dietrich/MM glamorous? Compared to Sherry they were road kill. It wasn't just that she was beautiful, smiling, graceful. She had presence, a natural spontaneous unaffected vitality that just overwhelmed me. I was more amazed than comports with conversation, insouciance, a cool and friendly first encounter. We went to the desk to check in, but she had not given them a deposit and unfortunately all rooms were booked. She suggested a not too distant alternative and I lugged my bag the half mile to the hotel. After some settling in we said our goodbyes and she said she could meet me after work around 5 PM tomorrow. Next evening we went to an upscale bar frequented by prosperous Chinese and Americans. On Saturday we went sight-seeing, had lunch at a waterfront café, talked and smiled a lot, me uncertain what to make of the situation. Next night we went to a sweat box dance bar, the floor packed with mostly svelte ladies, one eyeing me very agreeably. The noise was relentless. We had a few beers and some sandwiches. She went to dance while I stood observing the crowd. She could move her stuff in a very lovely way so as to suggest it was available upon proper vetting. I was a bit jealous. But then I was being ogled by a young girl who would serve any short term purpose I might have in mind.

In the course of random conversation Sherry described the overall business situation and standard practices of the executives she worked with. Her company produced windows express made for enormous high rise apartment and commercial buildings throughout China. Her contacts were mostly multimillionaires who offered her an apartment, car, stipend and paid vacations just to make herself available during their periodic business trips to Shenzhen. She would decline the offers without offense and keep the business relationship intact. As further introduction to the mores of contemporary Chinese, we had lunch with a friend of hers from college, a professional woman, married with children, who had a college student boyfriend who turned up weekends from Beijing to service her. Her husband had his set of playmates and they lived amicably but quite separately, just to keep the kids and family assets intact. Sherry invited me to her apartment for lunch, where I saw her enormous daughter, and made a feeble play for pussy. I hadn't got anywhere in that line with her (during the visit I did have two *seitensprungs* which were delightful and made up for lack of success with Sherry) so I revised my return ticket for 4-days early and left.

Our goodbyes were not stricken or tearful to say the least, and perhaps humiliatingly casual from my standpoint since I sort of adored her but had no idea how that could be converted into a physical and marital relationship. Back in California I continued to write her, offer trips to

Europe or California, but she replied agreeably and evasively. In her last message she said a school mate of hers had moved in with her, suggesting another possibility, a possible lesbian preference, if not physical then emotional? I painted her portrait based on a photo she sent. She asked: *Can you sell it?* So typically mercantile Chinese. Why paint if you can't sell?

Sherry evoked an abstract, insatiable and unappeasable yearning, stronger than desire or lust, untouchable, unlike love. Too much like a Goddess to be constrained by the pathetic yearning of a mere moral like me.

My internet search resumed. Many lovely women, but my eye was taken by **Linda** in Tianjin. Her photos were fetching and she had a direct and encouraging manner. She wanted to marry and she wanted me to come to Tianjin and do just that. Such decisive and unequivocal wordage had a favorable effect. I liked her looks, I liked her determination and I was willing to give it a shot. I required a *jurat* statement of single status certified by the State of California and processed through the San Francisco Chinese Consulate. Elaborate procedure but reassuring for the lady in question. She also wanted a ring, so I fished through my inherited collection and found a diamond cluster ring of Renee's grandmother that might serve. (Linda later had it appraised with disappointing results.)

I flew to Beijing where she arranged to meet me and drive to Tianjin. I got to the reception area and she was there, recognizable but averting her right side because she had a sty on the right eye. I sized her up favorably. Good figure, slender and easy to handle. I didn't mind the sty, assuming it was a result of stress, doubt, worry connected with our meeting and presumed marriage (totally without acquaintance or familiarity). We rode to the hotel in a car driven by a friend of hers. I put my arm around her and got as close as a total stranger would be able. Very nice hotel with an Elvis Presley theme bar (large blowup photos on the walls) and a Harley Davidson fishtail in the entry. The room had a large double bed, comfortably furnished. We went for dinner, an ample buffet, and returned to the room and got ready for bed. I liked what I saw. Her 37 D's bouncing amorously as she removed her bra, the delicious curve of her thigh and buttocks and a tattoo dragon on her lower left abdomen, a kind of symbolic Fafner guardian of the divine treasure as it were (excitement plays odd tricks on the imagination). The domestic preconditions established previously made this intimacy comfortable, unhurried, savored because of the foreseeable and inevitable outcome. I showed her the requisite letter, consular validation, and heirloom ring. She hesitated, not wanting to appear more interested in appraising its market value than enjoying its infinitely greater value as a symbol of honorable intent and conjugal love. She put on her nightgown and we went to bed.

In the morning we went to the registry office and filled out the forms, took the photos, signed the documents, were handed certificates, and civilly declared man and wife. I noticed how out of date their record keeping was, everything typewriter hard copy, filing cabinets full of typed forms and carbon copies. Nothing on computer or central database, nothing electronically filed or registered. This impression misled me as to the true level of computerization and centralization of such documents and proceedings in Chinese provinces. Married, we returned to the hotel. I said I wanted to visit Qingdao. The hotel had a booking agent who arranged two roundtrip tickets, booked a hotel, and arranged rental of a car and driver to take us around for a very reasonable price.

We got to Qingdao, and after a very long drive from the airport checked in to a large pretentious hotel, probably reflecting what Chinese architects thought was Western sophistication in the early 1990's when China was just opening to the world economy. Our driver and his wife met us the next day and suggested we might prefer something closer to the water and downtown. I agreed, we checked out and drove to a boardwalk hotel near where I lived in 1948 and the beach on which I regularly rode horseback. Marvelous! To see the bay and walk along the boardwalk brought it all back, except then there were no hotels, just rocky cliffs and shore line. The hotel was rustic, woody, charming and we got a large room with a large double bed and a large window from which to view the scenic bay and boardwalk. We walked for a while and then ordered dinner at the outdoor café (see photo). We spent several days wandering the city, beaches, monuments, looking for the house I lived in sixty years before (long gone), admiring the high rises, busy highways and streets chocked with cars, and the endless supply of pedestrians filling every nook and cranny. Linda liked wading in the bay. We had lunch at a seafood restaurant that served fresh catch of the day, including lobster. We looked at apartments, having considered that I would not mind living again in Qingdao if she couldn't get a US visa promptly. The hotel had a party of American college students getting their first taste of China and presumably part of a language study program although no indication of attainment in that skill was evident. They were a mixed bunch, somewhat noisy because they were mostly encountering each other and not the Chinese. The bed as mentioned was huge, a delightful playground. Our being married of course removed all constraint, doubt or concern. She was an eager, passionate, cooperative lover (There! There!), her 'Please do me!' look was irresistible. God I love that country.

The second night, Lucy of April bliss showed up for dinner at a local restaurant with a young college student! Lucy worked for a dating website and somehow Linda was acquainted with her and asked her to provide translation services (the student), if needed. So I end up meeting the lady I had been with three months before. I wasn't sure whether Linda knew this and was playing the game, or whether she didn't and I would have to. In any case, Lucy gave no indication we knew each other and we did the translation inquiry straight. I was taken with the friendly and attractive college girl who apparently was not indifferent toward me. For some reason I assumed that she was Linda's daughter (I had not met that article yet) and began flirting hoping I could get together *a trois* later with her and Linda. Lucy played the game straight and so did I.

Four weeks gets to be a long time and we enjoyed an amazing variety of experiences, not least the fatal (eventually) crash of her sister's husband within two days of my arrival. He was a truck driver on the insane roads of modern China. He was admitted unconscious to a local hospital and we accompanied her sister to visit and console. Chinese medical services are a bit shocking to someone used to the sanitary even sterile standard of cleanliness and hygiene in our hospitals. The doctors of course set the standards for health care. They endure years of penury as students/interns to finally achieve the title: MD. Standards are maintained by board reviews and rigorous medical supervision and constant training. Once 'doctored', the intern can look forward to years of ample income and prestige. They are supported by a nursing corps, rigorously trained and dedicated, and by orderlies who provide workaday support.

China is opposite. Doctors receive modest income and little prestige. The hospitals are notably deficient in cleanliness and hygiene, to a degree that would lead to closure in the US, and there is no nursing corps to care for patients. Family members are expected to feed, bathe, attend to patients and provide constant vigil. Patients sleep on crude metal beds four or more to a room, where congestion, noise, and smell of relatives cooking noodles and chatting endlessly is overpowering. Linda's brother-in-law was a big guy, 6'2" 190 pounds, who was in coma and never regained consciousness. At one point a doctor ordered an MRI scan of his brain, so we wheeled his bed into the corridor, across the pathway to an adjacent building where the MRI was completed. We then wheeled him back to his assigned room, nearly tipping him over on the uneven pathway. When I first saw him, I concluded he was finished. Three days later my diagnosis proved true.

Linda has a daughter, then 18-years old, planning to attend a university some distance from Tianjin. She was tall, very fat, homely (like Sherry's) as were so many children in Mao's one-child China. Too much anxiety raising just one leading to indulgences whose adverse effects were so apparent in the fat selfish monsters they produced. Linda had to accompany her daughter to register so I had a 4-day respite to wander and explore downtown Tianjin. When she returned we met a number of her friends. Lisa was engaged to a German fighter pilot now employed in setting up a factory for manufacturing Airbus jumbo jets. Lisa was shapely, but large, and he was burly, so he enjoyed picking her up and carrying her down the sidewalk. Lisa and he had been living together for seven months. His wife in Germany filed for divorce, so happy ending in sight. Lisa was over forty but had had a facelift and looked terrific. Another friend was engaged to a cop from New Haven Connecticut on vacation in Tianjin and also planning to marry when she received a visa and could go to the US. Together, we visited a German and English speaking bar which bored me stiff since I never wanted to see an American or European while in China. We also met a couple working in the government who drove us to outlying areas for shopping. She looked like something out of Ancient Egypt, straight black hair and bangs, black mascara eyes that never blinked, over an expressionless but relentless look. She never smiled and probably figured I was in this thing for the ride not the duration.

Linda's sister, as I said, is a knockout. Personality, beautiful, great body, intelligent and talented as I soon found out. We went to a Karaoke 'establishment', a house with a number of rooms equipped with karaoke speakers and TV monitor to project lyrics and suitable visuals. Also there were her sister's 'friend' (no sex just buddies) and another couple plus a single guy who kept telling me how much he liked Americans. Everyone could sing except me. Linda was good, very interpretive. But her sister was unbelievable. She could easily be a professional, well supported voice, throaty vibrato, attitude to give the words and music juice, and fascinating to look at. Eventually we left, the single guy insisting that we meet again. All I could think of was how can I get Linda to bring her sister, now widowed, to the US where we could live a trois. An entourage of three men and Linda's sister accompanied me to Beijing airport. I planned to return early in 2010. I liked Linda. So long as we were in motion things were fine. Linda was the only person I met in China who read for pleasure, not just information or study. But our inability to converse severely limited our prospects. She had no English and I had very sketchy Chinese. Without constant diversions and readily translatable reactions to them, the mutuality simply couldn't be sustained. Humor especially requires some conversational bond, and lacking frequent humor a relationship has little to smooth the path forward. She eventually filed for divorce, and I resumed my search on China Love Match.

Weiwen, adopted English name Vivian, lived in Shanghai, was divorced, about 38-years old when I met her in 2010. She worked as accountant at a construction company. We 'met' on CLM and arranged to meet. I arrived at Shanghai airport and was very pleasantly surprised to see Weiwen talking on her cell phone, an avocation worldwide. Incredible body in tight-fitting black leotard showing her figure in complete outline, enough to make a grown man cry. I knew whatever happened it would be a very pleasant trip. We went to the hotel near the center of the city, very well appointed with high quality furniture, a large bedroom and bath with adjoining sitting room.

She owned a large apartment, three bedrooms one bath, close in to the city. She lived with her son, then 15-years old. She had divorced her husband because he beat the son and was shall we say inconstant to her. I visited her place a number of times, but for the two weeks, with one exception, I stayed in my hotel and she stayed in her apartment. We visited sights, shopped, meandered, and conversed as much as her nonexistent English and my fragmented Mandarin would allow. So long as we were in motion and visiting various locations it wasn't a major handicap. I got along with the son and helped him with English lessons. As time passed I suggested that we might marry. She should come to California and we would see. She agreed, and apparently that was the key to our last night spent together in the hotel. She clinched the deal by letting me fuck her without condom! She had all the requisites for an easy visa: property, steady job, family and no obvious intention of becoming a drag on the US economy. I sent her money for the plane ticket and she arrived in San Francisco in January, looking good and ready.

In addition to touring the SF waterfront and other scenic spots, we drove to Monterey during which escapade my BMW-7 had a nervous breakdown. (So much for German engineering, plus I discovered how much of the body work and grill was plastic.) First the starter, then the electrical system shut down leaving me without lights at twilight in Carmel, twenty miles from our motel in Monterey. Next day the electrical system recovered although the odometer was permanently shut down, without any regret on my part. Despite this alarming uncertainty as to our ability to return to Oakland, we enjoyed the trip. One evening after a delicious lobster dinner and wine on the wharf we returned to the motel and I took a shower. She was in view of the small bathroom so I gave her as much of a show as possible without seeming intentional. She saw me nude, well-tanned, fairly trim and nicely lit, which seemed to have an inspiring effect. She attacked me in bed, the details of which remain classified.

We visited Golden Gate Park, the art museum and flower garden, and then had lunch at the Nanking Bistro run by Chinese from Shanghai. Renee and I ate there many times on outings to the museum. We ordered a favorite, walnut prawns, and on a visit to the restroom Weiwen got into conversation at the cashier counter with the owner and an old guy who looked 60-years old, apparently a waiter. It was old home week, fellow Shanghai denizens and dialect filling her in on how they made the transition from China to California, encouraging her to do the same. Also the seed of a surprise some three years later when I reconnected with Weiwen in California.

We were not especially suited to each other. I was a bit too complicated and autodidact to inspire confidence or enthusiasm and she was so obviously distant from my interests and experiences and preferences. I did kind of love her or wanted to, and I wanted her in the literal sense, but her response level excepting a few occasions of genuine sexual arousal was more A-B than A-Z. I felt that she was uncomfortable with me, although willing to marry. There was no mating of minds, no juice from her side to ignite my own. I was unable to make the relationship with Weiwen sing. But more about Weiwen later.

I returned to China Love Match search and found **Yanfeng**, a delicious irresistible photo. I recalled Vijuan's warning that most photos are 15- to 20-years ante, but I did not learn that was true of Yanfeng until I met her at my hotel in Shenzhen in May 2010. Our correspondence was abetted by her friend who was fluent in English and worked as a lawyer or at least a legal assistant. Savvy, skeptical and very well versed in the art of erotic composition, she made Yenfeng's messages (who couldn't speak a dozen words of English) sing with love, lust, and longing. I was primed for the encounter of a lifetime.

I booked a hotel downtown and had arranged to meet Yanfeng the evening of my arrival. Duly registered and established in the room, I waited for the knock which came about an hour late, around 8:30 PM. I opened the door and two women, one obviously Yenfeng a few pounds larger and a few years older than her photos, and a rather incisive lady who looked critically at me. Clearly precautions were in order before Yanfeng would begin this relationship, if relationship there was to be. We introduced ourselves and I smiled encouragingly at Yanfeng. Her friend asked to see my passport *'just to verify a few things since you can't be too careful.'* I had taken precautions and doctored my passport birth date from 1938 to 1948 and Xeroxed a copy. It would look phony on the passport but was convincing as a copy. I fumbled around and said I had a copy if that was OK. She agreed and verified who I was. Reassured that I wasn't a serial rapist, both ladies chatted agreeably and then the friend left. Yanfeng apparently was pleased at the prospects of our encounter. Occasionally a guy will find in the course of his erratic love life a girl who is so eager and willing that his surprise briefly interrupts his play, but only briefly. The flashing green light to quick and vigorous engagement surprises. Yanfeng was a sexual rabbit, got very hot very fast, breathing hard and complying fully with my intentions, a kind of carnal heaven on earth.

316

Yanfeng came from Sichuan, the remote eastern province that supplied workers for the industrial coastal cities. She worked at WalMart, the ubiquitous discount store in China. She lived with her mother in a rundown part of Shenzhen, which I never visited. Her sister had married an American who worked for the Feds in Washington and lives in Maryland. Yanfeng had little formal education but she was enthusiastic and spontaneous, had great energy, a primary source of charm. We wandered the shopping district of Shenzhen, ate in noodle shops. Weekdays she worked 10 AM to 7 PM and would come to the hotel with carryout. While she was working I wandered on my own getting many impressions of contemporary Chinese life.

Once a family seated at a street corner, father, mother, small boy and teenage daughter, solicited donations to relieve their financial hardship. I smiled and the mother got up and approached me. *'You want to take my daughter back to your hotel? $50.'* The daughter was a bit plump, not awful looking, but I was already occupied and didn't want to concoct a major problem dragging an underage teen back to my room, possibly leading to a police raid and worse. Sex for sale was common, professional or amateur. I walked by a massage parlor where a few rather attractive ladies waved at me to come over and review the talent. Another parlor on the main drag also had girls who looked the worse for wear standing in front. A couple of Arabs entered eagerly and the girls followed them in. Several streetwalkers turned up around 6 PM for the early trade. My two weeks were up and we headed to the bus station and my ride to Hong Kong airport. Yanfeng couldn't go to HK, she didn't have a pass, so we bid fond farewell with promises to meet again soon, a commitment I sincerely felt at the time but withered in the coming weeks.

Huong Mei lives in Maojing, a seaport town on the Southern coast used mainly for oil imports. I contacted her on CLM, attracted mainly by her remarkable breasts. We corresponded and I arranged to meet her in Shenzhen. I also tried to send her travel money through Moneygram unsuccessfully, which proved irritating to me and more so to her. I did get to Shenzhen, so did she, and we met at my hotel.

 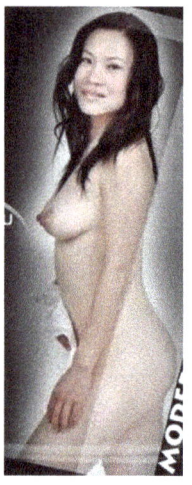 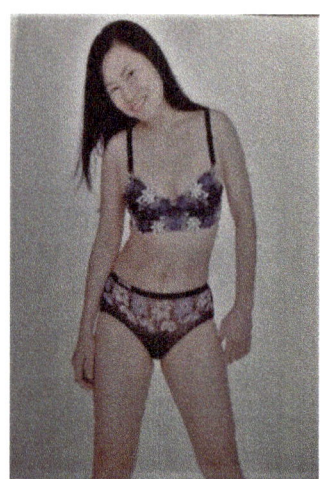

We had exchanged photos, she of her modeling days in her 20's and 30's. The photos she sent were ten or more years before but sufficiently promising to make the play attractive. We had dinner and returned to the room, which had twin beds. She undressed, got into her nightgown and crawled into her bed. I observed the process as discretely as I assumed necessary, but she seemed perfectly willing to show what she had without inhibition. Reasonable for a model who did underwear and nude poses for magazines. I got into my bed and assumed that was it. Soon she got up, came over to my bed, pulled down her nightgown and thrust her right tit in my face. *Is this what you want?* Indifference was hardly appropriate so I started licking her right nipple, which was rich and chewy. She then turned and went back to bed. So much for that. Next morning we had breakfast at the hotel across the street and decided to switch. Next day we got on the bus for the 7-hour ride.

Maojing is by comparison to Shenzhen or Shanghai very small. It had no taxis, only motor scooters on which one sat sidesaddle holding the driver around the waist in a precarious whirlwind through the town.

I stayed at a hotel while Huong stayed at her apartment, not an ideal situation for me. We went to tea with several of her friends one night. I took to one of them and Huong said she could fix me up, a bit acrimoniously of course. I demurred. *'YOU are the one I came to be with'* sort of reply. I was beginning to feel trapped, with no cell phone and unlikely satisfactory outcome to this muddled adventure. For one thing the photos were at least ten years ago. She had become rather more 'solid' and although her breasts were marvelous she was not the Spring I expected from my favorite chicken. She also was holding sex ransom. She wanted me to buy her a car before any approach to consummation. Approximately a $6000 proposition.

We had dinner with her daughter and her boyfriend. He was a very agreeable passive guy who worked for the Post Office. The daughter was plump (common enough for that generation throughout China) good looking, very smart, projecting a restless unsatisfied mood. She spoke English without a trace of accent, much like a California Valley girl. I was astonished and complimented her profusely. She was also studying 'business' in some form and I suggested she could easily get employed by an international corporation given her flawless English. That forced an anxious look from the mailman boyfriend who obviously would never leave his zip code. It also induced a thoughtful look from the daughter as she evaluated the secure but dull future with the mailman as compared to an exciting adventure in the world of financial predation. Huong and I drifted around for a few days. I got to know the hotel maid who seemed wllling ($75 US), but eventually I told Huong I would go back to Shenzhen, get the money from the bank, and return to buy the car she wanted. For some reason she thought that sounded like a great plan so I bought a single bus ticket for Shenzhen and kissed her farewell (for good).

Upon return to Shenzhen I stayed at the original and much less expensive hotel. I called Lucille, a lovely slender girl who worked in the family furniture business. She arrived in elegant fashion despite the humid 90-degree heat and we had lunch. She was pretty, well groomed, small, well proportioned, spoke no English and was therefore a prime candidate for marriage. We toured a museum of Chinese art and visited a bookstore which had an outstanding collection of piano music. I bought a volume of Chopin Preludes, reprinted from the original upscale German edition, for about $4.50 US. We returned to my hotel, but too much to hope for, she declined to visit my room and look at my etchings. I said I would like to see her again. She said definitely, but she had business in Hong Kong and wouldn't be back for three days. She said she would call me at the hotel when she returned. Promising.

Three days is rather long in terms of a two week trip of which 6 days had already lapsed, so I thought of **Jinmei** and gave her a call. She answered to my surprise, no notice having been given of my arrival in Shenzhen. I said I arrived to see her, was sorry I hadn't called or written ahead, and asked if she could meet me at my hotel, address provided. She said she would be right over. Beautiful Jinmei lives in Shenzhen, works as a doctor. She is from Inner Mongolia. The doctors who ran her clinic absconded with about $7 million of the annual budget a year before I met her. They finagled a transfer of funds to a Canadian account and then beat it. The Chinese government protested to Canada but there was no extradition treaty which would have made arrest and return to China possible, so the caper succeeded. As a result the clinic was unfunded and Jinmei was temporarily unemployed, although some arrangement was made to keep her income coming.

She graduated from Beijing University (the Harvard/MIT of China) Medical School, then was briefly married (four months) to a fellow doctor. When I met her she was 41 years old. She was beautiful when I met her so she must have been a Goddess at age 25 or so when she married. She never remarried. She mentioned a wealthy cousin in Macau who wanted to marry her but he traveled constantly and she didn't want a weekend husband. She hinted at a few older men she met at medical equipment shows in Hong Kong. She was very enthusiastic and professional about doctoring so maybe she had little interest in enlarging her off-work activities. She was connected somehow to medical instrument/equipment purchases for hospitals in China and attended a number of international fairs in Hong Kong where such stuff, much of it German made, was exhibited.

As mentioned, she agreed to come to my hotel. It took almost two hours. I had assumed she lived within the Shenzhen transportation services area, so had no idea what could take so long. Packing, shower, makeup, selecting the right outfit? Later I found out why. She lived in the most squalid outlying area of the city, accessible only by hourly busses and only from 5 AM to 11 PM daily. Her 'apartment' was more squalid than the Krushchev ones in Russia. A single-hole toilet in the center shower drain!, hotplate for a kitchen, small icebox, a cot bed, windows looking into the kitchens of her squalid neighbors, and no air conditioning to mitigate the miserable humidity and heat. She was a doctor but I forgot how little doctors earn in the Peoples Republic of China. Later I stayed at her place two nights and then got her to decamp to my hotel. But I am getting ahead of my story. I had almost given up when there was a gentle knock at the door. I opened.

First meetings between strangers are a mixed bag. Some are immediately disappointing. One assumes a smiling/welcoming/approving attitude until able to withdraw gracefully. Sometimes expectations are mostly met, so any qualifications or deficiencies can be disregarded on balance. One simply revises one's criteria to ignore the less optimum attributes presented in some particulars, and continues with an amended but not unfavorable evaluation of whatever other charms the lady presents. In fewer cases all foreseen qualities are fulfilled. No qualifications, compromise required. That is how I felt when I met Vijuan in Harbin.

Then there is Jinmei, where much more delightful presented itself, exceeding whatever I imagined or hoped for. Her online photos on China Love Match might have been taken with a telephoto lens. Impossible to get a clear impression of her appearance. She looked good at 100 yards. One supposed she wouldn't disappoint at 10. But I didn't prioritize meeting her because Huong's obvious pneumatic charms were explicit and easily identified. Jinmei was a bit of a guess. So when I saw this gorgeous smiling lady carrying her overnight case standing in my doorway, I felt an overwhelming confusion of joy/lust/love/amazement. Interpreting her attributes, she was elegantly dressed, every bit the refined lady. The overnight case an unspoken guarantee of further delights, her enthusiastic smile and '你好' greeting, her responsive joining in the impulsive welcoming hug I gave her settled everything for me. I was going to marry this girl.

We went out for dinner. Upon returning to the hotel, the desk clerk said I had several messages. A Miss Huong in Maojing had called. We returned to my room and the phone rang again. I answered and the desk clerk said Miss Huong was on the phone. I took the call, reassured her I would return tomorrow, and resumed my 'discussion' with Jinmei in my broken Mandarin, who seemed not the least taken aback, in fact rather amused by the interruption . Next morning we went to the hotel across the street for breakfast. By now I had quite a reputation with the desk clerks at my hotel. They handed me written messages and told me that Huong had called seven times to find out if I had a woman in the room. She excoriated the clerks and insisted they constantly inform her of my activities. As a precaution I checked out of the hotel and took a room in the hotel across the street. Jinmei was mildly amused at this hassle, taking my side now that we were well on the way to marriage and bliss. And that was basically true. As you see from her photos, she was a knockout and she had decided that I was definitely her husband (present or prospective) and would be a devoted and as I found out later a tenacious wife, for better or worse. We stayed in the busy eastern part of Shenzhen, mostly shops and noodle joints and many toothsome young girls. We shopped for clothes. She tried on dozens of dresses, skirts, jackets seemingly for hours. Never bought anything, but teased clerks with the prospect. After my visit to her dreadful apartment we decided to look an apartment near downtown. Time was running out on my 20-day visit so we planned for my return in October with the prospect of visiting Hohut, Inner Mongolia, and her mother and relatives. I wanted to marry her, she wanted to marry me. What could possibly go wrong?

Of course I had a few loose ends. Linda was resigned that a visa and reunion were unlikely and filed for divorce which required written consent from me. One difficulty was that the divorce proceedings, involving rather inexpedient Chinese legal procedures, were taking longer to conclude than my intentions required. But ambiguity seldom dissuades impulsive desire and I relied on assumptions that soon proved invalid. I returned to Shenzhen in October 2010 with my single affidavit. We stayed at 'our' hotel and shopped for gifts for her mother, sister and other relatives for the Autumn festival celebrations that literally drove one billion Chinese to hit the road simultaneously homeward. We just managed to book airfare to HoHut and could barely carry the mass of packages to the domestic airport. That we got to our destination was a complete surprise to me.

Nei Mengu (Inner Mongolia) looks a lot like Montana without the Rockies. Rolling grassy hills, China's cattle country where they produce the lean, tough, lousy (no feed lots) so-called beef served throughout the country. The cities are modern enough. In fact Nei Mengu supplies Beijing with much of its food supplies, armadas of trucks cram the four lane highway to the Capitol City, often bumper to bumper for miles with hours even days delay in getting there. We piled our junk outside a bus terminal while Jinmei bought tickets to HoHut our destination. The airport was twenty miles from HoHut so we took a bus, arrived at a hotel outside of town center and settled in. The first night we had dinner with her mother, sister, and related spouses and children. Very pleasant. Sister was totally unlike Jinmei, rather homely plump taciturn. Mother was short small plump and in no way accounted for Jinmei's looks or personality. The father who might have provided the missing genetic link was unfortunately dead. Next night we had dinner with her sister, her husband and her daughter. We went to a small noodle shop where everyone stared at us (not many if any Americans visit the area, at least not the noodle shop) but provided brisk eager friendly service to our party of five. Every time I happened to look in the direction of the kitchen I saw five smiling faces shining like new copper Lincoln pennies looking back. The husband brought a flask and offered me a nip which I declined. He looked half lit already, probably not uncommon among husbands throughout China. Very friendly guy but perplexed as to why I was there in the first place or perhaps more likely why he was there. Obviously not accustomed to the requirements of social occasions, just smiling in invincible silence nursing his flask devotedly. The daughter, a high school student, was cute and fun to kid, but not in a position to relieve the parental monotony.

The next day we went to the HoHut regional administrative center to begin the marriage process. The center was large, iron gated, with a sentry who snapped to attention when our cab entered or left the compound. Our driver liked Viennese waltzes which he played on his taxi radio during our trip from the hotel. I first noticed that every office had a cot for taking naps, unusual to someone accustomed to Western bureaucrats who strive to look overwhelmed with work, never to suggest an idle moment. Endearing and civilized, allowing Chinese a rest period in full extended position. There were technicalities about photos and visits to several offices. We eventually got to the registry, where Jinmei's sister dropped two packs of Marlboro cigarettes on the official's desk, given without comment received without notice, guanxi gifting just a matter of course. He took my passport and other documents and got on his computer. This was the first sign of my major miscalculation. I had assumed that if Tianjin used paper forms, carbon copies, and clunky metal filing cabinets, surely remote Nei Mengu must be the same or worse. Nothing so advanced as computer data storage was evident in Tianjin. Too late. He entered my passport number and there emerged information about Linda and Tianjin, however it got there. Perhaps divorce proceedings involving a foreigner were recorded in Beijing where computer documentation would be common. I had not mentioned to Jinmei the Linda event, assuming the divorce was completed and anyway no record of the marriage would be available. The lights went out and the fun began.

In law, intent is a factor with respect to a crime. If murder is impulsive, spur of the moment, even accidental, the degree of the crime and punishment provided under law is correspondingly mitigated. Usually one cannot be prosecuted simply for intent, deliberate or inadvertent, although threats can lead to restraining orders. In this case I had not actually married Jinmei. I intended to and explained that a divorce was in process and I assumed it had been completed, etc....etc.... I didn't intend to deceive. So much for the defense. In China, laws and enforcement are much less refined. Things tend to be more black and white than shades of grey. I wasn't sure exactly what charge might be brought against me and I was free to return to the hotel without special comment or restraint. Jinmei took charge from that point in dealing with the authorities on my behalf. So I heard second hand what they were up to and the steps I should take to get the hell out of there. Justice in China is mainly a question of money and power. The latter buys immunity or forgiveness. The poor go to jail. As a foreigner, I was a cash cow of sorts, difficult to imprison but easy to blackmail. After all, I couldn't get out of China if they chose to keep me there. Jinmei did describe in graphic detail the horrific conditions prisoners faced in Chinese jails. She cited the case of a Greek lothario who was sentenced to three years in prison for deceiving a trusting Chinese girl. Of course the deceptions by Chinese girls of Western suitors were equally if not more frequent but not directly subject to Chinese judicial relief. Jinmei presumably did everything possible to prevent serious consequences, because they allowed me to leave HoHut after paying a $3500 fine. That wasn't the end of it but it did get me back to Shenzhen, five days before takeoff. When I returned to California, Jinmei sent me a summary of the situation.

You say you have divorce information in Shenzhen. Please forward to my phone. You cheat the government of Mongolia. You are deception. You will be sentenced. You will be fined $100,000. Government of Mongolia call you. You do not listen. Please understand. You are making mistakes in Mongolia, very serious. You must deal with. Do you want police chase? Do you want to be sentenced?

You get the idea despite the fractured English. So what exactly was my state of mind? Since Renee died in June 2004, I had been drifting and disoriented. Online dating sites provided diversion and contacts. A kind of electronic river of adventure that attracted me, being without rudder or anchor to direct or stabilize. I had piles of emails that defy summary but mostly amount to the humbug every man-woman encounter requires to start with. They seek true love, looks and money don't matter. I seek a good heart and loyal friend, even though looks and a hot body are what I want. In 2010 I was 72-years old. I had never thought chronologically, but this was a fairly advanced age to attempt major sexual escapades. I did notice that my ardor was more initial than sustained. After a few rolls in the hay I began to feel uninspired. With nothing to do but eat sleep and fuck, one soon turns what should recreation or dessert into a treadmill or junk food.

Given Jinmei's letter and likely formal official retribution, the situation required careful consideration. I couldn't risk internment in China, but fortunately there was no extradition treaty with the US to enable that threat. I had already paid $3500 for my miscalculation. And I had not actually committed a formal felony, only what I considered a misdemeanor--almost but not intended nor actual bigamy. But the aggressive tone of Jinmei's letter was open to two interpretations. She was genuinely concerned about my well-being and dramatically emphasized the dire conditions of Chinese prisoners as an inducement to pay fines and avoid repercussions. There was also a suspicion that she might have been induced to abet a fraud by getting me to pay fines that would go into the pockets of the regional police chief, a cut given to Jinmei of course. Fear is the best form of coercion, the victim overwhelmed by panic loses all rational control. I wasn't there yet and unlikely to be.

Another factor was the total lack of official communication to me directly as to the nature of the violation and its consequences, a formal official charge in writing, or any accounting of my earlier payment of fines. All I was expected to do is send money without any idea of who gets it and what formal accounting is made. Paying without a receipt much less depositing without a receipt is not good business and suggests more fraud than law enforcement. Chinese are expert racketeers and as likely to be so in official positions as not. Foreigners can be conned to the extent possible without any accounting to higher authority, personal cash flow especially for police, party and other controlling officials beyond trace. Over the coming months our emails hashed out the pros and cons and gradually attenuated my devotion as compared to my sense of survival. Sad to give up such a beauty but the search could continue closer to home.

I headed into 2012, scanning China Hook Up, a Bay Area dating site. I met Holly, a lovely slender lady living with her computer geek son in San Mateo. She was about 5'5", 105 pounds, great shape, attractive face, mild sweet voice and temperament and very poor English. We met a few times, but she was so unacquainted with American ways that I could never quite avoid getting her flustered and anxious. Any physical contact seemed to come as a complete surprise. Although divorced with a son, she seemed to be as amazed as surprised that a man would actually want to touch her. There were other brief contacts, but the most amusing and confusing was between two ladies named Lili who lived in San Mateo and Burlingame. Lili Lee lived with her daughter in a very large elegant house in the latter city. Her photos showed her at some distance in the hallway, obviously not gorgeous or slender but possibly OK upon closer inspection. **Lili Ma** lived in San Mateo and had just one photo equally ambiguous as to detail but more promising as to attributes. I conflated both in emails and assumed at one point they were the same person. I eventually got together with Lili Ma one Sunday afternoon in June near a Safeway in San Mateo. She drove, I drove, and we went to a nearby restaurant for a snack and chat. We hit it off and met a few times for a movie and dinner or both. She had a fetching figure, a charming smile and willing look but skeptical and not ready for fast forward. We went to the beach south of Half Moon Bay, lay on a blanket along with 40,000 other people. I looked at her back sleeping and fell in love. Eventually we spent a weekend at a motel on the shore. Thereafter she came every Friday night to my house and returned home Monday morning to work as a care giver for a senior retired Army guy.

She mentioned a number of former boyfriends. A Greek software businessman who had good taste and a big income but was too busy to pay as much attention to her as she would like. There was an American she thought would marry, but who ran off to Shanghai to marry a website acquaintance. Sixteen months later the woman parted from him with a substantial sum of his money. He called Lili to renew the association, but a woman scorned is a woman lost. She also did modeling for a fashion photographer who paid her for shoe modeling shots and took her to Los Angeles where he paid for a screen test. He also took fetching photos not intended for commercial use. I am realistic. The past is prologue but of no significance. If they got to play in her sandbox, so what? I wasn't anyone to complain. I spent the summer and fall of 2012 and the spring of 2013, with Lili, visits, trips to the beach, opera events, restaurants, Monterey. I arranged for my sister to visit in June and she served as witness to our civil marriage in Oakland June 23, 2013.

I once tried to define marriage, something I always wanted. I wasn't suited to playing around even though I did some of that. I always wanted to love and care for someone who felt the same about me. Marriage is a civilization built day by day from shared opinions/laughter/concerns/ intuitions, deep soul love, reading in bed together never a forced or contrived feeling simple quiet gentle indestructible. Above all laughing together every day and many times. And crying tears of joy and sorrow. The only thing that matters in life, if you are lucky enough to find it. I found it a second time with Lili. We traveled to Paris in 2014, stayed in an adequate apartment near Place des Vosges. Did the grand tour and ate often in a local Chinese restaurant. I first went to Paris in 1969, De Gaulle had scrubbed it clean of the black coal dust that covered and defaced the magnificent public buildings. Several times after that the city still looked beautiful, but in 2014 it was back to grime, Arabs and Africans creating their special level of mayhem, and the locals obviously no longer in charge of their destiny. *Dommage.*

The following year we took a cruise from LA to Cabo, Puerta Vallerta (*of Night of the Iguana* fame with smoldering Burton and Ava Gardner and somewhat less overheated Deborah Kerr) and other coastal pit stops. Mexico and Mexicans have charm of sorts but I wouldn't want to live there, although many expats on social security from Akron and Spokane and so on lived there and provided guided tours. I bought two pair of huaraches, a reminiscence of the ones I wore when I attended Fallbrook HS in 1952-53, a golden age for California. We went with another

couple, a friend of Lili's and her American husband. I dreaded the idea of being locked up on a boat with thousands of strangers for seven days, but it turned out to be delightful. Princess Cruise had a beautifully appointed ship, outstanding entertainment (great Mariachi trio for one), a marvelous buffet for breakfast lunch and anytime, and a truly elegant dining room with white tablecloth, silverware, wine and cuisine (not just chow). I was a convert.

We went to Las Vegas, the inevitable, once with our cruise friends and my sister Linda and her husband Harold Wolfe. Not entirely copasetic, given my iron-whim sister who had arbitrary opinions of what should happen and little tolerance for what actually does. Too complicated to explain in detail. We did spend a fortune on 'haute cuisine' that fell notably 'bas' at a franchise restaurant of a TV chef whom my sister (she got certified as a chef in Denver) watched devotedly. But what the Hell! Vegas is for fun and we managed to have some. A second visit was provided by Lili's nephew Michael, her twin sister's son who was devoted to his aunt. He was a successful banker in Nanjing age 30-years, and had an expense account which we molested so far as possible by staying in luxury class (American Lincoln not Italian Ferrari definition of the term). We saw a big show at a big casino which excelled athletically but lacked ultimate point. Lili's daughter came along and I was able to observe her sweet buns (albeit in thin panties) rubbing each other in one of the shortest miniskirts I have so happily seen. She moved to another hotel to avoid further displays. Michael bought an Armani suit in which he posed for business publicity photos in San Francisco before returning to his Heimat. I tried my hand at Black Jack, first ever gambling and won $157. Quite a boost. I had read up on the game and realized that you don't play your hand, you play the dealer's. It all depends on his going bust. He has to play every hand below 17 and has to hold if he gets 17. If he gets 13 to 16 there is a good chance he will go bust. Not as interesting as computer chess but you can actually win (or loose) $$$ and it is an exciting way to kill time.

EPILOGUE

This capsule history leaves out many sidebars and characters. Hugh Barbour Hutchison (1901-1974) is one. A member of the Society of the Cincinnati (SOC), scion of a pre-revolutionary Herndon Virginia family, a flaming queer and exemplar of that remarkably pervasive demographic in Washington, New York City, San Francisco, and LA. The Society was formed in 1783 by officers who served with General Washington, membership restricted to male descendants. In 1938, the local residence of a member from Massachusetts, Larz Anderson, at 2118 Massachusetts Avenue, was bequeathed by his widow as a national museum and headquarters for the SOC. Built in 1905 as a 'Florentine Villa' in the middle of WDC, it cost $750,000, structure and all furnishings, about the price now of a 1-bdrm 1-bath condo in San Jose, a suburb of SF. Unexampled splendor and appointments for a wealthy diplomat who served in London, Paris, and Rome able to entertain at a European aristocratic level.

I met Hugh at a party given by Miss Janet Fish, whose brother Hamilton was also an SOC member. At the time I was 16-years old attending Georgetown University in 1954 (way too soon for college!). Hugh invited me to a party at the SOC, where several **Star and *** Star generals in uniform looked around bewildered, possibly disoriented, by the opulent setting and, in several cases, fairly decadent ancestors of our founder's Army. Just an insight into the 'aristocracy' of inherited wealth and social prominence that lurks behind elegant curtains and lead glass windows in residual elegance in our major eastern cities. Hugh broke his right arm, incapacitated by a large cast for driving and signing checks among other deficiencies. Miss Janet Fish asked if I could help him from time to time. I drove him occasionally after class and acquired Power of Attorney so I could sign his checks. We had dinner fairly often and he was invariably courteous and grateful but as was perhaps inevitable, he made an inevitable play which I eluded. I was not aware of how widely distributed this proclivity was. He was a convert to Catholicism, not sure whether sins of the flesh having less stricture than sins of the spirit in the canon induced such conversions, or whether the implicit tolerance of deviance among members of all-male fraternities denied (technically) hetero relief made the church attractive.

I was grateful for this early monitory introduction to the large number of straight-looking men who were definitely louche. Hugh retired in 1956 from his career as hearing examiner at the Federal Communications Commission, moved to Copenhagen, and then Dublin, Ireland, a seemingly unlikely deer park for homosexual diversions. He was friends with Julian Green (1900-1998), also gay and from a Virginia 'First Family', who moved to Paris after WWI, where he wrote novels in French about amorous and other inversions in the faded drawing rooms of pre- and post-Bellum South, as well as journals, plays and other novels. Julian Green was the first non-French national elected to the *Academie Francaise,* in 1971 to replace deceased Francois Mauriac. A remarkable achievement. The *Academie* was established in 1635 by Cardinal Richelieu, limited to forty members, called 'Immortals', duly elected by peers to serve as a Supreme Court to maintain the purity/integrity/'frenchness' of France's language and culture. Green's novels, if written in English, might have gone on the shelf with *Uncle Tom's Cabin and Gone With the Wind,* as epics of Southern society. His French, uniquely brilliant, entertaining, diverse, won him laurels in a country jealous of its prestige and presumed superiority. He was devoted to the Confederacy and never ceded his US citizenship. In 1996 he rejected the 'Immortal' honor, stating he was a loyal American and felt it was not honorable to take such an entirely French honor as a foreigner. The homosexual tendency among Southern writers and their literary themes took better known form in Tennessee Williams.

Gerald Richard Perreau-Saussine, film actor name Peter Miles, was a student in Georgetown College a member of a circle of aesthetes that included students from the School of Foreign Service. He was slender, fey, an elusive personality, a bit hermaphroditic in manner. His major cachet was to have a poem published in *Poetry* magazine in 1957, *Swimmer Emerging.* His father left Japan in 1938, the year Gerry (as we called him) was born, and settled in Los Angeles.

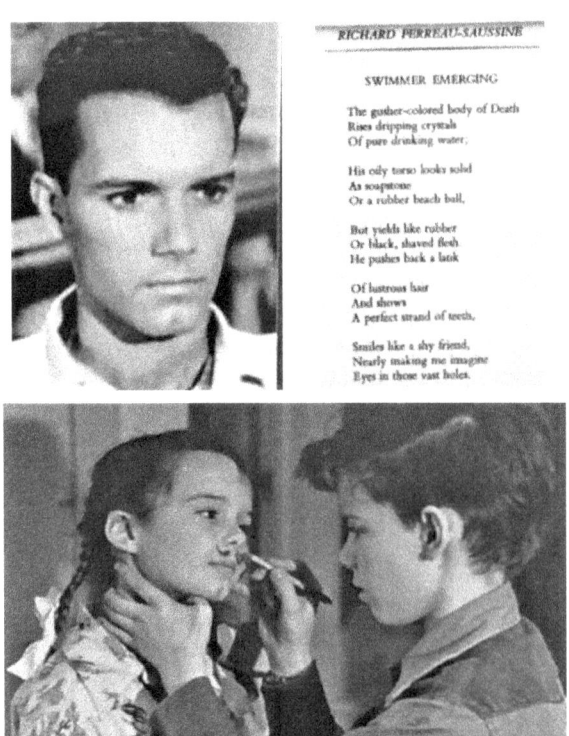

336

As early as 1943, he and his sister Gigi (right photo) were under contract as child actors to MGM. His film credits are numerous, his first film as son of Humphrey Bogart in Passage to Marseilles 1944 continuing until the early 1960's when both he and Gigi discontinued fading acting careers. He appeared with many major stars: Judy Garland and Fred Astaire 1945, Joan Crawford 1947, Myrna Loy and Robert Mitchum 1949, Roy Rogers and Dale Evans in 1950, Robert Taylor in Quo Vadis 1951. He and his sister Gigi were virtually adopted by Samuel Goldwyn, she appearing in the latter's 1946 film Enchantment with David Niven and Teresa White. Sam gave Gigi equal billing with the main stars in lead-in credits although she played a short role as the 8-year-old version of the heroine. Much of Gerry's film career happened before he entered Georgetown, almost as a has-been! Gerry appeared in TV series with Betty Hutton 1959-60 and in Father Knows Best, Perry Mason, the Lone Ranger, and Sunset Strip. Gerry was also a screen writer of modest scale. His novel 'That Cold Day in the Park' of 1963 was made into a film of the same title in 1969. Sam Goldwyn, an almost parental friend, twice presented him a Samuel Goldwyn Creative Writing Award. Incredible that from age 5- to 25-years old, he was constantly in the company of major movie stars and cast in parts with many of them. The last thirty years of his life were much less dramatic. He later taught in Burbank public schools and died age 64 of cancer in 2002. Among his close associations was Cary Grant, with whom he cruised Hollywood for partners, both gay, Cary more now and then as with Randolph Scott. Jerry is completely forgotten. Early glory and late oblivion. But what a ride!

I turned 80-years old in 2018, a further move in the endgame chronologically, although I never thought of life in numerical order. I was feeling time's cruel blade however, and became interested in reconnecting with past acquaintances. I managed to connect with Jack Ellenberger, an unflattering beginning to what turned out to be an unpromising excavation of past encounters. Jack was bitter about his 'release' from the law firm in Washington where he worked as librarian for a number of years, digital computer referencing replacing the skilled hand of manual librarianship. Now living in New York, 87-years old and in poor health, tended by a nurse, he didn't remember me at all. I called him again in 2020, but he was incapacitated as his nurse explained unable to speak, soon to enter the great unknown. Belatedly following Harry Jacobs, his buddy of Georgetown days, who died in 2010, a Catholic Priest of all things. .

Ephron Catlin returned my phone call much to my surprise. He lives in Houston Texas. He said he got fed up in 1987 and left New England for good, excepting a Bar Harbor Maine family resort he and his two brothers inherited jointly. He had left Army Language School in 1962 as I did (the last time I saw him), went on a grand tour that included the Soviet Union where he was 'detained' for two weeks, their records showing our ALS attendance. He was supposed to have a cushy job with Gillette and apparently got into medical equipment sales that included the Soviet Union where he visited frequently and nearly mated an adhesive woman, probably a KGB operative, her passion for him a bit outré to be believed. The KGB may have been impressed by his Boston Brahmin connections and background hence the effort to seduce. The Houston thing seemed odd, the worst climate in the US. Full of himself as ever, no further contact after the call. My second lesson in how irrelevant the past is, quite reasonably, to most people.

Tell Schreiber son of a Hollywood executive and ex-ALS student made a career in theater in Washington State. His actor son by a Jewish lady in New York co-starred with Angelina Jolie in SALT. Tell didn't reply to my Facebook approach. I called Bill Crumb's widow. Their daughter had married a Marine who performed in the Marine Band for White House events. Not much aftermath from our last encounter in 1992.

Brent Primus, surviving brother of Richard in Minneapolis, was solo running the family law firm, involved in Boy Scouts with Hmong refugees and still giving seminars as expert in the legal complications of the railroad industry. I remember the bright lively kid of 9-years old and the young head of the law firm of the 1990's, become a large, fat, dull Midwesterner in a baggy suit somewhat addled by years of professional repetition.

Strangest of all, I was able to track Harriet Mether, last seen in 1961 just before I left for basic training. She married Richard Rosenberg in 1964, an instructor (still working on a PhD) at Mankato State College in southern Minnesota and distant relation of Julius and Ethel Rosenberg, both executed for treason in 1953. He later transferred to Penn State College in Altoona PA and an unremarkable career as a third tier academic bureaucrat about whom I could find no records. They remained for decades in Altoona where Harriet was an itinerant art teacher in grade and high schools throughout the State. She had two sons, the first in 1967. She died, age 82, in January 2019. Harriet was a prominent member of the Guild of American Papercutters, a nonprofit organization of the Commonwealth of Pennsylvania! That it was a guild was unsurprising (any activity apparently now has its organization), that it was non-profit was implied. Largely a hobbyist collective with a 'museum' in the large Victorian house of a devoted member, it didn't attain sufficient status to become a marketable diversion.

The Harriet I knew was enchanting, elusive, inexplicable. She had been a shadow of regret for years, an extraordinary girl at 23-years, as described in earlier pages of this memoir. For years,decades, I held her memory in my writhing soul, that I had lost her that I would never be with her that I failed in some way to overwhelm her as she overwhelmed me. The photographic record is perplexing. For two or three years1959-1963, including the time I knew her, she was beautiful, clear evidence for my adoration. Not so before or after.

The photos are roughly 16-years to 80-years old. And now looking at the erosion of beauty over time and the eventual ravaged age, I wonder how I could have been so enchanted by her, like some potion-besotted character in Shakespeare's Midsummer Night's Dream. If I reverse telescope the photos I can just barely recover the impression of her face at 23-years. But not reconcile. Unimaginable or unrecoverable from the photos of her later life. The enormous brick pile building of her apartment has been demolished for contemporary apartment buildings and offices. No trace left of the scene of our romance. I often thought of her as a successful actress, her voice, enthusiasm and animation so ideal for such a career. That she ended teaching crafts to grade schoolers and doing cutouts, weaving fabrics and making graphic prints must have drawn on the practical, hands-on tactile side of her soul. One chooses a path that seems congenial. She was self-driven and what she chose must be what her view of destiny conceived. I doubt she stayed with her husband. She was an entirely free spirit unsuited and disinclined to perpetual relationships. I know in retrospect we never would have made a life together. This (see below) is the Harriet I knew and loved. This this is the Harriet I lay in bed with. Mesmerized by her wonderful voice, the green-rectangle flecked light-brown irises of her expressive eyes, the russet hair and delicious skin, the pursed lips I so loved to kiss, the lovely breasts, the russet bush exposed as she stood naked in front of the fireplace, the flicker of burning logs warming her skin, and the delighted gasp as I entered her sweet body, the eager adventure of her love making ('stroke it more, stroke it more') as she fulfilled her intent to begin a career of sexual exploration of which I was the first.

Harriet Mether

I have witnessed the decay and ruin of San Francisco since 2000, to say nothing of urban California and for that matter the world. Lili and I have a secure bond and a working marriage that provide us both with a refuge, sounding board, and source for renewal in the face of whatever screwball happens outside our perimeter. 2020 gave us corona virus, a kind of modern plague of Egypt without a promised land to go to. There is a kind of completion. I have done everything I want to do, been everywhere I want to go, known everyone I want to know. My living room is my Shangri-La where I can ride the magic carpet of music, memory, imagination through time, to that distant place and long past moment when perfection of being occurred between Harriet and me, in a broken down brick tenement of inconvenient utilities, dirty windows, soiled curtains, and wrinkled sheets, holding each other, where we shared an ideal of beauty and love I wish could have been frozen in time, a perfection Harriet and I had together, then left behind a millennium ago.

> *Where have all the flowers gone?*
> *Gone to graveyards every one.*
> *Oh when will they ever learn,*
> *Oh when will they ever learn?*

www.ingramcontent.com/pod-product-compliance
Lightning Source LLC
Chambersburg PA
CBHW051132120626
46547CB00012B/767